"Vicki's personal experiences as a LEO wife and profound research shine through in this incredibly practical resource. This book is an unparalleled tool that delves with unbridled truth into the heart of issues facing law enforcement officers and their marriages. I highly recommend it for all officers, spouses, and pastors or counselors who serve this unique subculture."

Jonathan Parker
Pastor, Cop Church Chattanooga (www.CopChurchChatt.com)
Founder, Covered Law Enforcement (www.CoveredLawEnforcement.com)
Chattanooga (TN) Police Officer

"Very inspirational read! It comes at the perfect time when there are so many broken hearts in America from all of the senseless deaths and emotional pain. Thank you for writing this!"

Deputy Chief Eddie Reyes; Alexandria Police Department (VA)

"Victoria has once again used her God-given talent to produce a work that is relevant, relational and resourceful. She uses her passion, wisdom, and creativity to reach out and touch law enforcement officers, their spouses, and families right where they are. She provides the help needed to grow relationally and professionally. Her insight is invaluable. I am proud and honored to recommend A Marriage in Progress."

Chaplain Dale Henderson, Centurion's Faith
Deputy First Class, Forsyth County Georgia Sheriff's Office

"A Marriage in Progress is about conscious living and loving and setting intention for marital awareness. Marital awareness is to marriage what situational awareness is to good officer safety; they both identify elements of awareness and consciousness to be successful which enables one to survive and thrive from the beat to your own backyard. This is an excellent book, Victoria. Bravo!"

Barbara Upham, Lieutenant (Ret.), California Highway Patrol

"Law enforcement officers are highly trained to perform the nature of their job and how to physically survive lethal encounters. However, they and their families receive little to no training on how to survive a relationship/marriage directly affected by the job. The very nature of the law enforcement profession can prove lethal to a marriage if officers/dispatchers and their families are not trained in relationship survival. A Marriage In Progress gives marriages the training to survive. Victoria Newman delivers her message not through theory, but as a law enforcement wife on the front lines of her marriage and her husband's police career. She shares relationship survival tactics from living them. Do not become a statistic of law enforcement divorce—read this book."

Todd Langus Psy.D., Law enforcement therapist and former police officer,
drtoddlangus@gmail.com.

"A Marriage in Progress is a great example of the transparency that not only Brent and Victoria live but transparent examples of others in different situations and how they have lived life. While being an officer is a paid position, it is really a calling with specific training for all life situations. Due to the nature of this training, marriage is really difficult. It takes two people to make a marriage work. Victoria uses her passion, experience and wisdom to provide practical help for law enforcement marriages, but frankly the information can be used in all walks of life. I recommend this book to help each marriage partner gain a better understanding."

Darrel Billups, Th.D.
Executive Director, National Coalition of Ministries to Men

"Victoria Newman has shown tenacity and fervent dedication to the writing of this book. As I read A Marriage in Progress, I saw it not only as a book for law enforcement, but also for counselors and the public to better understand what happens behind the scenes. It is my hope and prayer that when each person reads this book they have a better understanding of what it is like behind the badge, but also that they will come to the realization that there is hope in situations that seem hopeless. Victoria gives that perspective."

Rebecca Parkey, MS, LMFT, LCMFT
Licensed Marriage and Family Therapist (MO)

"A Marriage in Progress has the ability to change and impact the lives of not just the law enforcement officer and his/her spouse but their children, grandchildren, family, friends, and the list goes on. Victoria's unique perspective, understanding of the dynamics of a LEO family, and willingness to be a positive force for marriage is desperately needed in today's culture. I love how she tells it like it is and doesn't pull punches. She shoots straight and tells us the truth. Thank you, Victoria, for the hard work and willingness to be transparent for the benefit of us all."

Chuck Gilliland, President of Fellowship of Christian Police Officers
Sergeant, Dallas-Fort Worth Police Department (TX)

"Victoria knocks it out of the park with A Marriage In Progress. Drawing from her own experiences and those of the many others whose lives she has touched, Victoria has put together a "must read" not only for those in law enforcement and their spouses, but for anyone looking to gain a better understanding of the unique challenges in a law enforcement marriage. Her insight and wisdom have helped many and with this book, there are sure to be many more."

John Caprarelli, Los Angeles Police Department (Ret.)
Author of Uniform Decisions

"A Marriage in Progress is one of the best police family resource books I've ever read. It's as if Victoria wrote the book about my life as a police wife. The book is so excellent and interesting, I couldn't quit reading it. I would highly recommend this book for every police family if you want to strengthen or improve your marriage."

Linda D., National Police Wives Association

"Having worked for four different law enforcement agencies, three SWAT teams, and numerous protective details, specialty teams and the military, I was used to change, transition and struggle. On a SWAT team you learn to fill in the gaps as they occur; you learn to lead, follow, or get out of the way during high stress and critical incidents. If an operator goes through the door right, you buttonhook, cross left or blow by—it's what specialty teams call fitting into the stack or reading the need. It's second nature to read the tactical terrain and react correctly with continuous training, coaching and experience. Few couples approach their marriage with this same tenacity, this same high visual horizon and dedication. It's what we do for our careers, but not often for our marriages. A Marriage in Progress takes us to a place where we can walk it through, chalk talk the event, and allows us to practice to correctly fit into the marriage stack—to read the need to survive in marriage."

SSG Emmett William Spraktes
California Highway Patrol (Ret), NREMTP, Tac-Med instructor
California National Guard (Ret), Author "Selfish Prayer" www.selfishprayer.com

"Victoria offers practical advice from personal experiences she and her husband share on how to have a successful relationship in this truly trying lifestyle. She shares these nuggets of pure gold wisdom in a down-to-earth, true-to-life, completely genuine way that reveals her heart and passion and feels like talking to a trusted friend. As counselor, spouse and officer spouse, and fellow relationship advisors, we appreciate the necessity to be vulnerable. Sharing hardships in our relationships as well as successes give a true sense of hope—no fluff, all real—but in a way that is truly enjoyable to read. As fellow Christians, we very much appreciate the boldness with which Victoria incorporates her faith as a building block for the success of her marriage—again, a true sense of hope and truly inspiring. A Marriage in Progress is a real expression of this life and is a great resource for officers, spouses, chaplains, counselors, and anyone in a law enforcement relationship—personal or professional. However, many of the basics of this book can apply to any relationship! It's just that good."

Mendi Keatts, MS, Therapist; Chaplain, Wives Behind the Badge, Inc.
Lt. Stephen Keatts, Roanoke City Police Department (VA)
Creators – P.O.L.I.C.E. Families

"Victoria Newman's writing approach translates into sense and sensibility on paper. You will feel an ease in reading while at the same time experiencing many "Aha" moments. Another must read by an amazing author."

Melissa Littles
Author, *Bullets In The Washing Machine*
Founder, The Police Wife Life, LLC.

A MARRIAGE IN PROGRESS

TACTICAL SUPPORT for LAW ENFORCEMENT RELATIONSHIPS

VICTORIA M. NEWMAN

Dedicated to my amazing parents

Gary and Mary Campbell

Through whom
over 50 years of unwavering faith and committed love
have shown me what home is.

And for generations of proud Americans before them
whose blood runs through our veins

Living quietly, Working diligently
Loving deeply, Learning consistently
Serving God faithfully.

May the legacy live on.

TABLE OF CONTENTS

FOREWORD

Other than the ultimate training manual for life—the Bible—what you hold in your hands is the most important book you will ever read as a law enforcement officer. I do not say that lightly. As the Editor in Chief of Law Officer Magazine, full time police officer and college professor, I have literally read thousands of articles and books on the profession. While criminals are thought to be our biggest threat, this could not be further from the truth.

I have been in police supervision, middle management and now upper management for over two decades. In that time, I dealt with personnel issues on a weekly basis. Without a doubt, the largest threat to our safety, security and well-being as officers is not the evil that lurks in the shadows but our own illusion of our behavior. We justify poor work performance by blaming bosses. Although our marriages aren't great, they will do considering our schedule. We may abuse alcohol or barely sleep but that is because of the stress of the job. We consider financial burdens part of the profession. We justify not spending time with our children because of various plausible reasons. While you may not fall into every category, at a basic level you have to recognize much of this within the law enforcement profession whether it is yourself or those you work with. To some degree, we all bear these issues and we have accepted them as fact for as long as I can remember. Hollywood glorifies it and we pretty much believe it.

Until now. A Marriage In Progress by Victoria Newman will change lives across our profession. It would simply be impossible to read the words on these pages and not be changed. From improving your marriage to being a better parent, employee, and even financial manager, this book covers more ground than anything available today. It is relevant, detailed, and brings a credibility that our profession desperately needs when discussing these very tough issues. Victoria Newman is a profound author, speaker, mother, and wife and has chiseled her view through decades of marriage to a California Highway Patrol Chief. Admittedly it has not been easy. She documents the struggles within their relationship as well as the impact and toll she saw the job take on her husband; which ultimately collided with home life. Her personal story is intermingled with sound research, outside sources, and testimonies of others in the profession. Chapters conclude with questions to be answered, discussions to be had, and direct applications for life, career and family.

As courageous as it must have been to write this book, it will take much more than that for you to read it. The voices in your head will tell you to close the book almost immediately—but you must not. Law enforcement has been defined by our past and current transgressions for far too long and this book can turn it around. You need the contents of this book whether you think you do or not.

The tipping point is here for law enforcement and it rests in your hands today. I urge you to read this book, give it to others, and watch everything you thought was normal change forever.

Major Travis Yates, Tulsa Police Department (OK)
Editor in Chief, Law Officer Magazine

THE MAN
BENEATH THE BADGE

The badge reflects its golden gleams, earned and tried and purified

The uniform pressed and creased, clothes authority, rescuer, defender of peace

The armor confidently strapped in place, vested plates guard and shield

The man stands tall and strong with chiseled face, steady, solid, sure, ready

The calling to respond and aid, serve selflessly, sacrifices made

The heart sometimes broken, sometimes full, drives him forward, onward

The will in control, resolve, conviction, discipline and volition

The soul moved by mercy, accountability, knowing humanity, charity

The courage results and rises in danger, overcomes anger, wins

The love of God and family, motivates, hydrates, sustains.

vmn
11/15

TRAINING IS EVERYTHING

"We are what we repeatedly do. Excellence, then, is not an act, but a habit."
- Aristotle -

We received calls from eight couples in two months. They were people we knew who read my first book, A CHiP on my Shoulder. The reason? They were having marital problems. Because my California Highway Patrol husband, Brent, and I were open and forthright about our struggles in the book, others felt comfortable confiding in us. For weeks we listened to stories of serious communication issues, affairs, fights, and parenting problems. It was exhausting.

We had a free night at home so I popped in a movie. I chose Fireproof. I'd seen it before, but after hearing about so many issues, I thought a story about a marriage saved would be encouraging. Brent was on his computer in the other room, listening.

Toward the end of the movie, the main character, Caleb, knelt by the bedside of his wife, who was bitter. Their marriage was nearly over for many reasons, but he'd taken on a 40-day challenge from his father to actively love her no matter the response. The process changed Caleb, but his wife wasn't easily convinced. In tears, he apologized, recommitting to love her despite her filing for divorce. I was in tears, too.

I heard a voice from the kitchen, "We are trained NOT to go there."

Huh?

"What'd you say?" I asked.

Brent went on to explain that a level of vulnerability like that could be death to a police officer. Officers are trained to shut out feelings so that they can be objective, read the situation, and respond appropriately. There is a purposeful silencing of emotional reaction and a building up of skills to take control no matter what madness or sadness is taking place. Their lives depend on it.

This conversation stuck with me. Could it be that one reason law enforcement officers struggle to have good marriages is that their training works against the connection and vulnerability needed for intimacy? The more I talk with police wives, officers, and those who counsel them, I think this is true in many ways.

Are the people who are sworn to protect, at times making deep sacrifices for our community's well-being, doomed to unhappy and unhealthy marriages? Is it almost impossible for a marriage to make it if at least one person is a cop? Some say that it is.

Marriage is difficult. Merging two individual lives into one life together takes grit, humility, and commitment. It's tough work. It takes trained effort. But it is not impossible.

As an officer, you were educated and trained to do what you do. At the California Highway Patrol, all officers first undergo cadet training at our live-in academy. One of Brent's favorite things is to visit the academy on the first morning cadets report. They are given explicit instructions and then put under intense pressure while they attempt to follow those instructions. It is an exercise that is designed to humble them, get their attention, and orient them toward success in the months to come. After a grueling 27 weeks, the officers that emerge are completely different, having been educated, trained, and even transformed by the process. They are prepared to take on the complex and difficult duty of policing in the 21st century.

Most couples (of all occupations) don't get training to do marriage well. Some clergy have a short process of premarital counseling as a requirement for their services, others don't. Engagements concentrate heavily on wedding ceremony preparation, and then that day comes and goes. The couple is then given a license to live happily ever after until they die. That's a tall order given what life hands out for anyone, but add the complications and risks that a crisis-driven career creates—well, there are a lot of broken marriages.

Cops are cops through and through. It's not just a job, it's an identity that tends to affect all of life. It's an inherent calling to something significant, meaningful, and difficult; therefore relationships differ from others who are not in law enforcement. With these realities in mind coupled with a strong support for police officers, this book approaches marriage through principles of law enforcement training, concepts, and police culture to strengthen relationships.

I am not an officer. But I have lived the life with my officer, eager to understand who he is and what makes him tick. My first book, A CHiP on my Shoulder, was about my own experience as a cop wife and conversations with other spouses. I saw consistent themes—same issues, different details. It was written primarily for spouses and supports both the law enforcement career and the family. But it takes two people to make a marriage work. CHiP was directed toward spousal roles, difficulties, influence, and inspires spouses to accept and work towards a great life together within the confines of a law enforcement career. Your perspective as a peace officer is very different, and therefore a different approach must be taken.

I am writing to you, a peace officer, with respect and full support. This book is based on surveys from over 930 officers and spouses from all over the United States and Canada, and interviews with over 75 officers, spouses, therapists, and dispatchers. Examples are included from my own marriage—things Brent and I did right, and things we had to learn. It includes extensive research and provides insight gleaned from many years of involvement with police families. I had several key law enforcement officers, spouses, and therapists review this manuscript. Their feedback was thoughtfully incorporated. It was important to get this right.

All of the stories included are true to the best of my knowledge. Most names mentioned are pseudonyms. I have been given permission to use their stories or quotes, with the exception of anonymous inclusions from the online survey.

A Marriage in Progress was written with all law enforcement families in mind. There are many non-traditional relationships that make up the law enforcement community, and so the principles and stories are written to be universal. There are also many officers who have been married more than once. This book is not about what you should've done in the past, but rather what you can do now. Any current long-term relationship can benefit.

At the end of each chapter, you'll find a question or two for personal contemplation, a thought to discuss with your spouse, and an application suggestion. Any good training manual is useless unless there is an implementation of the information. Every chapter concludes with a quote of support for police from well-known people. Finally, if you find you need a break in between some of the more intense sections of A Marriage in Progress, refer to the Comic Relief section after chapter twelve.

Thank you for what you contribute to our communities. You sacrifice a lot for this career. You shouldn't have to sacrifice your family, too. My hope is to provide perspectives, tools, and motivation specifically designed to encourage, equip, and empower you to thrive in your marriage and family. If you find this to be the case, it is then up to you to put these concepts into practice.

Mindset determines actions. Consistent actions determine habits. Habits determine outcomes. That's training for a marriage in progress.

CHAPTER ONE

THE JOB:
ITS CALLING AND COST

"The mystery of human existence lies not in just staying alive,
but in finding something to live for."
Fyodor Dostoyevsky, The Brothers Karamasov

I've invested over 27 years of my life to supporting, loving, and respecting my husband, Brent.

The patrol was the first decision we made together as an engaged couple. Five weeks after we were married, he reported to the California Highway Patrol (CHP) Academy in West Sacramento, California, which is a live-in academy. Every weekend I washed and ironed his cadet uniforms and then kissed him goodbye as he left each Sunday night to make the two-hour return trip. Every Friday night I anticipated his arrival home.

After six months of training and a celebratory graduation, we left family, friends, and all that was familiar to report to his first assignment in Los Angeles—three weeks before Christmas. We learned to live, drive, and thrive in the great metropolis, blending into millions of anonymous people.

Between his shifts, I listened to stories of ruined lives, stupid people, interactions with Los Angeles Police Department and Los Angeles Sheriff's Department, and the humorous escapades his fellow cops entertained while arresting drunks, treating the injured, and dealing with the poorest behavior humanity can offer.

I also watched him change.

I wondered if these changes were normal, so asked a wife of Brent's classmate if she noticed anything different in her husband. "I have no idea what you're talking about," she assured me. Embarrassed, I turned away, thinking there was something wrong with me. With us.

Three weeks later I learned that this same woman left her husband, which resulted in divorce. She just didn't want to talk about it, didn't want me to pry, and probably had already made up her mind that she was done.

This wasn't going to be my story.

There are many casualties of a career in law enforcement. Lots of spouses have left and filed for divorce. Some have stayed only to become hardened and bitter. There are many children who started out excited and proud to be the son or daughter of a police officer, but years of absence or harsh treatment have made them angry and estranged.

There are also many police couples that have grown old together, enjoying retirement in their latter years as they've weathered years of the good and the bad. There are many children who've followed in their parent's footsteps, either becoming peace officers themselves, or marrying into the Blue Line Family. Many police officers are amazing parents.

So what's the difference between relationships that turn out well and those that don't? This is a question I've been asking for years, especially in preparation for this book. Interactions and interviews with many police families have given me much to ponder—in my marriage, and in the marriages of others.

I've learned there's a lot we can do to prevent from becoming tragic statistics. Instead we can thrive in our family lives, actually growing through the journey; celebrating milestones together like retirement and enjoying grown children and grandchildren.

Brent and I were blessed to bring four awesome people into this world. Their lives enrich ours and create balance and perspective. The CHP has always been a major part of this crazy life we lead. We are blue and gold (CHP colors) through and through.

This journey hasn't been easy, and there have been many bumps along the way. But we've done it regardless. Not perfectly, but well. You can too.

Who You Are, What You Do

I love uniforms. Pressed creases and shiny accouterments that sparkle in the sunlight. The mixed scent of leather and sweat. The faint creak of freshly polished shoes and the swish of the gun belt as officers prepare for duty. These senses bring comfort to me.

Each badge or shield represents a soul, an oath, and a determination. The leather represents protection and sweat reminds me of the sacrifices. The shoes carry that officer into some dark places.

Every May, law enforcement agencies across America honor those who've made the ultimate sacrifice. I appreciate not only those who have given all, but those who have sworn to protect and serve, and risk life and livelihood as a protector of our society's peace and order.

You are more than a uniform. Your contribution is vital to our communities, restoring peace to disorder. But we also ask a lot of you, probably a higher standard than anyone else. In A CHiP on my Shoulder, I wrote:

"To be a cop is to be many different occupations all at once. He/ she has to be an athlete, a soldier, a scientist, a researcher, a paramedic, a NASCAR driver, a gun expert and marksman, a counselor, a chemist, a diplomat, a wrestler, a runner, a mechanic, a writer, and a lawyer. He must have a mother's intuition, the nose of a bloodhound, the patience of a farmer, the compassion of Mother Teresa, and the tenacity of a 2-year-old. He must make peace out of chaos, comfort the anguished, discern criminal behavior from stupidity, and make split second decisions that may have life-altering consequences. He's expected to be polite when verbally abused, keep people safe in dangerous situations, respect those who disrespect him, and understand the intentions of those who are misbehaving. He must constantly confront evil, and remain unsullied. He must be quick to respond, though sometimes the calls stack up.

He must be able to speak police shorthand on radios that may be difficult to hear, especially when in heavy or fast-moving traffic. He is constantly second guessed on his actions, criticized for his demeanor, mocked for his diet and feared for his authority. He's a threat, a target, a punisher, yet is a rescuer, a protector, and in some cases, a savior.

"Given these considerations, society's expectations on our law enforcement are just short of impossible. But day to day, they report for duty, not knowing what the shift will offer. They put on their badges and try to do the best they can to fulfill the expectations of those they serve." (p. 76-77)

The Job You Love

With these responsibilities, there are benefits.

Cops talk about "drive the car, shoot the gun." Some of the fun things that draw people to a career in law enforcement are weapons, radio equipment, computers, special details, vehicles, dogs, and protective gear. This is a definite benefit to being a peace officer.

You receive a salary for a job that will continue to be a need. Obviously some departments have more resources than others. But the fact remains, there will always be crime, and therefore there will always be a need for the law enforcement profession.

What you do matters, even when you have doubts that you're making any impact. My guess is that this is important to you. The very make-up of a peace officer is motivated by a sense of meaning, making a difference in the lives of others. Making the world a little safer because a criminal is off the street. Feeling deep pride when you arrest a dangerous thug who's eluded justice for far too many victims. Or the satisfaction of coming to the aid of a family in trouble on a dark night. Law enforcement is a meaningful career.

I was reminded of the awesome responsibility our husbands have.
When they put on that uniform and badge every day and go out into
what is sometimes a very frightening world, remember that they
have taken an oath. An oath not just to protect and serve.
That oath also includes the promise that when they are spit at,
yelled at, and called horrible names, they are expected to stand
there and take it without fighting back. An oath that requires
them to treat not only the public, but their friends and family
with respect on or off duty. That is a HUGE load to carry every day.
It takes a very special person to be able to to this job.
Please remember this the next time he comes home grumpy
or has to stay late. We need to be their soft place to land.
Connie, CHP wife

You have the power to affect life change. Recently Brent received a call from a colleague, Ron, from years past. Ten years prior, Ron's son had been arrested for DUI by Brent's officers. When Brent learned that the suspect was Ron's son, he notified him and offered support. Now, many years later, Ron thanked Brent, and showed him pictures of how his son had grown up, joined the army and fought for our country in Iraq and Afghanistan. He said the arrest was the best thing that could've happened to him. His son had been on a track of destruction when the arrest occurred. Justice intervened, changing the course of his life. Now that is meaningful.

"People sleep peaceably in their beds at night only because
rough men stand ready to do violence on their behalf."
George Orwell

When Kim from Georgia was with a small agency she arrested a young, black male for breaking into a school and stealing food. It turned out his mother was a druggie and wasn't caring for him, so he tried getting food for himself. She ended up arresting his mother and got the young man into a home with his aunt. Just another day on the force. Fast forward years later.

Kim was working a breast cancer fundraiser and ran into the kid's aunt. She told Kim that her nephew had gotten his grades up, graduated high school and went on to college. She believed it was because of what Kim had done for him that day. The young man credited Kim for helping him get his life on track. The aunt hugged Kim, and with many tears declared that she had saved his life.

Mike had been chasing and arresting a juvenile named Joe for several years. Joe was a frequent flyer on the verge of committing some serious crimes. Just before Joe turned 18, Mike arrested him and talked to him about how his life was going to change once he became an adult. Mike didn't see Joe again. Several years later, Mike received a letter from Joe, who had moved to Arizona and became a deputy sheriff for Maricopa County. After being on for five years, Joe got hurt on the job, so became an investigator for an attorney's office. He thanked Mike for that talk—it had completely changed his life. He wanted Mike to know he'd made something of his life and thanked him. Mike kept that letter posted in his locker to remind him every shift that, "I'm here and I can do some good."

Years later, Mike was rear ended while out at a traffic accident and was forced to retire because of his injuries. When he cleaned out his locker, Mike was very disappointed when he couldn't find the letter. He thought back to Joe's words and example of moving onto something else after he was injured, and was personally inspired. The favor was repaid, and the help came full circle. "If you can help one person, your career is worth it," says Mike. "Fortunately, in my 27 years, I was able to hear from several that I had helped. That makes all the difference."

Almost every week I hear about acts of compassion police officers do for people. George built a wheelchair ramp for an elderly man with cancer. Derrick bought groceries for a homebound elderly woman who had no food at Christmas, including a beautiful poinsettia. Michael took a wayward young man and spoke truth into his life, meeting with him on a regular basis for several years. That man is now a model citizen with a job and a family, making contributions to society instead of wasting his life behind bars.

How many people can say they've made a profound difference in someone's life? You're there when people are at their worst—a little compassion goes a very long way, whether you're able to see the result of it or not.

There is a sense of pride in this profession, and accomplishment when you've earned the right to wear the uniform. You are among the two percent of the population that is trained to do this job. If you had landed in any other profession, you may not feel the same satisfaction, because this profession is tailored to who you are.

But this job also introduces a host of challenges.

Individual Challenges

Job stress is high—dealing with mad, sad, and bad people day in and day out takes its toll.

Department politics creep up here and there, depending on the leadership. We all know it isn't a given that all cops make great leaders. This can be a source of significant stress.

In a career that is physical and deals with crime, the risks of injury or death are higher than with other vocations. Add the fact that you work long hours without breaks, eat poorly or too much, and the risk increases. Fatigue, too, is a powerful and silent enemy that increases your risks for injury or illness.

Without proper prevention and intervention, your health will suffer. A lifetime of eating fast food, pounding energy drinks, and lack of exercise can pack on weight and raise blood pressure, increasing the risk for diabetes, heart attack, cancer, and other diseases. Out there on the road you are also exposed to hazardous materials, smoke, and other substances that can affect your health. Coupled with the long-term health effects of hypervigilance, which I explain further in chapter two, you have a higher risk of suffering health consequences.

> *"It is easily forgotten and often overlooked that it is an awful life*
> *experience for a police officer to be placed in such a situation.*
> *It is an often unappreciated role these men and women step into.*
> *Many folks don't care to see them around when all is well.*
> *Few really want to do the job that they hold, and are all in an*
> *uproar when they are not there when we really need them,*
> *and heaven forbid that they should be allowed to go unwhipped*
> *after they make the hard and unpleasant choices."*

Judge quoted in his ruling in a lawsuit over a
fatal shooting by an officer

If that weren't enough, you must endure accusations, intense scrutiny, and even prejudice. Although this isn't anything new, the intensity seems to be at an all time high. The Ferguson Effect has been taking a toll on departments across the country, as the media and others question and critique every tactic and decision of those who protect and serve. The in-your-face lack of support by some citizens and lawmakers who cower to their demands intensifies an already difficult job.

Relational Challenges

All of these individual challenges contribute to problems at home. Moodiness, conflict, and poor communication result from stress and fatigue. Many cops have a tendency to isolate when things pile up inside, which in turn is misinterpreted by your loved ones as apathy. They are unintentionally hurt, and if there isn't intervention of some kind, bitterness can develop.

Peace officers have been trained to compartmentalize on duty. Shut down emotion. Distrust. Hide, stuff, downplay and ignore feelings below the surface. But if this compartmentalization is continued into off-duty life, it can be detrimental to connectedness with others you love. They will misunderstand, take on responsibility for, fall victim to, and eventually suffer under the weight of unresolved soul wounds. More on this later.

Physically, your job sometimes requires you to be away from your spouse and children. Unfortunately you're going to miss some of those important moments.

> *"On Christmas Eve, we both had simultaneous arrests,*
> *arrived at the jail to say, 'Merry Christmas!'"*
> Amanda, Texas

This career may also affect your sex life. Images you've seen or crimes you've investigated can seep into your mind's eye at inopportune moments, and take away desire for sex. Stress is not exactly an aphrodisiac, either. Intimacy suffers when we fail to voice what's going on beneath the surface.

Unless you are just starting your career as a police officer, you already know the challenges. But what you may not know is how to combat them. The chapters that follow are designed to equip you and your family to communicate within the realities of these challenges.

A Few Words For Women Cops

Several years ago I went to a women's retreat in the mountains in the middle of winter. It doesn't snow much in the lower elevations in California, but the night before we were to leave, it dumped several inches. To get home, we had to maneuver a steep, windy road that was covered in snow. We inched down the mountain until all traffic stopped. There was a vehicle that had slipped off the road and was stuck. A couple of deputies had tried to pull the car out, but they became stuck themselves, blocking the entire road. Everyone waited. After a while, a tall, confident woman in a CHP SUV drove up, took charge of the situation and had everyone unstuck and out of the way in ten minutes. She told everyone who was waiting that she would lead us all down the hill in a caravan. It worked! It was a proud moment for my beloved CHP, and for women.

If you are a female police officer, you've proven yourself as a comrade in a male-dominated profession. You've endured the training, and you've gone through the rites of passage. You've earned the respect even though you might've been doubted. And you've made the profession better by bringing the thoughts and perspectives of a woman.

> *"Women entering law enforcement today still have the opportunity to be groundbreakers and influence law enforcement, both tactically and politically. They can be role models for young women. They can modify some of the rigid authoritarian practices that have contributed to negative public opinion and distrust of the police. They provide a needed service for women who are the victims of rape or domestic violence and find it hard to confide in male officers.*
> *Culturally conditioned to be nurturers, women are uniquely suited to deal with quality-of-life issues and relationship building, which are the cornerstones of community policing— the wave of the future."*
> Dr. Ellen Kirschman, I Love a Cop

Not a lot of women can do what you do. Myself included.

You have toughness about you—inner strength that rises beyond the normal emotional tendencies that we celebrate as women. You must have inner confidence that takes the flak that comes from others and renders it powerless. It is a beautiful thing to behold when a woman in uniform blends her femininity with command authority.

"The reality is most females are simply smaller in stature and weaker physically than their male peers. Everyone knows that, even if it's not politically correct to point that out. I'm 5'3" and 135 pounds, built more like a gymnast than a prizefighter! But what I lacked in stature, I made up for with tenacity and a quick wit. I became quite adept at verbally convincing people just how capable I am."

Crystal, Montana

But some of the traits that make you a great cop can be the very things that work against your relationships at home. For one, the strength and confidence you exude may be intimidating.

I had a conversation with a female CHP officer about A CHiP on my Shoulder. "I'd love to say that I had someone to read your book," she sighed. "But I don't want to marry another uniform. And they are pretty much the only men who can handle a female who's a cop. So I shall probably remain single."

Anne from Ohio commented, "My ex didn't understand my job or my schedule and having to work second shift and holidays with Tuesdays and Wednesdays off. I carried a gun and he didn't; it bothered his ego."

The crazy schedules and long hours are difficult on a relationship in any marriage. But as an officer you are a strong woman; you know how to assert yourself, especially in confrontations. If your spouse is intimidated by your strong personality, conflict arises at the very core of who you are as an individual. Competition is a complication that makes it difficult to mesh and morph and live an intimate life together. But it is still not impossible.

I recently met a female police officer that's been married for over 20 years to her high school sweetheart. I asked her what the secret was to the success of her marriage. "I don't know, really," she said with a twinkle in her eye. "We've been together since we were kids. We can't imagine life without each other." After a few questions, I surmised that since they knew each other so young, they were used to adapting to change throughout their time together. He respects what she does, and vice versa. They had learned to accept each other as cop and non-cop, finding that common ground.

They figured out early that mutual respect is key to marital success, as are attitudes and actions that communicate respect.

Karen was working graves. Working as a flight paramedic on a CHP helicopter, a terrible thunderstorm ripped through the area, forcing them to land. At the time she wasn't carrying a cell phone, and thought her husband Mike would be asleep. She didn't want dispatch to call to wake him up to say she's okay. She'd weather out the storm and get back up in the air. Well, Mike stayed up worrying, and was livid when she returned because she hadn't called to let him know she was OK.

Just because you're the protector in your profession, doesn't mean your non-cop spouse won't try to protect you. Most men traditionally take on that role, and even though you are not a damsel in distress, this is a completely natural thing for a guy. If you take this as an insult or as evidence that he doesn't think you're good at what you do, you may need to rethink. He knows you can take care of yourself, but I don't have to tell you there are some really bad people out there. Like a woman at home who sometimes worries about the what-ifs her husband faces, your spouse is not that different. It's not a question of your ability; it's the realities of life and risk on the street. And the fact that he cares for you.

Character On Duty and Off

It takes great character to do what peace officers do. It takes discipline, self-control, patience, and tenacity. You have a sense of altruism, but it is balanced with courage to speak truth and require accountability to the law.

You are trained to run to chaos. You feel fear like others, but an inner character dares death, steps in and up to the task at hand—to protect and serve in the ways in which you were trained.

I think back to my husband's training. At first, academy personnel knocked the wind out of him and his classmates. They stripped the cadets of the faulty foundations they had come in with. Pride. False sense of ability. Selfishness.

The instructors put the cadets in impossible situations and demanded they perform despite the obstacles. There was a purpose: to make them teachable and trainable. Then the instructors began to rebuild them. To give them tools and instill a will to survive, take charge of chaos, and to respond appropriately under severe conditions. By the end of his training, my husband was rebuilt and ready for action. He was a trained observer. He knew what to do in crisis. He was confident.

Training instilled discipline and built character, driven by a sense of duty and honor. The way we practice our lives determines how we will respond to crisis. Our character—the things we value, the integrity we live out, and the conviction that there are some things worth fighting for and against will step up—or not—in the midst of the trials that come our way.

The following is an unofficial working list of advice some of the instructors at our California Highway Patrol give to our cadets. It is lovingly referred to as The Rant:

- Look at the bad guys professionally, not personally; it's your job to be the good guy, and their job is to be the bad guy.
- Be a quiet professional: tit for tat just leads to trouble.
- Live the job—this will keep you alive.
- Be gracious with outside agencies, their uniform doesn't matter when you're in a shit storm and need help.
- Be grateful...do you really need to be that toxic person at work that spreads cancer?
- Your employment is NOT an entitlement.
- You wield a lot of power; you've been entrusted with a lot of power. Don't muck it up!
- If you do mess up, OWN it. Lie, and you'll lose everything.
- Lead by example, good leadership is also good followership.

- Bitching doesn't solve problems; it compounds them.
- Other officers need tough love sometimes.
- Carry your pistol every day. Don't leave it in the car with your badge and ID.
- Be patient with people...even stupid people.
- Don't ever forget the excitement you have right now and your passion for the job.
- Don't let others influence you into a wrong moral/ethical decision.
- Start your 451/457 NOW.
- Don't live up to your paycheck (spending).
- Don't fish from the company pier, or date people you arrest.
- Agree on rearing style before marriage and before children.
- Communicate to future spouses the expectations and non-expectations of personal life—it is a crisis-driven career.

Heroes are made in the quietness of soul resolve, in the mundane episodes of repetition, and in the decisions made day to day. Then, when duty calls, the choice is made to respond, simply yet readily. But does this character extend to your off-duty time—in your family?

Do you discipline your time to build up your spouse and kids? Do you use self-control in your attitude and tone of voice with them? Do you follow through with that sense of altruistic duty when it comes to your marriage? Are you patient?

There are many officers who will readily reach into a fiery vehicle and pull out a kid trapped in their car seat. But ask an off-duty cop to dig deep and save his marriage? Not as instant and dramatic, but just as heroic.

Will you be a hero in character to your spouse, to your kids? To those who look up to you? In uniform and out? There's not much difference in the call. Who you are off duty is the same as on; you just wear different clothes. It is vital to your relationships to take the instilled discipline, built character, and the fierce dedication and apply it at home. This attitude may not make the six o'clock news, but there is a significant contribution to generations to come.

Proactive vs. Reactive Marriage

Most marriages are lived day to day. A couple lives life, responding to whatever the moment holds. The next day is the same. And the next day. No particular goals or plan, just chillin' through life. This describes a reactive marriage. When conflict arises, it is met with reaction to the symptom. Depending on personalities and temperaments, this may or may not go well.

A proactive marriage is different in that there is purposeful attention paid to the relationship on a week-to-week, year to year basis. There's a vision—a thought process on what you want to build in your life together. Having an excellent marriage comes from proactively building a foundation of shared knowledge of each other, tailored communication, and time spent investing into you as a couple. There's an investment—placing a priority on building a life together purposefully. Then you as a couple plan how to accomplish the vision.

Your career and training are largely proactive. You're not just a first responder, although that is part of it. You train for the possibility of what could happen so you're ready to deal with a situation if and when it does. You have methodical ways of investigating; you have a plan. If you're working the road, you do a sweep of your beat—making sure there aren't stranded motorists or other problems. Perhaps you do community events, reaching out to the public to create supportive mutual trust, which pays off in the long run. Excellence in policing comes from proactive training—building a foundation of knowledge and tactical know-how for what could happen.

Our relationships are similar.

Some of Brent's and my most memorable dates are when we dream together. We talk about things we want to do or create and why. Goals. Plans. What we envision for our children and us. We've done it for years.

Nowadays, we reminisce about how things were when the kids were small, and laugh at how we would do things differently. We are starting to talk about what to do when he retires. We talk about dreams and plans for our money. We talk about things we want to do with the kids now that they're older. That's proactive.

Brent and I share a Google calendar. His events and reminders are in green, mine in blue. Every day there is a name in green across the top of the day—my name or one of our kids. This everyday note to Brent is the reminder to interact proactively in some way with that person. A text, a date, a phone call; it is a reminder to engage in relationship with one of us directly every day. This is proactive.

As law enforcement families, we must be proactive. We've got to build up each other and our relationships when we have the chance, because there are seasons of this career in which we run out of steam. Like when money is tight and the kids are being chronically naughty, or when someone has a health issue. Or when there are protestors in Ferguson or New York night after night and it's mandatory overtime for weeks. Or when there is a serial rapist that you're one step behind and you won't give up the chase. Or when your spouse is working long hours on their own work project and it's wearing on you and the kids. That time spent building into you as a couple will sustain for awhile until you can pick up more time together later. Relationally speaking, running on empty for long periods of time leads to brokenness, bitterness, and parting ways.

Dispatchers: Heard But Not Seen

A group of us listened intently to a recording of the radio traffic of an on-duty incident. The dispatcher's voice was smooth, professional. He responded clearly as the officer announced he was attempting to pull over a suspected stolen vehicle. Silence. Then, something illegible came across the radio. We had to rewind it a couple of times to understand that it was an 11-99 plea from the officer. But the dispatcher picked up on it immediately—professionally and calmly initiating radio protocol, sending officers his way. It was hard to listen to the rest, as this call ended in losing an officer to a gunshot to the face.

The dispatcher wasn't physically present at the scene, but this dispatcher was the calming, professional presence that brought in the cavalry. In the chaos, his mind was sharp, his words crisp, and those who heard it later were amazed.

Telecommunicators are the unseen partners on the radio—they are listening, responding, giving officers the support they need to do their job on the streets. But they don't get the satisfaction to visually see the outcomes of the calls, or the end results of what their work produces. Once the phone is hung up, the emphasis goes to the officer who is there and on scene.

Like law enforcement officers, there are only about two to three percent of the population who can do this job. Dispatchers have a high turnover rate within the public safety profession, about 17-19% according to the Journal of Emergency Dispatch. "In other words, two out of every ten telecommunicators leave the profession each year. A telecommunicator's career averages two to three years. Reasons for high turnover include: low knowledge, skills, and abilities (KSAs) of applicants leading to costly errors and terminations; the 'adjustment factor' or inability to conform to the demands of the profession; disciplinary issues; stress; low pay; scheduling conflicts and rotating shifts; workload; lack of leadership; inefficient training programs; and limited promotional opportunity."

"I have a baby, and there's a dog barking..."
(Insert airhead accent here).
The dispatcher sighs and responds,
"Well, I'm really glad that your ovaries work,
but our officers are at a head-on fatal right now.
You'll have to wait."

Dispatchers deal with the self-centered underbelly of society and they hear the most precious angels on earth. They don't get out much—working in a close environment for long hours. They go into the job with a wide-eyed sense of wanting to make a difference. They have the morbid sense of humor and tend to harden with time, just like officers.

This book is addressed to peace officers, but much of this book applies to dispatchers as well. Many times dispatchers are underappreciated and overlooked when it comes to the realities of law enforcement. And the difficulty they go through on the other side of that radio goes home with them.

> *"I like that it's never the same day twice. Every time I pick up*
> *the phone it is something different. I never get bored.*
> *I talk to the ebbs and flows of society. I talk with everyone—*
> *a WWII vet who is having a heart attack but doesn't*
> *want to bother anyone, to a 12-year-old reporting child*
> *abuse because her parents took away her phone."*
> Dispatcher, California

Dispatchers work shift work. This affects their families.

Dispatchers want to protect. Serve. See justice and diligence prevail. Help people. The motivations are very much the same as officers; the role is different.

Since dispatchers only hear what officers and the public relay, they tend to develop their own visual ideas of scenes. Most of the time they imagine things worse than they are. There are calls that stay with them, just like officers.

They hand over most of the control to those who are on scene, many times not hearing the outcome. The stress is significant.

> *"Dispatchers don't give themselves enough credit.*
> *One job is the emergency, the next is the nut case,*
> *the 911 little kid, and you have to be able to get the information*
> *quickly and then make split second decisions. There are a lot of*
> *people who cannot do that job. Kudos to you!"*
> Kim, California

Kudos to those who are dispatchers. Thank you for holding officers in your capable hands. Thank you for what you do, and the sacrifices that go along with your service.

*"My hubby is so modest and reserved, he would never tell
anybody this. There is a female dispatcher that he got to know
during a special assignment. He was chatting with her and learned
she's going through a very tough time with a nasty divorce and child
custody fight. The lawyer's fees have set her so far back she's two
car payments behind and if she loses her car, she'll lose her job.
He bought a sympathy card and drove to her watch office and gave
her a card with a $1000 check in it to cover her car payments and
more. We are by no means wealthy, but we received our tax returns
and I always count that as "extra" money. He asked me ahead of time
if it was okay and I said yes, of course. It really touched me that he
reached out to this single mom who is struggling. He said, 'she has my
life in her hands every day.' I want dispatchers to know how much
you are appreciated."*
Marci, Spouse, California

. . . .

Think: Why did you go into law enforcement? Was it what you expected?

Debrief: What are difficulties in your relationships that seem to have their root cause in your job? What burdens are placed on your family by your job?

Strategic Action: Consider options to ease the burdens of your job on your family. Sometimes small changes can make all the difference.

*"You couldn't pay me enough to be a law enforcement officer.
Their job is a tough job. You have to solve people's problems,
you have to baby-sit people, you have to always be doing this c
at-and-mouse game with the bad guys.
My respect for them is immense."*
Christopher Meloni

CHAPTER TWO

IT'S ALL ABOUT YOU!

"I go to work to escape home. I go home to escape work.
At all times I'm where I want to be."
Rob, Officer, Livermore Police Department

Every single one of your relationships has one thing in common: You.

Everything you do, everything you are, everything you go through, and everything you choose has a lasting impact on those you share your life with. Whether you like it or not. Whether you acknowledge it or deny it. Whether you trust others with yourself, or choose isolation. Who you are affects others—positively and negatively. We are interconnected. We are accountable to one another.

Every relationship begins with what we can control: self. There are strategies you can put into practice in your relationships that will make a positive difference and can influence your family in a positive way.

At the beginning of any journey of transformation (like civilian to officer), it's important to evaluate your mindset, and change it from self-focused individual to team member.

If you embrace the realities of who you are, what you do, how it affects you naturally and negatively, then you can learn to change your tendencies. You can evaluate your weaknesses, bolster your strengths, and learn new techniques that will help all of your relationships.

With the right training.

Your Family Needs You

Dr. Todd Langus, a former police officer who is now a counselor to first responders and military, says, "Cops are so willing to give everything for their work. They're trained for it. But there is a separation—a missed application of integrity, dedication and honor at home. We handle home life like we approach a call—a 20-minute fix. Out on the road, this will work. At home, very little is fixed in 20 minutes. That's just a Band-Aid."

You are a rescuer. You want to right wrongs and correct behavior to bring about peace and justice. There are policies and procedures. You apply your training by administering the proper protocols and you solve problems. Then you're on to the next call.

> *"Everyone thinks of changing the world,*
> *but no one thinks of changing himself."*
> Leo Tolstoy

Relationships aren't about rescuing, or fixing. They're about interaction. Listening is crucial—often longer than you deem necessary. Relationships are about understanding and relating; changing your own behavior or attitude to relate better. Communicate better. Love better. You are needed by your spouse and by your kids. Not to rescue them. Not to fix them. But to love them. Actively. Inconveniently. Purposefully. Unselfishly. Consistently.

But to do this, you've got to start with you. Self-awareness is first on the list.

Be Self-Aware

"I just don't realize when I'm being a dick," said the retired chief of police.

"Can I quote you on that?" I joked.

He went on to explain that he used to come home in a mode of operation in his demeanor—and his loved ones would suffer the effects of this demeanor. In other words, he was grumpy, and didn't realize it.

"How can you not know that you're being a jerk to your family?" I challenged.

The other cops at the table took turns defending his point, giving me examples of how eight to twelve hours a day they deal with people and have a certain way they relate to customers. They speak clearly, assertively, and authoritatively. It's second nature.

When they are at home, they continue to speak assertively and authoritatively, and this offends. Jared said he didn't realize what he's doing until his wife came back with the same tone, and that jarred him. It was a wake up call, and he gave her future permission to let him know when he reverts back to that mode.

Later, another officer came to me privately.

"Years ago, when I was a Marine, I had no idea I was being such a jerk to Carissa. One day she was at the store and I was cleaning up around the house. I came upon her diary, and opened it to see what it was. I was shocked to read about how I had been treating her. I had no idea. When she returned home, I apologized. Since then I've tried to be more self-aware."

Impatience. Harsh words. A tendency to interrupt or argue with your spouse or kids. Brusqueness. Bossiness. Irritation. Correction. Criticism. You are in tune with it on duty; you're paying attention. But if you aren't self-aware, this may be what you portray to your family.

Even if you aren't aware of it, this wounds your loved ones. It may be just a graze, but it still hurts. Add together enough of these minor injuries, and you've got a problem. They can be internalized as intentional disrespect or lack of love, or seen as fighting words to retaliate against.

If we aren't aware of the dozens of tiny wounds we cause, there is, of course, no apology. Resentment builds a wall that separates and protects the victim; and then distrust sets in. Over time, resentment compounds into bitterness. Depending on your loved ones' personalities they will withdraw or come out swinging. At the least, they will lose respect for you and dismiss you as a total insensitive jerk.

Talk to your spouse about this. Ask them if they see this tendency in you, and how it affects your relationship.

"Police work is on my husband's mind a lot."
Jamie, Texas

Avoid Isolation

Sometimes our marriages operate as two separate people living alone in our homes. Police officers have a tendency toward this. Your job has trained you to keep the things you deal with and see inside—you don't want to relive it, and/or you want to protect your family by "not bringing it into the home." On its face, this seems like the right thing to do. It's a form of protection. It's an attempt at keeping the home free and innocent.

Truth is, you will inevitably bring your job into your home—because those images are inside you, and have imprinted themselves on your mind and your soul. Refusing to acknowledge, relive, or share the things that are bothering you inside will isolate you from your spouse and other loved ones. I think of it as a retaining wall erected so the insides don't spill out.

Seems like a good idea—and you've got to do this on duty. But instead of the images of the street, you're introducing confusion into your home. From a spouse's perspective, this is worse. Not knowing what you are dealing with separates, and more often than not we misunderstand. If you don't tell your spouse, he/she may misdiagnose the problem, and that compounds hurt feelings. If you're bothered by something, tell your spouse, even if it's something generic. You never know, she just might surprise you with insight, or bring comfort to you in a way you didn't expect.

Understand that over time, unresolved issues and images grow and fester and come out in other ways. If there's pain, you may be tempted to self-medicate. And then you've got another problem.

The other thing that isolation does is keeps you from knowing anything other than your own point of view. When you've talked with witnesses about a crime or an accident, there may have been discrepancies. As you know, the witnesses may not be lying; they just saw the incident through their own point of view. They missed details. They misinterpreted actions. Their recollection was skewed. Even though you are a trained observer, you still have limits to your point of view. Getting others' points of view is crucial, whether it's on the job, or an issue at home. You'll be much closer to knowing the complete truth.

Having people you trust to run things by is how you fight isolation. In Brent's and my years together, I have been one of a handful of people he debriefs his life with. He has friends that are law enforcement and others that aren't that he will talk to. At times in his career, I have been the only ears that hear him. Other times I just don't cut it—he needs a different perspective, or someone more objective than I. This has been something that has sustained Brent, and strengthens our relationship.

Fight Hypervigilance Intentionally

I attended Dr. Kevin Gilmartin's training on Emotional Survival for Law Enforcement. It was the first time I heard him teach in person.

He presented the parts of police officers that others rarely see: the biological and chemical reactions to what they are trained to do, the responses that affect their bodies short and long term, their attitudes and decisions toward the job, and their relationships at home. It was excellent information.

At the break, I spoke with him. The exchange was maybe two minutes in length. But it rocked my world.

Let me back up a bit. A month prior, I attended a conference in Canada. One of the presenters provided information from Gilmartin's book. She gave a great summary of hypervigilance, which is the biological process a peace officer undergoes while on duty, which heightens awareness, thinking abilities, and quick response to anything that arises. She explained that once the shift is over, the body needs to recover, which means off-duty, the body goes into an exact opposite/depression-like state to offset the affects hypervigilance (Gilmartin calls this the hypervigilance biological rollercoaster.) After her presentation, the law enforcement wives had several questions, mainly about how to explain and train their children to understand and accept this phenomenon. I purposed to ask Dr. Gilmartin exactly that.

"Kids should not even be aware of hypervigilance," he asserted in response. He then shifted and sighed in frustration, "Spouses can be the biggest enablers..." I didn't hear anything after that. Enablers?

By then a crowd had gathered. The lady next to me winced. Embarrassed, I excused myself. Later, after three hours of traffic-laden processing in the car and a tearful conversation with Brent, I realized something: I'd used hypervigilance as an excuse for some of the bad habits in our home. And not only was I not engaged in the fight against the hypervigilance rollercoaster, I'd actually resigned myself to it, and joined in with both feet.

I'd believed and taught law enforcement wives about the need to understand who our officers are, how the job affects them, and then deal with it. That isn't the entire picture. We need to understand hypervigilance to not just deal with it or make excuses, but rather join in on the solutions. As a spouse, I am the heart of my home, and my husband's best friend. I'm his backup at home—and the negative biological effects of hypervigilance take place at home.

But it's not just spouses who are responsible to fight against the negative affects of hypervigilance. It's your battle to fight.

Gilmartin didn't write his book so that police families could just understand hypervigilance and make excuses. Gilmartin wrote his book so that we understand hypervigilance, and fight to end it. Your health—physically, emotionally, and relationally—depends on it. Our marital wellness depends on it.

Gilmartin gives some recommendations to combat the hypervigilance rollercoaster. For detailed explanations on these ideas, pick up a copy of Emotional Survival for Law Enforcement. I've added some further tools that my husband and I have implemented in our lives, as well as ideas gleaned from other sources.

If your spouse isn't on board with this idea of hypervigilance or just doesn't know about it, read Gilmartin's book together and talk through it. When he's in your area, get a babysitter and take your spouse. Let your spouse know this isn't an excuse for unpleasant behavior, but the first step in understanding the biological tendencies behind the behavior.

It is your body's natural tendency to go to a depression state after a prolonged adrenaline hike. Once you understand the cycle, ask for backup, and then change it.

Weapons to Fight Hypervigilance

Because hypervigilance is a biological phenomenon, you need to first combat it with diet and exercise.

Whoever does the shopping at your home is key here, but you also make choices of where and what to eat on duty. Brent regularly gives me ideas of what he likes to take to work, and I make sure we have it on hand. He also gave me full permission to try new healthy recipes regularly—as long as I don't use eggplant or dump a bunch of random ingredients into a casserole dish. This has worked well for us.

Ted, a lieutenant with the highway patrol, has taken the idea of exercise to heart. He joined a spin class at his local gym to sweat out the stress. Month after month of consistent exercise not only brought about great results in his weight and stress level, but also provided a trusted social group. He cycles with these guys regularly in the gym and on trips. Ted has also developed deep trust in others that are not in law enforcement.

"Don't forget the push-ups, or you might be pushing up daisies sooner than you'd like."
Chuck Norris

Another recommendation by Dr. Gilmartin is to have other roles and hobbies in your life other than your career.

For Brent, an important role is coach on our son's baseball team.

Brent loves baseball, connecting and teaching kids, and has built a strong bond with our son over the years. For others it may be a runner of a relay team, or four-wheelin' on the weekends, deep sea diving, or cooking for guests. Your roles as mother, father, wife, husband, or mentor build into lives, providing balance in your life, and keeping you from sitting in front of the TV or computer for hours at a time.

If your family is complaining that you spend too much time flipping through your phone, take them on a walk or get out a board game. If you are regularly eating dinner in front of the TV, choose to shut it off and sit around the dinner table. Look your family in the eye and ask, "What was the high point of your day, and the low point of your day?"

It makes every difference for not only your individual wellness, but for your family's wholeness.

An additional way to fight negative hypervigilance tendencies is to renew your mind. As a cop, you are constantly dealing with bad people, sad people, and mad people. Day in, day out. Year after year.

After awhile, it tends to give you a warped sense of who actually makes up our world. It's natural. If you are dealing with liar after liar, you begin to surmise that everyone is a liar, including your wife. If you are dealing with sex offender after sex offender, you begin to think that everyone your daughter wants to date is a potential sex offender. And so on.

Having balance in your life through roles that aren't job-related really helps, but I think cops need more than that. You need counter intelligence.

Dr. Caroline Leaf, in her book, Switch on Your Brain, talks about how recent research is showing that DNA actually changes shape according to our thoughts. "Toxic thinking wears down the brain. The Institute of HeartMath, an internationally recognized, nonprofit research organization that helps people reduce stress, discusses an experiment titled, 'Local and Nonlocal Effects of Coherent Heart Frequencies on Conformational Changes of DNA.' This study showed that thinking and feeling anger, fear, and frustration caused DNA to change shape according to thoughts and feelings. The DNA responded by tightening up and becoming shorter, switching off many DNA codes, which reduced quality expression. So we feel shut down by negative emotions, and our body feels this too. But here's the great part: the negative shutdown or poor quality of the DNA codes was reversed by feelings of love, joy, appreciation and gratitude." The constant negativity you encounter on duty will affect you long term if you don't take steps to counter it. This is biological, natural.

Think about it. You receive information every shift. Much of that information is negative. You train for contact with perps who want to kill you. You have to examine disgusting crime scenes for evidence and clues. Those of you in the jails are consistently dealing with criminal minds that hate you. On the highways, people you pull over are constantly coming up short in terms of decency and morality. But this isn't the total picture of our population.

Here is a list of things to plug into your life that will counter the information you receive on duty.

- Seek out things that are true. You've been trained to investigate. You look for crime and who committed the crime. What about investigating things that are good? I know people who love knowledge. They read books. They learn about the craft of making knives. They look up how to make scrambled eggs by Gordon Ramsay online. They try out new things, like snowboarding, or sailing, or photography.

- Seek out someone who is virtuous. Someone who lives a principled life, a rich life. Someone who has been through some things and gleaned wisdom. Later in life I spent more time with my grandparents. As I shared my life with them, they shared their stories and their wisdom with me. I came to appreciate their long-term perspective, and the peace they had in their faith. Spending time with someone older and wiser is a great way to keep a balanced perspective.

- Seek out someone who is positive, honorable, and has a good reputation. Brent is always looking for new books on leadership. He's amassed a great quantity of papered ideas from leaders of past and present decades. But some of the best advice and perspective came from his meetings with a retired CHP Commissioner and Sacramento County Sheriff, Glen Craig. Before Glen passed away in 2015, Brent had lunch with him on several occasions and ran scenarios by him. Brent asked lots of questions, then sat back and received Glen's wisdom. With this interaction came a renewed sense of purpose and encouragement. He came home refreshed from a simple hour of sitting with a great leader.

• Seek out involvement in things that have an innocence or purity about them. Small children with their sense of pure wonder of the world come to mind, as well as animals that trust so readily.

Evan, a retired cop and military hero shared with tears in his eyes, "My children sustain me." There is something about the bond with your kids that is rejuvenating. I've seen Brent come home from a rough day on-duty, pick up our little blonde daughter, and melt. I've seen his stress disappear while he wrestled with our boys on the living room carpet. I've learned that this is something he needs when he comes home, no matter what we've got going on.

Another idea is shared by over 85,000 police officers worldwide. These officers have chosen to get involved with the Special Olympics Law Enforcement Torch Run. This is where officers carry the Special Olympic Flame of Hope to local, national, and international games, raising money and awareness for Special Olympics along the way. There are many ways officers have gotten involved; not just the torch runs, but through polar plunges, Tip-A-Cop fundraisers, and truck convoys.

At one of these local fundraisers, an amazing little athlete by the name of Karissa swam in a local pool for twelve hours. The Roseville Police Officers' Association was present, SWAT guys, K-9 officers, and other representatives from other departments in the greater Sacramento area. At one point, Karissa grew tired and needed a break. Bo, a retired K-9 from the Galt Police Department, jumped in and swam for her while she rested. It was one of those moments to never forget.

The innocence of these athletes restores a little something back into the soul. If you are interested in joining this amazing community outreach, see the Resource Guide at the back of this book.

• Make time to pull out of the ugly, and spend time in the lovely. Chances are that you spend hours of your day/night in the ugly parts of town on duty. Graffiti. Trash. Filth. But beauty is not far, even if you're working Los Angeles or New York or Detroit. There are pockets of beauty just a drive away. Take some time and get some fresh air near the ocean or in the trees. Take the family—make a day of it.

• Strive for excellence on duty and off. Higher education. Seminars. Marriage retreats. Conferences away. This has been something Brent and I have done throughout our marriage. We've both taken classes, gone to seminars, joined Bible studies, went to conferences, and went away on marriage retreats. It wasn't every year, and not all were designed for our marriage specifically, but it was a way to engage our minds. Striving for excellence in different areas of our lives also gave us opportunities to talk about deep issues and how they pose obstacles within our lives.

• Lastly, make it a practice to look at things in a positive light. If something or someone is worthy of a compliment, let the praise come. If you like something that your spouse does, voice it. If you are impressed with an action or a word by your spouse, or if your kid comes clean right away instead of shifting blame or lying, say it. Encouragement covers a multitude of mistakes.

"When you make a conscious decision to focus and redirect your attention correctly, you change physical matter— your brain and your body change in a healthy way. Purposefully catching your thoughts can control the brain's sensory processing, the brain's rewiring, the neurotransmitters, the genetic expression, and cellular activity in a positive or negative direction. You choose!"
Dr. Caroline Leaf, Switch on Your Brain

Get Some Rest

The typical cop gets four to six hours of sleep per night. This isn't enough.

"The feeling of being tired and needing sleep is a basic drive of nature, like hunger," says Dr. William C. Dement in his book, The Promise of Sleep. "Your sleep drive keeps an exact tally of accumulated waking hours. Like bricks in a backpack, accumulated sleep drive is a burden that weighs down on you. Every hour that you are awake adds another brick to the backpack: the brain's sleep load increases until you go to sleep, when the load starts to lighten." Our bodies generally need one hour of sleep for every two waking hours. Some need more, some less. When you are working long shifts with little sleep in between, you are carrying that heavy load of bricks with you, making everything you do just that much harder.

There are nights when your responsibilities make it impossible to get more than four to six hours. But there are also distractions that you can set aside to give yourself another hour or two. Here are a few tips that will help you to get more/enhanced sleep:

- Watch caffeine, nicotine, and alcohol consumption. Alcohol tends to make you drowsy at first, but can interrupt sleep later in the night.

- Create a bedtime routine. Take a shower, listen to soothing music, or concentrate on breathing/relaxing once it's dark.

- Having sex at bedtime makes tension disappear, and sleep more sound.

- Create a cool, dark and comfortable sleeping area. The bed should be comfortable; it's worth the extra money for a better mattress and pillow and softer sheets. Keep the room cool, and shut off any light in the room. If you're sleeping during the day, invest in panels that keep out light or use a mask. Perhaps a fan will help keep family noise from interrupting your sleep.

- If you snore or stop breathing while you sleep, look at devices or seek a doctor's help. Sleep apnea will inhibit good sleep, and can lead to heart problems.

- Regular exercise helps you sleep.
- Use the DVR to watch favorite shows at a time more conducive to sleep.
- If you can't sleep because of something on your mind, get up, write the problem out, set it aside, and purpose to deal with it after you've had more sleep.

A tip for fighting fatigue on vacations is from Annette, whose husband is a farmer. Whenever they go somewhere on vacation, she doesn't plan anything for the first two days. She found that her husband needed to decompress and catch up on sleep first, and then he was good for the activity the rest of the vacation. Rather than disappointment, she manages her expectations, and everybody wins.

The other reason to get more sleep is because if you don't, you are chronically grumpy, and this breaks down relationships. If you are exhausted, self-awareness is just about impossible. Your thought processes are hampered. There isn't energy to engage. If your spouse and children are part of the problem in getting more rest, explain that like them, you need sleep, too. Your moods, safety, relationships, and long-term health are on the line.

Acknowledge Your Soul

Katie heard sobs coming from the laundry room. She opened the door and saw her mother sitting on the floor crying. She knelt down and hugged her. "Mom, what's going on?"

Her mother, a Montana state trooper, tried to stop the tears, but they just kept coming. She went on to share with her daughter that she was first on the scene of a horrific motor vehicle accident the night before. She described the scene with a far-off look in her eye, and talked about the victims. The tears streamed again when she admitted that she accidentally stepped on the family dog that had been ejected from the car and died.

Sooner or later, every cop realizes that some calls just don't go away. What you do with that knowledge has far and reaching consequences for the ones you live with.

It is a common assumption that cops can handle whatever they come across. Just look at RoboCop. Or Jack Webb. If you can't handle it without emotion, you're weak. Unworthy of a badge. You just pull yourself up by your bootstraps and deal with it, right?

Wrong. You can see, hear, smell, and taste. But when it comes to feeling, you limit yourself to the outside of your skin. You are not a robot. You came on this job to make a difference in the world. But many times the choices people make determine terrible outcomes, and you can't do a thing about it. There will be tragedy, death, and human suffering. As someone who cares—wants to do something about it—this is a hard one to reconcile internally.

> *"If you always do what you've always done,*
> *you will get what you always got."*
> Anonymous Survey Response

This is where training works against you off duty. On duty, you're trained to set aside pain to get the job done. There are heroic stories of officers who are severely wounded and return fire. Adrenaline kicks in, and a lot of times you don't realize the extent of injury until it's over.

But what happens when an image or an odor brings about pain?

I call these soul wounds. And much of police training in years past (and in some places, present) has been to train the body and train the mind to silence the soul temporarily so that you can do what needs to be done to get the situation under control.

Your training is repetitive—silence the soul. Push it aside. Wipe it away. Repeat. So then when you're off duty, what do you do? Drown it with a rum and coke, and then a shot of tequila? Swallow it with a second hamburger and large greasy fries? Silence it with the pursuit of a pretty waitress? Some just ignore it until they want to put a gun in their mouths.

Harsh? Yes. But this is a very real problem.

You have a body—arms, legs, torso, etc. You also have a soul. The soul is the unseen force within you that commands your body to fall into line. The soul is what you think (your mind), what you want (your will), and what you feel (your emotions).

Your mind, your will and your emotions determine your course of action. The soul leads the body. It's a crucial component of who you are; yet there is little training on how to guard, nourish or restore your soul.

If you break a bone, you go to the doctor and he sets it and then mobilizes it until it heals.

> *"Emotional trauma isn't a weakness; it's an injury to the brain and spirit, to a person's ability to effectively process traumatic circumstances. And it is not a sign of weakness to seek help from a trusted coworker, a chaplain, a peer support team member, or a counseling service. It is a sign of courage. In fact, allowing yourself to hurt because you won't seek the help you may temporarily need is a tragic sign of weakness."*
> Captain Dan Willis, Bulletproof Spirit

If you have an injury to your soul, what do you do?

In preparation for Selfish Prayer , my client and I interviewed Matt, a flight medic who suffered from multiple soul wounds from his time in theater. I'd seen pictures of Matt when he was deployed, but who answered the door was someone completely different. He'd gained weight, lost his hair, and blinked profusely when he spoke of Afghanistan. He had gone into law enforcement briefly when he returned from the war, but when a co-worker got in his face, he had a very strong urge to kill him on the spot. Thinking he might actually pull the trigger next time, Matt laid down his badge and gun for good. At the time of our interview, he hadn't worked in awhile. He was diagnosed with Post-Traumatic Stress Disorder and was undergoing extensive therapy.

One of the main stressors for this medic was a notorious battle in which cries for help were downplayed and ignored. There were men who died that day, and Matt listened to them call for help over and over until they spoke no more. He wears a bracelet that bears the name of one of the men who died in that battle to this day.

After our interview, we set up a critical incident debrief of sorts with several of the men who were a part of that battle. At the time, three and a half years had passed since they were in Afghanistan. We met up at the CHP Academy, gave the veterans a tour to break the ice, and then the rest of the weekend they talked through their recollections. During the tour, Matt's wife and I discussed his condition. "Has he said much about this battle to you?" I asked.

"No. I'd never heard a thing about it until you showed up."

"I'm sorry," I said quietly.

"Don't be sorry. Are you kidding? This is really, really good. Good for him, good for us."

Wounds to the soul affect the individual, the job, and the family. In addition to PTSD therapy, this debrief was a key that unlocked the way to Matt's healing, and a deeper understanding from his wife.

Your soul is as real as your shooting hand. On duty, your mind is trained to think a certain way, your desires are shut down, and your emotions are irrelevant. But off duty, this won't work for long. It's important to acknowledge this part of you, and then learn to feed it, treat its wounds, and then guard it.

Your loved ones will thank you.

. . . .

Think: How self-aware are you?

Debrief: Ask your spouse how self-aware you are. Keep it humble; keep it positive. This conversation can only improve your communication, no matter the answer.

Strategic Action: Look at the list of ways to renew your mind off-duty. Brainstorm a couple others. Choose one idea each month for the next three months Look at the list of ways to renew your mind off-duty. Brainstorm a couple others. Choose one idea each month for the next three months and incorporate it into your off-duty time. If it makes a difference, email me and let me know (victoria@how2loveyourcop.com). I'd love to pass along your story (no names, of course).

"In my public service, I treasure my friendship with law enforcement officers. I admire what they do and support them in every aspect of their job. I have always looked upon law enforcement officers as my friends."
Dirk Kempthorne

CHAPTER THREE

YOUR BACKUP AT HOME

"My wife is committed to always having my back. If I have a bad day, she will listen and just sit with me. I recently was involved in a shooting. She has been loving and supportive and always there when needed."
Michael, Officer, Illinois

It was Mother's Day and the Hadleys were getting ready for church. The phone rang. Rick, a police officer in Indiana was called out to an accident. Carrie packed up the kids and went without him. At the restaurant after church, the hostess asked how many were dining.

"Three for now, and hopefully a fourth later," Carrie answered. Her son, Noah, chimed right in and said, "My daddy is a policeman." Sister Noelle added, "My daddy is a hero." This was her favorite phrase, and was inscribed on the necklace she was wearing.

Carrie and the kids sat down, colored together, laughed, and enjoyed lunch. Afterward, they headed for the bowling alley.

Rick finally joined them midway through the game, and all had a great time as a family. A little later, the kids and Rick presented Carrie with a necklace and bracelet for Mother's Day.

"I couldn't love my family any more," Carrie commented later. "I'm so thankful for our time together, even if it's half hour lunch dates. I cherish every moment with them."

What an amazing attitude!

If you've got a spouse who understands who you are and supports what you do, hold onto that person and don't let them go. You've been given a gift that is worthy to be treasured.

Many are those who thought they wanted to be married to a man/woman in uniform. Many are those who couldn't handle it.

A cop wife friend and I joke about how at the orientation before the Academy there are some girls who prance about in heels, dressed to kill, lots of make up, leaning on the arms of those about to enter into law enforcement. Six months later, there aren't many of them left. Those that attend the family panel have a quiet strength about them—they've weathered half a year of absence, some as single parents, and they learned about sacrifice. They've supported their loved one through a transformation of mind and body, and celebrate their accomplishment.

It's a good start.

> *"When you come home, you really have to switch partners.*
> *You gotta leave some of that stuff behind. For the most part,*
> *that shift is over; your next shift is here."*
> Mel, Retired Patrolman, Married 25 years

Being the partner at home of a police officer is not for the faint of heart. It requires inner strength, deep commitment to you and the job itself, and the creativity, flexibility, and tenacity to make it all work.

The Demands on Your Spouse

The first thing your spouse has to deal with is your schedule. When there are just two of you, this is a little easier. If your spouse is working a nine to five job and you're working swings, you get to see each other for a few hours three to four days a week. It requires purposeful planning and expectations that are realistic. When kids' schedules are added to the mix, life can get insane. I've heard police families talk about creative solutions, but inevitably this really affects the spouse.

When our daughter was born, I quit work to stay at home. This made things a lot easier for our family. But many couples can't afford this.

"I am fatigued by being the default parent all the time," says Lisa, wife of a CHP officer and mother of small children. "When there is a kid sick, I usually take the day off. There are days I am just holding on until he gets home for a break or to use the bathroom by myself, hear myself think, or make dinner without burning it."

"Then, BAM, a 'Going to be late, headed to jail' text comes in at 5:45 and I have to regroup, muster the strength, and push through until bedtime."

Is this fair? Perhaps not. But it is reality; one I have experienced more times than I can count. Many wives experience the same thing. Again and again. One way to help your spouse unwind from this, especially those wives who stay at home with the kids, is to get them out of the house on a regular basis. Being at home can be distracting as there is always something to be done.

Another reality for spouses is the assumed risks that come with your job. There is a shadow in the back of your spouse's mind that there may come a day when you don't come home.

One summer day my cousin and I and our kids went horseback riding. We had a great time, stopping at Starbucks afterward, and laughing all the way home. Until I turned onto our street and saw a black and white parked in front of the house. My stomach tightened.

As I pulled into the driveway, the officer looked up briefly and then put the car in drive. I breathed a sigh of relief when he pulled away. He wasn't here for me. Thank God...

I think every spouse fears that scenario. A uniform at the door and an escort to the hospital. It's something we dread, something that we know is a possibility. Even though most of us get used to it and don't think about it day after day, there is always the what-if.

And then something hits close to home to bring it to the forefront.

Recently we lost two Sacramento-area deputies to the same suspect in a several hour shooting rampage that spanned many miles. That night, I posted my feelings on Facebook, and it resonated with almost a thousand people (most of whom were spouses):

"As I prepare for bed, I wonder at the day's happenings. It weighs heavy. I think of two women who will cry themselves to sleep, knowing that there are cold sheets an arm's length away, and as they reach for his pillow, drinking in the scent of him, knowing that, too, will fade away in time. I think of six children who will grow up without their fathers, and in that is profound sadness.

In that moment, I am overcome with thankfulness that my Chief is nestled next to me, worn by the day, but safe. Yet there is a sense of guilt for that thankfulness as I mourn for Mike, and I mourn for Danny, two men whom I've never met, but will attend their funerals, and cry, and feel the loss to our Blue Line Family.

I also think about the female officer I saw on TV today who was crying while trying to fill out her report. And I think of Danny's partner and his wife, who I've come to know and love, and wonder how many nights they will be awake replaying October 24, 2014. And I think of Mike's mother, who 26 years ago TODAY, lost her husband in an LODD. I wonder at the tragic irony, and can only imagine the depth of her grief.

I know the risks of this career, and I've felt and dealt with my fears through the years. But it doesn't mean that I ever get used to it. So, I will allow myself to shed some tears, and come alongside those left behind in the days to come, and we will never forget."

After that shooting, a deputy's wife thought she'd have an open house for any wives who wanted to get together and just hang out, talk, and support each other. Sixty women showed up.

"Every shift he puts on his badge, willing to go above and beyond the call of duty to protect and serve others. He is a true hero, from doing something simple to make a citizen's day brighter to his willingness to lay down his life for others. I believe there is no greater love."
Heidi, Kansas

There are other realities of being a law enforcement spouse. We know there are lots of women who are attracted to your uniform and will come onto you even if you're wearing your wedding ring. When you come home aloof or withdrawn for weeks at a time, that thought crosses our minds.

We sleep alone a lot of the time.

If you're on call or on special call out duties, we parent alone much of that time.

"My husband has a hard time figuring out how to balance his duties to his family and his duties to the public," says Eva from Maryland. "He feels compelled to help others before himself—and by extension, his family—at all times, even when the badge is off. Meanwhile, the children and I don't recall ever agreeing to come in second place."

When you're out of balance, we're out of balance. We take up the slack a lot of the time. But your job is not an excuse to get out of family obligations or to help out around the home. When you're home, engage in the family activities.

Most recently, we've been dealing with a new phenomenon: cop hate. You see it. You hear it on stops. You somewhat expect it. You understand it and try not to take it personally. But spouses do.

The protestors offend us. We're caught off guard when a friend on Facebook posts an anti-cop comment. We sadly hit the delete friend button. We get angry at the "Hands Up, Don't Shoot" campaign.

Livid. Because we know you and love you. We watch you be gentle with our kids. We know your heart and we see what motivates you. And just like you have a deep desire to protect, so do we.

In some ways, and some days, spouses feel like they are fighting for you and your marriage, and your kids. Here is a poem that describes that fight.

Warriors at Home

We are the warriors behind those who go to war.
While our officers battle on the streets, we battle from within our homes. We are the strong back up forces that support, equip, and empower our police officers out on the street.
We stand.
We know who our officers are and who they are not, yet we stand with them through the darkest of hours and the brightest of victories.

We are proud.
We love the uniform and all it represents. We know the need, we see the sacrifice, and know what our officer did to earn his uniform, his badge, his gun, and pride in who he is.

We support.
We know what they go through; we know the cost. We let them lean on us for what they need so they can do what they do out there, coming home at the end of the shift.

We defend.
We battle the questions. There are those who are against our officers, who hate their authority, who take away their freedoms to wreak havoc on our communities and families. It's hard to hear the criticism, even from those we are close to. But we stand up for our officers anyway, sometimes silently.

We battle.
We battle moods. We battle our own reactions to those moods. We battle the long-term apathy that comes with such moods.

We make do.
We explain to our little ones why their daddies or mommies aren't there. We've already wrestled with this in our minds and hearts. It's not how we'd like it to be. But it is reality, and the first thing a cop spouse must do is to accept things as they are, and then make do.

We go alone.
We get in the car and go to birthday parties, school plays, and church services. We get dressed and put on makeup and smile and do this out of survival. We would prefer to go with our officer—but instead we just go.

We are loyal.
We care about our officers, and we are in their camp. We love them fiercely and defend them to those who would dare speak or act against them.

We persevere.
At times it is tiresome. There are times when we are lonely, and we are exhausted, and we are done, and yet we wake up every morning and do it again. And again. And again.

We love fiercely.
This is our motivation and our perseverance.

We cry.
Tears are not a sign of weakness. They are a sign of strength. We acknowledge that sometimes life sucks, and we are not made of stone. But we are still strong—strong enough to let ourselves be soft when we need to be.

We cope.
When things go sideways and catastrophes happen, we learn to roll with it. We cope. We make things happen. We thrive when others only survive. And we do what we must.

We trust.
We believe in the training and abilities that our officers have. We trust them to be safe, and to be vigilant. We trust their partners to watch their back, and their leaders to do the same. We choose to trust in the face of fear.

We face hard moments alone.
We take our kids to the doctor, and take the phone call of bad news. We walk on eggshells when our officers are bothered by something and wait patiently for them to spill the reason. We face hard moments knowing that our officers will be there, eventually.

We work hard.
We clean and cook and plan and flex and work because we believe that what we do matters to our officers. We work hard to make a safe place for them to come home to, day in, day out, year in, and year out.

We do without.
We are lonely, we are underestimated, and we are thought of as weak. But it takes an amazing person to do without and creatively thrive anyway.

We mourn.
We put on black and we tuck a handkerchief in our pockets and we stand with our officers and mourn those who made the ultimate sacrifice. We hurt with our husbands, and feel their pain, and let the tears flow when they're not around. We feel the pain, too.

We fear.
There are many unknowns that we face. Will he come home? Will he be faithful? Will he be safe? We have no guarantees. We endure close calls, hospitals, and the what-ifs.

We fight.
But we fight anyway. We fight for our marriages. We fight for our families. We fight for our rights. We fight our own emotions and we fight with our officers. There is no place for us on the sidelines.

We are warriors.

We are strong.

There may be some who don't feel that this poem describes their life with their officer. But the majority of cop wives have seasons that are included here. I have gone through these seasons. Do I think about it all the time? No. Am I bothered every shift? Nope. But over the years, hard times come and go. It is then that I feel like I have to fight for my marriage.

Getting Your Spouse on Board

Everything mentioned in this chapter thus far is under the assumption that your spouse understands your job and your commitment to it, and supports what you do. But this isn't always the case.

I've had some pushback on my book for spouses. The number one complaint is that I place too much emphasis on your job and its importance, and that I advocate strongly that spouses need to support their officers. I acknowledge that I am guilty on this point. But there was a time in my life where I had no idea what the heck I was doing, didn't understand the ramifications of Brent's job, and how it affected him at different stages of our life together. I just knew that a few of the other spouses were struggling and ultimately leaving. And actually, who I married was different than who I was living with.

I loved my husband, and wanted to be the best wife I could be. But when it came to understanding him as a patrolman, I was clueless. I guessed a lot. And I made many assumptions that had nothing to do with the truth. Frankly, I wish I had my book twenty years ago.

> *"Date nights are pretty impossible with two kids, our schedules and finances. We have turned our date nights into ride alongs. Grandparents take the kids for the night and I get to be the passenger. We get a lot of time to talk and hang out. He gets to show off, I get to meet his buddies, and I get to grab a bite at his favorite to go place. It's not fancy, but it's fun and a great way to understand everything my LEO goes through in a night."*
> Elle, Idaho

My guess is that your spouse loves you dearly, but finds himself/herself puzzled or frustrated from time to time. Here are a few things you can do:

Education is first. If you want your spouse to get on board, share with them about what you do. I will talk about family readiness—the preparation needed to enter into a law enforcement career as a family—in the leadership section. I got this idea from researching military families and what they undergo in connection with deployment. The United States military recognizes the need for families to understand the expectations of their servicemen, and how that would affect those at home, especially when they are deployed overseas for long periods of time. They educate them on protocols, expectations, and resources that are available to help them while their family member is away at war, and after they come back.

The difference here is that you are not deployed overseas for a year at a time; you are deployed every day into nearby communities for 20-30 years. There are complications for both types of deployment, and I'm not saying that either one is worse than the other. My point is that like military families, law enforcement families also need to be educated on protocols, expectations, and resources available to help them throughout the seasons of their officer's career.

Because many of our departments are not providing this kind of training, you'll need to educate your spouse:

• Bring home any information from work (such as End of Watch packets or written policy) and go through protocols with your spouse. Take the mystery out of what happens if. Make sure you have copies of insurance policies (and if you don't have one, you must get one), updated beneficiary information, and all information in a file readily accessible by your spouse. If you want to prepare even further, talk periodically about funeral and burial wishes.

• Three books that may help your spouse: Emotional Survival for Law Enforcement by Kevin Gilmartin, I Love a Cop by Ellen Kirschman, and A CHiP on my Shoulder by yours truly. There are other really great books for spouses that are listed in the Resource Guide, but these here are the most informative on police culture and behavior and how that relates to the spouse. These books are a chance for discussion and a way to discover that you are similar to many other peace officer families.

• Keep your ears open for support groups, conferences, and seminars that will educate and encourage your partner in this role. Law enforcement conferences for couples take place all over North America. I have included some in the Resource Guide, but do a Google search for more.

"I feel safe and protected in the presence of my partner,
even when we are apart. I know his car goes fast,
his friends are always near, and his response time is quicker
than that of a 911 call. Years of living in fear with countless
sleepless nights, always watching my back even into adulthood,
I will never forget the exact moment he helped me to see
what life is like without all my fears. For that, he is my hero."
Laura, Oklahoma

Communication is the second thing that is important when getting your spouse on board.

Talk about your job and why you love it. Help your spouse to understand your motivation and the parts that are difficult. Brent took time with me over the years to help me understand the CHP and its mission. I grew into a wife that is absolutely blue and gold—and it made his life just that much easier. It also gave me a better attitude toward him regarding the sacrifices I had to make at home.

Day to day communication about the ups and downs is crucial. Your spouse may not be up to the gruesome details of an accident or crime scene, but he/she will be very open to hearing about the fact that you were bothered by a death you investigated. If your spouse understands that you are wiped out by the stress or grumpy because your sergeant is riding you, he/she will be better at supporting you or giving you space, and making sure you get your sleep.

Appreciation sprinkled consistently throughout the week-to-week grind is a key ingredient to gaining support from your spouse. If you were late getting to an event because of an end of shift call and she laid out a change of ironed clothes, thank her. If he covered picking up the kids because you were delayed at the jail, tell him thank you. It's easy to take each other for granted when you're not paying attention. Not paying attention on duty could get you killed; not paying attention in your marriage could kill it. Keep up the observant behavior when you're home, follow up with appreciation, and you've changed the whole dynamic.

"Divorce is not an option.
Many people ask me about the divorce rate with
peace officers, and I just laugh and say,
'Divorce? NO. Murder? Yes.'
This life comes with dark humor,
and it's necessary to my sanity."
Denise, Deputy Spouse, California

How to Love and Respect Your Life Partner

Whether your spouse is supportive of your job or not, there are some key things that you can do that will make every bit of difference in the tone at home. Each one of these points requires that you decide in your mind that you care about your family, and want to make sure they know and experience that care on a regular basis. Complacency kills—but proactive action produces life in your off-duty hours.

• Prioritize your spouse above everyone else.

Yes, everyone. He/she takes precedence over kids, co-workers, parents, and even beat partners. Why? Because she/he is your counterpart in life; your other half, so to speak. Two individuals, one life. If either of you feels that someone is more important than each other, commitments wane, walls go up, and trust deteriorates.

"Why do you demean your spouse?
You demean the respect others have for you."
Stephen, Lieutenant, Virginia

• Be thankful for who she/he is.

An officer in Duluth, Georgia called his wife at 0300. "Honey, I need a ride home. I had a chainsaw thrown at me from a moving vehicle and my baby (car) is out for the count."

She got out of bed and drove to the station. She chuckled and cursed all the way there. She stayed up to listen to the story, and then yawned all day. It's not every day that a spouse gets that call in the middle of the night. I hope this officer thanked his wife for the good deed.

When a couple has been together a long time, it's easy to take each other for granted. Little things that don't take much effort hold such importance. Like saying thank you for something she does every day. Last night Brent thanked me for doing the laundry. Do you know how many loads of wash I've done in the last 27 years? Thousands. But when I washed bedding today I did it with a spring in my step. Just because I knew he paid attention, and he was thankful.

• Be kind.

Kindness matters and can be shown in word and tone. Communicate in a way that shows you see the recipient as a unique human being and that you care about them. It draws them to you. Protective walls come down.

Kindness can be shown in actions, too. My father-in-law is a retired cop. He's masculine, terse and to the point, and gives everyone crap just to test them. But then out of nowhere he'll give a smile or a hug, call the ladies good-lookin'. He'll surprise my mother-in-law with a special dinner or party or generous gift. He'll occasionally call us and offer us something he saw in his travels. He'll encourage our kids with a few well-placed words. He is rough on the outside, but tender and kind inside. It endears us to him.

You can be who you are and still be kind.

• Listen as if your life depended on it.

You're tired after your shift. You've expended all the words you have for the day. But there are those at home who want to share their life with you through their stories and thoughts. They don't want you to fix anything, just to listen.

Listening with the intent to understand is difficult at the outset, but also a source of renewal for you as the ones that you love most share their lives with you. Quality of love cannot be achieved without accomplishing this.

• Appreciate your history.

After you've been married a little while, it is good to talk about the good old days. Brent and I talk about our life together before the kids showed up—how there were no cell phones, and that we didn't own a computer. Somehow it validates the time we've been together and how we've weathered the changes. The kids enjoy talking about it, too, and gives them perspective. Once in a while, we'll talk about the circumstances surrounding their birth, or a significant memory they were present for but don't remember.

It's great to reminisce about time on duty with your buddies. Do it with those at home, too.

• Let your spouse in emotionally.

Understand that when you are silent, your spouse will fill in the blanks. He or she will usually be wrong about why you're quiet, or internalize a problem that doesn't exist. You don't have to have a long, drawn out conversation every time. But trust your spouse to see the you that is beneath the skin.

> *"Once you begin to share your real feelings and fears with your spouse, it relieves you of the burden of always having to seem undaunted by the traumatic things we are exposed to from time to time. It allows you to strip down that wall of invulnerability at home, while still maintaining control while at work. Home can then be your oasis—your safe haven to recharge your battery. We all need a place where we can drop that 'tough guy' persona for a while so we can rejuvenate."*
> Tom Kenney

• Set boundaries.

Balance is key for good relationships, but it is elusive. There's a constant working to make sure that you're not over-invested in police work (as tempting and natural as that may be), and not under-invested in the people that you live with.

There are also boundaries that keep you safe with others. You adhere to officer safety rules and procedures to increase the probability that you will return home at the end of your shift. Wearing your vest, watching your speed, approaching a car on the passenger side away from traffic. If you want your family to be there waiting for you, set time limits with others, set touching boundaries and cell phone boundaries and location boundaries for your own safety with those who may want more from you than is healthy. More on that later.

> *"You may need to unwind when you get off work.*
> *But your spouse needs to unwind as well."*
> Mendi Keatts, POLICE Families Class

• Every so often, splurge.

I scored big when it comes to this area. Brent is awesome when it comes to splurging on me. It's not all the time; otherwise we'd be in trouble financially. But once in awhile, he will put time, effort, and money into making memories.

On our 25th wedding anniversary, he took me to where we met—the church in Chico where we first laid eyes on each other, and eventually were married in. We walked around and marveled at the changes over the years, and talked about warm memories. Then, in a picturesque place, he dropped to his knee, pulled out a ring, and asked me for another 25 years.

Oh yeah, he did well. It's times like this when I feel cherished and appreciated. Your spouse will, too.

• Value his/her contribution to your family and to the world.

Greg came home after a particularly trying day. He had dealt with the molestation of a five year-old girl on duty and it permeated his mind. His wife set him down with seriousness. "We have a problem," she began. He braced himself. "The last two weeks I've bought chicken at the grocery, I've realized it is spoiled." He waited. "The chicken is bad!" she complained.

There were many thoughts that came to the forefront of Greg's mind. *Well, then go to another store! he wanted to say. You mean to tell me you're worried about spoiled chicken, when I witnessed a little girl's life change forever? Do you understand the evil I am dealing with?* was another thought.

Unless you are married to another first responder or medical professional, chances are that your spouse isn't dealing with life and death matters. They aren't driving around saving people in their time of need. Their sphere of influence may not be the community as a whole, but rather the classroom, a store, or even one child at home.

But your spouse's contribution is still important.

"The world is made up of all kinds of people, and they make our lives what they are," says Karen, a retired highway patrolman. "I worry about cops who are all high and mighty because they're wearing a uniform. Heroes come with all kinds of capes. There are so many people who make this world go around. We've got to get off our high horse and take time to value that other person at home. If we don't get this early on in a marriage, that could get really ugly."

"He's so wrapped up in telling me about his exciting day and doesn't really ask about my day or the kids," says a cop wife in Arizona who stays at home with the kids. "By the time he does, it's kind of small on the scale in comparison."

Emily from Maryland has the same dilemma. "He has a hard time recognizing that I do anything productive or important when he isn't around to see it. The fact that I've molded my entire career, home life, and child rearing around his schedule makes most of my effort practically invisible. It gives him the feeling that he is the only person really working—

and then I have the nerve to expect him to help out when he comes home tired."

This is a complaint from many spouses. Many husbands come home with the attitude that what they've done that day is more important than what their wives have been doing all day. But let me say that as you have been responding to calls and crime all day, your spouse has been responding to the needs of her own career and/or children.

Brent and I went to a marriage retreat several years ago when I was at home with the kids and homeschooling. One of the exercises did was marriage mapping. We put together a timeline of our relationship—beginning to present. At first it was fun as we divided the years up by where we lived on the patrol. We popped in the kids, his positions, and then sat back. Suddenly I felt invisible, and got upset. On the page were some really cool things, but my name wasn't labeled with them. It took some work to remember things I'd done during those years to represent my contribution to our family. Most of my days were spent quietly, without anyone seeing what I'd done.

Now if we were to do this exercise again, I would label my family's accomplishments as part of the work I'd done quietly in our home. When my oldest daughter graduated Summa Cum Laude from college, I had to take a little credit as I'd taught her to read, to study well, and kept her healthy physically, emotionally, spiritually, and relationally. The same goes for the successes of our other children and even Brent's successes. To quote a sappy cliché, I was the wind beneath their wings. I see it now. Unfortunately I didn't see it then.

• Maintain your character and integrity.

Stay true to who you are, and the morals that guide you. Walk through life with your conscience intact, on the job and off duty. Everything else hinges on this principle. The decisions you make, the words that you say, and the wisdom that you implement into your life will carry over into all aspects of your life, especially when it comes to those at home. A spouse can weather all storms when she believes and trusts your character.

As a police officer you are a vital member of the Blue Line Family.

But understand that your spouse is as much a member of this family as you. Your support at home is vital to your safety, your well-being, and is the greatest motivation to come home after every shift. Your family is your backup at home.

A Spouse's Calling

Perhaps you were drawn to law enforcement because of the benefits and the satisfaction of making a good living. But there are many police officers that were drawn to law enforcement by an inherent sense of duty. There wasn't any other option. This is considered a calling, or destiny. Lt. Col. Dave Grossman describes you as a sheepdog—a somewhat dangerous individual whose purpose is to protect sheep (most of the general public) from wolves (those who want to devour sheep). A dog is by all accounts a predator like a wolf, but has a different inner drive to protect. You were inherently called into this line of work because of who you are.

But what about your spouse? He or she married into this line of work (unless your spouse is another officer). Is there a call for the spouse?

Since our early years in Los Angeles, Brent has been good to remind me often, "I can't do this without you." I responded well to that. Because of the way I was raised, I believed in his mission as a highway patrolman. I knew early on that his calling was crucial to California's peace and freedom. But over time I realized that I, too, had a calling—to support the thin blue line with commitment, understanding, and in my attitudes and actions as a cop wife. I wrote about this in A CHiP on my Shoulder:

> *"Your guy can go through the academy, he can train, and he can save lives, but there is another side of him that really needs you. Your respect can bolster his confidence. Your support can give him that extra emotional stability that he will need as his job wears him down. Your love can break down the walls he'll be tempted to build around himself when what he sees hurts his sense of how the world should be. It may seem a little overstated to some, but when I say you are a not-so-silent partner behind the badge, our everyday reality shows it to be true."*

My initial call to the thin blue line didn't arise from who I was as a person; it was driven by a deep love for my husband. It developed into a calling, as I perceived the importance of my work within our home and how it affected Brent on and off duty. Your spouse could be unaware of the affect their support of you (or lack of support) has on your work, or be totally unprepared and in some cases, unwilling, to answer his/her calling as a police spouse.

For the last several years, there have been groups of all kinds that are agreeing with this idea. A healthy home life is extremely helpful to an officer while he is on duty; a home where relationships are not perfect but healthy, where each person has a role and knows the expectations of those roles, and both operate with an attitude of not just me, but we.

Knowing that who you are and what you do is supported at home makes all the difference. But it works both ways. As spouses, knowing that we, too, have a calling that is valuable and vital to our families and the law enforcement community, is a motivating factor in how we conduct ourselves within this calling. Knowing we are appreciated by our officers (and their leaders) is huge for our overall morale, and motivates us to continue.

Merging Two Lives Under One Calling

Chances are that your spouse has his/her own career. There are children to raise. Life is lived one day at a time. Seasons come and go. Joy and pain. Passion and apathy. Ups and downs.

Uniting in purpose and vision in light of career and family is a lifetime process. Merging two souls together into one life takes time, effort and communication. Then adding little people into the mix complicates it all. I once heard a therapist say that adding one person to a family is more like adding two relationships to a marriage (mom with child, dad with child). Adding a second child adds three relationships (mom with child, dad with child, sibling with child), and so on. All kinds of dynamics are in the mix. A united family vision helps to frame those relationships and creates interdependence rather than a house full of individuals with different agendas. Then an understanding of roles and expectations within the ever-changing life you lead together creates stability. All of this requires consistent, purposeful communication.

Not easy for anyone. It just doesn't happen naturally. But when one is engaged in a career requires sacrifices, a thriving marriage and a family requires consistent and creative effort.

Two-Cop Families

Many cops are married to other officers, making you both police spouses. This dynamic can be positive and negative on a relationship.

First of all, as a couple you have a built-in camaraderie and understanding that others have to work at. Your spouse does what you do, so you share a common bond, off duty and on. There isn't a need to educate your spouse as to the police culture—they're a part of it. They speak in code. They understand the world like you do. Your life together has a theme that runs through it—and this is for the most part a good thing. But there are also challenges.

> *"I admit, coming home to a spouse that 'gets it' when you want to complain about the typical every day BS call is nice—not every person can look at a police officer's work complaints and see the situation in quite the same way. I don't get crap from my spouse for having to work holidays or weekends because he is in the same exact boat I am."*
> Barbara, Michigan

As in all law enforcement relationships, schedules are a constant exercise in flexibility. Steve and April work opposite hours so that they can manage their five-kid home together. Other couples purposefully work the same shifts so they can be together with their families as a whole. But inevitably, there will be something that doesn't work out.

> *"It all works until it doesn't."* - Renee, California

On September 11, 2001, Karen dropped her kids off at school. About the time she made it to work, the second plane hit. As the morning progressed, all aircraft were grounded except law enforcement. Karen, a paramedic flight officer, was ordered to hop a helicopter to southern California to patrol some of the bigger landmark targets. The problem was, her husband had just retired and his party was to be in a couple days. She wasn't happy. She boarded, on her way to the "happiest place on earth (Disneyland) while spitting nails." Until she learned that the pilot was missing his wedding reception. They both decided to quit complaining.

"We jump for joy when we get our work schedules figured out for the year, and realize our duty days don't coincide, so one of us can stay home with the kids while the other works," says Tiffany. "We routinely plan birthday parties and holiday family meals on days that don't fall on those particular 'special' days, and you know what? It works. My family embraced my weird schedule long ago, and is able to accommodate us most of the time. If we can't get together, Google Chat fixes the problem for missed family contact."

It's not just about special events, of course. The day-to-day managing of the home and family demands coordination. Some families are able to have dinner together because they work nearby and one can come home while the other is off. They take shifts as to who gets up in the middle of the night with sick or frightened kids. Some even rely on five-minute debriefs in the garage while one is coming home as the other is about to leave. Some will debrief on Bluetooth as they drive past each other.

It's a little chaotic, but it works. A little creativity, a lot of flexibility, a dash of humor, and soon you've got it working smoothly. And then things will change again.

IT HAPPENS

Kelly was on duty after one of her co-workers was shot. She was there to secure the scene until the shooting team arrived. Up drives her husband, Matt, who was on call. They worked together for about an hour, and then suddenly Kelly looked at him and said, "If you're here, and I'm here, who's got the kid?"

Kids of two-cop families have all of the benefits and difficulties of one-cop families, only double. But our kids also rise to the occasion, too.

Sam was on duty and Liz had just got home from the grocery store when she got a SWAT call out. She looked at her teenage son and said, "You've got the house. Put away the cold groceries, and I'll get back as soon as I can."

Several hours later, she is decompressing at home. She opens up the fridge and sees a can of sweetened condensed milk sitting on the shelf. She chuckled to herself—her son saw the word milk and assumed it went in the refrigerator. "My son was responsible," she laughs. "He said, 'I got this.' We have to train our kids to embody leadership that we have in the community because sometimes they have to step up at home."

"Finding daycare for four kids over the holidays suuuuucks."
Sarah, Officer, Michigan

There will be times when you both have to be on duty. This is where it is huge to have neighbors or family members take the kids. It's important to have a couple of backup plans on hand for when you both aren't available. Surround yourself with people you can depend on.

"We are a team at work and a team at home."
April, Dispatcher, California

One of the areas of difficulty for two-cop families is that work tends to spill over into private life. Beth and her husband Rick struggle with this. "I see this pattern we're developing, and over the last couple of years I've been trying to derail that train," she confides. "I recognize that without a good support system of friends, hobbies, interests, or activities outside of work, actual work stress just builds. It doesn't have anywhere to go. If you don't give yourself something besides work to think about or concentrate on, then work takes over. Everything. And it starts to come out in the home."

But it can be difficult for a two-cop family to find others they trust. One such couple has a daughter who is very involved in soccer. They attended a barbecue to get to know other parents on the team. Soon they were overhearing talk about a ticket one had been given, and the opinions about cops went wild. Our cop couple suddenly felt very alone.

Keep trying. There are those close by whom you can depend on, and grow to trust.

Working together on duty can have its difficulties. Susannah was on duty, and her husband, Alan, was working a traffic accident nearby. Suddenly the radio traffic increased. Susannah listened in horror as her husband's partner screamed into the radio that a vehicle had struck Alan. "I didn't know for several minutes if he was even alive. That was awful," she said. "He survived. He had to have his knee reconstructed and got a concussion. Has a nice scar on his head."

Then there is competitiveness that comes with being in the same career. Like who has the better story when you get home. Or the conflict you had on duty. Or who will make sergeant first. In these situations, be self-aware. You're on each other's team first—and take each other into consideration.

Whether your spouse is an officer or not, he or she is your first line of backup at home. The second line of backup is the little people in your home.

· ·

Think: What does my spouse do to make my job easier? Have I voiced or shown my appreciation for these things?

Debrief: Read this chapter together and ask your spouse what applies to him/her specifically, and what they disagree with.

Strategic Action: Take one of the bullet points above and put it into practice intentionally this next week.

*"My husband noticed I started buying grocery store
flowers for myself shortly after we moved to a new city.
I told him they were beautiful, made me happy every time
I looked at them, and were worth the (menial) cost.
Soon after, he started buying me flowers every week on
his last day of the workweek. Same flowers, same cost,
so much more happiness.
Always makes me feel loved and special."*
Patty, California

CHAPTER FOUR

LITTLE PEOPLE

"Ask them, tell them, make them: it works on the street, but not at home."
Unknown Spouse, Survey Response

I use the phrase "little people" to describe kids because of one reason: they're little people who grow up to be big people. As we parent, this is an important thought to keep in mind. Our children will one day have families and real jobs like truck drivers, nurses, lawyers, teachers, and yes, cops. They have feelings, dreams, and doubts, and want and need interaction with us. The way we parent lays the foundation for their morals, values, attitudes, and character. This in turn affects whom they choose as friends and how they'll spend their lives. No pressure!

I was on the phone with a pastor from the San Francisco Bay Area. He was interested in providing training and resources for police families. As the son of a police officer, he knew the challenges that come with the job. I asked him about his experience.

His voice went icy as he recounted the separation of his parents in third person language (a symptom of unresolved pain). He described problems he witnessed in his home, many of them related to his father's job. His parents were able to repair their marriage after a few years, but the hurt ran deep. This man was angry—still. After many years, he still carried the burden of hurtful memories.

On the other hand, Christa wrote a book called Blue Line Baby—Chronicles of a Cop Kid, in tribute to her father, who was a California Highway Patrolman. She gives detailed account of all kinds of experiences during his career. As we read her story, Brent and I laughed and cried through many of them, and marveled at how policing has changed over the years. When Christa and I later talked about cop mode and how that permeates off-duty life, she said, "That's the way it was because of who he is. And I wouldn't have it any other way."

That's quite a difference from the pastor's story. Bitterness or blessing—I don't have to ask what you want when it comes to your kids. But as a peace officer, your shift schedule works against your parenting. Fatigue works against your parenting. Your knowledge of crime. And victims. Your trained eye that finds fault and error. And above all else, your demeanor can work against you.

The good news is that many cops have been successful parents of little people that grow up to be upstanding citizens. Despite the challenges you have as a police officer, you can have great relationships with your kids. And if you have struggled or even failed up to this point, there's still hope.

Held to Higher Standards

Something wasn't quite right. Brian's "spidey-sense" was pingin'. Son Danny was given permission to longboard to a friend's house about three miles away. A couple of hours went by, and it was a really hot summer day. Brian had a meeting nearby, so he thought he'd pick up Danny as a "surprise" on the way, saving him from having to longboard home on a hot afternoon.

Brian pulled up in the driveway of Danny's friend. "Where's Danny?" Brian asked.

"Danny? Haven't seen 'im."

Brian's ears went hot. "He told me he was coming here a few hours ago."

"I haven't talked to him since yesterday," the friend insisted.

Brian dialed Danny's phone. No answer. The friend dialed Danny's phone, and he picked up.

"Dude, your dad's here. Where are you?"

Brian grabbed the phone and the cop tone came out. "Tell me where you are right now," he directed. In response to Danny's reported location, Brian ordered, "Okay. Don't move an inch. I'll be right there."

Brian drove to Danny's location, which happened to be his girlfriend's house.

"Get in the truck."

Danny did as he was told without a word, ears and chin low, transmitting clear signals of a guilty conscience.

"Give me your phone." Danny complied. It was launched into the back of the truck. The longboard flew there, too.

Girlfriend was history. Social life was done for the rest of the summer. Phone and electronics nonexistent. Danny was allowed to eat, sleep, and go to football and baseball practice. Period.

The story quickly spread to the rest of his baseball team. The story got better with time. "Dude, Danny's dad ran over his longboard! He broke his phone into little pieces!" While not true, Brian let those details go. Let them believe what they want. After all, the myth of what happened will be a great determent to further misbehavior.

Sometimes it's hard to be a cop's kid.

There's a standard in place to protect kids and keep them under control, to be sure they don't end up like a lot of the people they arrest. There are consequences at home, but that's better than jail, right?

Cop kids don't get away with much. Police officers are trained to detect deception and their kids aren't immune from this skill. There's also that sixth sense that comes with being an officer. Something doesn't seem legit, and then the interrogation begins!

There's also a network of information that gets around, especially in rural areas. If an officer's kid gets into trouble, there's a good chance the officer will find out. The standard is higher, and the kids find themselves accountable to everyone. That's a kind of pressure other kids don't typically face.

Realities and Realizations

In addition to this, you know what goes on out there. You see the evil underbelly and know that people are not always what they purport to be. Most will give the benefit of doubt, but not you. You know there are wolves in sheep's clothing—and they're everywhere.

"As police families, we tend to be more protective and we tend to see red flags or just get a feeling something isn't right with a neighbor or neighborhood kid. That friend's house down the street that our child used to play at, can't now because Dad's radar went off and it doesn't seem like a safe or trustworthy place to send our little ones," says Kim from Texas. "My daughter will get upset because she doesn't understand and we can't really say to her, 'because we think the mom is using drugs and the child is being molested, but we can't prove any of it.'"

You serve and protect those in the community. Your family is part of the community. The love you have for your family produces an intense instinct to protect them. You want to have control over your family's safety. It's natural, and you may struggle with this. What does protection without paranoia look like?

*"I ask myself often is this is the type of world that I want
to bring my children up in. I feel guilt and remorse for
bringing children into this awful place, but at the same time,
I love my children fiercely and can't imagine life without them."*
Dan, Officer, Arizona

As our four kids have gotten older, Brent and I have had many instances to deal with our kids and their safety. When they were younger, our girls were only somewhat aware of dangers. As they've gotten older, Dad has walked through several scenarios with them to keep them on their toes. Our oldest son is extremely aware of stuff that is going down around him, and has become savvy at protecting himself.

We've learned to educate our kids, train them to think and be aware, and prepare them to protect themselves. The way to do that is through communication, educating them calmly and firmly with age-appropriate information, affection, and humor whenever possible.

Two helpful tips to keep in mind about your kids' safety and conduct:

1 | Be positively engaged.

Kids' understanding of the real world and your intentions to protect them are best communicated in a tone other than the one you use on duty. While this may sound obvious, many law enforcement officers unwittingly slip into cop mode. Brent and I talk about people's choices and the consequences of those choices all the time. We talk about seat belts in the car. We pray for troubled kids in front of them. We get involved in our kids' lives, and make sure that kids come to our house often rather than our kids always hanging out elsewhere. When possible we make sure we meet the parents, and ask questions. We even voice our expectations to the parents as far as our children's behavior. This is a subtle way of setting the boundaries and subtly letting the other parents know that we are involved, care, and will follow up with our kids.

2 | Explain your expectations.

When our kids push back or ask why, we take it to a different level. Sometimes we voice our concerns, sometimes not. But we've made it a habit to firmly but calmly explain where we're coming from. They may not like it, but at least they know our reasons. It's also a good idea to proactively explain things in advance on occasion. This kind of communication builds trust over time, whether it seems so at the time or not.

> *"In our house we have rules and expectations that don't seem to exist in my daughter's friends' houses. Like bedroom doors staying open, and when you're outside, you play where I can see you."*
> Kristin, Texas

At no time do we make an apology for our standards or our expectations. We tell them this is the Newman way, and we refuse to compare ourselves with other families. Because of our confidence and pride in who we are as a family, eventually our kids adopt the same ideas.

Sometimes, however, there are times when you can't explain. When the Sacramento and Placer deputies were slain October 2014, it was all over the news, locally and nationally. James called his nine-year-old daughter who was walking home from school. "Hey, Sweetie, I need you to keep the television off this afternoon until I get home, OK?" She didn't like that. "Why, Dad?"

"I just need you to keep the television off until I get home. I'll tell you why later. Just don't turn on the TV, hear me?" She agreed reluctantly. Then later, James told her what happened. They watched the news together after he had a chance to prepare her.

"If we are going to survive this, you must realize that
FEAR IS NOT REAL. It is a product of thoughts you create.
Now, do not misunderstand me.
Danger is very real, but FEAR IS A CHOICE."
Will Smith's words spoke to his son in the movie *Earth*

Some of you will have kids that have a sense about danger that is built into their personality. Eight-year-old Landon's dad travels a lot. Sometimes at night his mom lets him sleep in his Daddy's place. One morning, Mom was making up the bed and found his play sword tucked in between the mattress and the bed frame. He was prepared to protect Mom from the bad guys! Landon may be a little warrior in the making.

We want to raise aware kids instead of fearful kids. That attitude starts with us.

At the time of this writing, our daughter is attending college five hours away. When she left, we were confident that she would be just fine. Why? Because over the years, she'd developed a pair of strong legs and a great right hook! She also had been trained by Dad to detect when something wasn't quite right, and get herself out of danger. She also carries a stun gun and pepper spray. She had the opportunity to use that training within the first few weeks of the first semester.

Evidently everyone in the freshman dorms go to parties on the weekend (you're not surprised). We have discussed alcohol use with her, behavior at these kinds of parties, and how to protect herself. Brent is also very good at telling both of his daughters how special they are, and that they didn't have to settle for second best when it came to boys.

She spent the first weekend alone in her room because literally everyone in her three-story freshman dorm was at a party. Because she is an extrovert, she didn't care for that. The next week she decided that she would go to the parties with her friends, but be the designated driver. At one such party, a guy who'd been drinking far too much came on to her. She was nice about it, but told him she wasn't interested. He didn't get the hint. He was moving in closer and closer, and she decided she'd had enough. He slurred, "Why are you playing so hard to get?" At that point, she stepped back, gave him a hard shove in the chest, and shouted, "Because I am hard to get!"

Booyah! Atta Girl!

Parenting Between Shifts

Shift work is hard on a family. Especially when you don't have seniority and get whatever is left. We don't have a long list of do's and don'ts for this issue. You just have to make it work creatively and with flexibility, communicating along the way. And then next month, when your shift changes again, you adjust.

If you don't have much time to spend with your kids, then the time you do have has to count. It has to be intentional. Keith missed his daughter's fifth grade graduation ceremony because he was on duty. But later, he picked up his daughter from home and went straight to Lowe's to buy a rosebush. They brought it home and planted it together. That rosebush now blooms and grows as a testimony to Steve's love for his daughter.

Dr. Gilmartin told me that kids should not even be aware of hypervigilance. Because hours spent vegging in front of a screen closed off from those you love are wasted. Hours that your kids need to spend with you, and you need to spend with them. On homework. Or talking through a problem with a bully. Or watching the video of their "missed note" at their piano recital. Or just a time of snuggling while you quietly talk with your spouse.

Every. Moment. Counts.

"Being around is not the same as being present."
Spouse, Survey Response

Momma Cop

As moms, you and I have that instinct that comes with raising little people. It's the fierce protective love that imbeds itself into our souls, dictating our motivations, and shoving aside our tendencies for selfishness.

As an officer, I imagine this mom instinct is particularly strong in the knowledge you possess of how bad this world can be. Even my Inner Grizzly has emerged at the times when I perceive my kids are in danger. All the more for you who protect people for a living.

Shift work is hard on a mom. Kelly from Texas says, "I find myself often shuffling kids to activities after two hours of sleep, only to get home in time to put on a uniform to return to work for an undetermined amount of time."

I've also talked with officers about how they've been able to work with the shift work to see their kids more. It depends on the dynamics—what shift you're working, how flexible your childcare is, and what your spouse's schedule looks like.

A lot of couples bear down and work opposite shifts so that their kids don't have to do childcare much, if at all. This is tough on a relationship, but knowing it is for a season and taking advantage of days off together can make it work in the long run.

It also depends on attitude. If you are consistently negative, this will be passed down to your kids. They know—their little (or not so little) radars are pingin' just like yours. They will follow your lead. If you are positive, they will enjoy the time you do have that much more.

Seasons of a Parent's Life

The big picture of parenting is to train a child to be grounded, moral, responsible adults. The journey is filled with years of trial and error, learning along the way for both parents and children. The way we parent changes through the stages and seasons of their lives, in purpose and approach.

Early Childhood

This stage is mostly about being present, being playful, and establishing perimeters. It's also an exhausting stage, physically and mentally.

"Toddlers require much more patience than felons."
Andrea, Highway Patrol Spouse

As a police officer that works long hours or is on call, the time spent with little ones can't always be as much as you desire. But when you're home, being present means paying attention, even when you're tired. Rejuvenate by engaging, especially when you don't feel like it.

"My husband was laughing at me when he came in and
saw me setting up Legos in rows and teaching our
one-year-old about cone patterns. She has a police
motorcycle Lego set and I couldn't help myself.
She still thinks the traffic cones are hats."
Christina, Wife of a Motor Officer

Brent loves little children—he has a way with them that is so precious. Recently we were talking with a mom in the parking lot whose deputy husband was out of town. They have three very active boys, ages six, three and 18 months. The boys were climbing in and out of the car, honking the horn, and were a little out of control, but Mom desperately needed to talk with me. So, Brent and another guy with us decided to keep the boys occupied for a bit. After about 20 minutes, I look over and see the 18-month-old in Brent's arms, head down and perfectly content. Our eyes met, and I melted at the sight of Brent's smile. It had been a rough couple of months at the department, and I could see the stress fading away, simply by holding a cuddly little one.

> *"Our 3-year-old son has fully embraced the life of an*
> *LEO kid. He calls police cars 'Daddy Cars' and*
> *will 'arrest' me or pull me over when we are playing*
> *in the house. He actually wrote me a speeding ticket*
> *this afternoon for chasing him too fast. He will pretend*
> *like he is going to work and will fill up his backpack,*
> *grab his pretend car keys, give me a kiss, and say he is*
> *off to work. When asked where he works at, he replies, '*
> *The jail. Just like Daddy.'"*
> Megan, California

School age

This stage is about education and character training. Our kids are involved, exploring new things, and learning about the world they live in through home, school, and their experiences.

Life gets a little more complicated for police families, as the kids now have their own schedule that more often than not conflicts with your own. This is where creative parenting is crucial. Set the expectation—you're not going to make every event. But you can make the ones you can attend all the more special. Your spouse plays a special role here. Use technology to record dance recitals, soccer games, and school plays and then watch together later.

Use time off to your advantage. Wash the car or do yard work together, and then grab an ice cream or a movie. If you have to run into the office for a short time, take one of the kids and introduce them to those you work with. They would love to see where you get dressed, or how the lights work on the patrol car.

"Looking back at my life with a mother as a police officer, I must say I am very proud that my mother worked her ass off to get her spot in law enforcement. I can remember her going to college at night, studying, and eventually leaving to attend the academy. I also remember watching her graduate from the academy alongside other fellow officers. That time without my mother was difficult; I was very young. But I do remember her letters she sent while at the academy and her phone calls that made me feel better about her being there."
Katherine, daughter of a Montana trooper

Our sword-wielding friend Landon had a police birthday party. His mom invited a few officers to come in uniform, and a retired K-9 did a demonstration. The kids and parents interacted with police on a fun level, building community and trust. After Nerf target practice and toy police car races, they were given junior badge stickers and sent on their way with awesome memories.

Jason and his wife decided that they would choose homeschooling as a way to spend more time with the children. They each take turns teaching in his off-duty time, creating some balance for the kids and much-needed breaks for Mom. Brent and I also chose to homeschool for several years; the kids were able to get that time with him no matter what shift he worked.

Officers can help with conflict resolution when the kids are in a disagreement. When Gary came home for lunch on duty, the boys had gotten into trouble. Mom was trying to get to the bottom of the conflict but it was frustrating. She asked Gary to step in. Moments later she returned outside to see the kids separated, individually questioned, and he had the truth based on testimony. Mom had to chuckle a bit, as Gary had used his investigative techniques in his parenting. Awesome!

Teenagers

Some people think that teenagers are somewhat of a lost cause. Not true. They are very eager to learn, just in their own way. Teenagers are a lot like toddlers. Both stages of life are transitional. Toddlers are transitioning from baby to child. They are very independent, trying new things on their own. They learn to walk, talk, dress themselves, and how to relate with other people—the basics of life as a child.

By comparison, teenagers are transitioning from child to adult. They are very independent, trying new things on their own. They learn who they are, where they fit in, how to dress, and how to relate to all kinds of people—the basics of life as an adult.

"My daughter was waiting for her dad to pick her up from practice. She was so mad because he picked her up in the patrol car. She phoned him and told him to go get his personal vehicle and said she would wait with her friends. He got on his intercom and called her out. He said he never saw her move so fast to get into the car!"
Joan, Texas

It's easy to see how toddlers need their parents to set boundaries to keep them from danger. It's also easy to see that when they don't want your help ("I do it!"), that's just not going to work out. Parents have to step in, despite the push back of very strong-willed and determined toddlers.

Teenagers are not that different. They, too, need parents to set boundaries to keep them from danger. In fact, I don't have to tell you the danger is even greater. Teenagers still need their parents' help, it's just a little trickier because they talk back, they're not always with you, and are even more independent. But we as parents still have to step in despite the pushback of very strong-willed and determined teens.

One of the ways that was effective to teach our kids some valuable life lessons was through volunteer work. They've learned about life outside of their protective cocoon, saw and felt the suffering of others less fortunate, and had to dig deep when out of their comfort zone.

At least once a year our church youth department put together a service trip. Our church is located in a wealthy area, so it is a priority that our kids see poverty and get their hands dirty. Brent and my oldest daughter went on a trip to San Francisco to serve meals to homeless people and halfway houses. It was a partnership with an inner city ministry and our church. On this trip, Brent was driving to a location in the Upper Tenderloin with six girls in tow. They turned a corner, and right in front of them was a knife attack happening in the middle of the street. The girls screamed in terror. Brent slipped into cop mode. "QUIET!" he yelled to get their attention. It was instantly silent. In a soft voice, he told the girls that they were to sit tight, make sure all the doors were locked, and then dialed 911. Within a short time, San Francisco PD showed up and took the perp into custody. The girls were fearful and shaken.

After Brent field-ID'd the suspect and provided a statement, there was discussion amongst leadership as to how to deal with the fallout. Some of the other parents wanted to just ignore the incident so that parents at home wouldn't freak out. But Brent saw it as a training opportunity. They pulled all of the teams together, let the girls tell their story, and then Brent explained things from a police perspective. He was able to educate the kids on how crime happens (it was a drug deal gone bad) and the risks drugs bring, and then talk about how to deal with something like this when face to face with it.

Powerful lessons for thirteen- and fourteen-year-old kids.

When Brent and our daughter returned home from the trip, they told me about the knife fight. I was concerned about her seeing something so violent and asked about it. She really wasn't traumatized by it—the debrief alleviated her fear. (Insert commercial here for Critical Incident Debriefs.)

Volunteer work is a great way to talk/serve with your teenagers (or younger). Once they get a taste of this, they've got a new barometer for fun. One of our kids told me that she would rather spend a week playing with impoverished kids in Mexico than party. Interaction, smiles and laughter versus a buzz that hurts in the morning—in her mind, there is no comparison. Volunteer service has been an important key to shaping our kids into who they are today.

One more thing on teenagers. They respond well to mutual trust and respect. Many spouses talk about how their officers will interrogate their kids, treating them like criminals. Fear does that. A lack of trust will do that, too.

> *"I have an 18-year-old daughter and there have been*
> *way too many times that I have went 'cop' on her when it*
> *came to places she had been and things she had been doing.*
> *Basically interrogating her like a suspect instead of*
> *trusting her like a daughter."*
> Phil, Officer, Georgia

If you've been educating your kids about the dangers that lurk nearby and showing your kids you love them through actions and words, you've built up trust. We take this very seriously in our home—because without trust, relationships can't be healthy. We actually talk about trust, how we've built it over the years, and how a simple bad choice can injure that trust. Explanations for expectations. Trust hangs in the balance.

The difference between interrogation and information gathering is tone. If your kid messes up, apply the discipline, talk it through until you can hug it out, and move on. "My teenage daughter and her soccer teammates decided to paint a practice field without consent. They were caught by the local PD," says a retired deputy from Minnesota. "I stopped to see the girls in uniform while they repainted the field and corrected their mistake. I believe they enjoyed me being there, knowing that they had done wrong, but I didn't hold it against them."

Your kids may make stupid choices. A little grace mixed in with consequences goes a long way to influence and guide them through it. Always keep in mind that your goal is to raise a responsible young man or woman, not a perfect one.

Young Adults

Many parents think that the teenage years are the most difficult for a parent. We've learned that the young adult stage is by far the hardest. Why? Because you no longer have control.

It's the stage of parenting where we have to trust in the training that we provided for our children over the years, and hope and pray they were listening.

They're making decisions—important ones. On their own. Understanding unfolds as their minds fully develop and life experience takes hold.

In this stage of parenting, we are letting go. Wow, that's a scary thing. Because they're still young, and they're going to make mistakes like we did. The last thing they need is helicopter-parents.

Because Brent and I are in this stage of life with our kids, I'll share three things that work for us:

Kids and Control

1 | Listen when they want to talk. More often than not it's when we're tired or distracted. It's inconvenient, but crucial. In fact, this is key to building relationship and lasting influence with your adult child.

2 | Resist the urge to deter consequences of their choices. Natural consequences are amazing teachers.

3 | Encouragement empowers. Double down on the positive— they need our support. Their future is bright, in spite of and in some cases because of a setback.

On duty you are trained to take control of the situations you're dealt with to keep the peace. When all hell breaks loose, you bring order to chaos by whatever means policy deems necessary. You don't have relationships with the people you are helping or arresting—it isn't personal. You have a job to do, so do they, and that's the way it is.

Your kids need a different approach. As little people who bear our names and are a part of us, they deserve our time, attention, and our best effort. This isn't always easy.

You do not control a relationship with your child. You influence your child. The difference here is the level of respect that you give each other.

We won't always get it right. But apologies cover a multitude of mistakes. It's never too late. And unlike the on-duty demeanor, vulnerability with your kids smashes down walls and creates intimacy. Close contact. Real interaction. Real trust.

Rules? Yes. Our kids need boundaries from which to operate from. But they also need to know that those rules are in place to protect them, not just to ruin their fun. They can only understand this within the relationship they have with you.

Final Thought

Police officers have an amazing capacity and perspective with which to raise kids. Your discipline and training, your knowledge of danger and safety, even your schedule can really be an asset to your parenting. It just takes a little balance, intentional effort and creativity, and a willingness to be fully engaged.

I'll finish with an incredible story of a little girl who loved her highway patrolman father and his helicopter. After living for years in a remote area we call a Resident Post, the family moved to a slightly larger town in northern California:

> *At nine years old, we moved to the big city. Redding seemed like a foreign country to us. We went from knowing every single person in our town to not knowing anyone. I went from being at the top of my class of ten students, to being a number on a roll sheet of 25. It*

was very scary for all of us, with the exception of my Father. He loved his new assignment.

H-12 was the California Highway Patrol's Northern Division Hughes 500 D helicopter. It was mainly used for search and rescue in that region as well as assisting allied agencies with locating illegal marijuana grow sites, suspect searches, aerial photography and air transport. My father raved about the beauty and excitement of flying above the northern California coastline--flying about 100 feet from the surf or over 300 foot redwoods with the skids about 20 feet off the tops of the trees.

As the flight observer, my father's job was to be the eyes of the bird. He was the spotter for all kinds of searches, as well as utilizing the searchlight that was a brightness of three million candlepower. On occasion when he worked a night shift, they flew over our house as my brother and I were playing down the street with the neighbor kids. My father always shined the spotlight on us to create a very Close Encounters of the Third Kind-scenario as he spoke over the radio loudspeaker saying, "Get home, your mom is looking for you."

Benton Air Park was only about a mile from our house. I usually saw when the bird approached for a landing. I often climbed on my bike and made the ride down the hill. The office was a temporary sort of building—very small quarters. It was packed with medical supplies, flight suits, helmets and a few desks for report writing. I usually waited while they were still in the bird, powering down and completing the flight logs. After they exited, I could then get off my bike and wait to be waved over. I was never allowed to approach without my father.

I loved the smell of the jet fuel and being close enough to see how many bugs were on the windshield. I waited patiently until my father gave me a rag to wipe down the skids and step-ups. Everything else was too fragile, but I had my job and I was proud to do it. He often quizzed me about the equipment on H-12. He explained how everything worked. Next time around, it was my turn to tell him. I loved knowing everything about H-12 and I wanted to fly in it so badly.

In 1979, I was enrolled in Manzanita Elementary School.

I was the weird kid. I went from being the top of my class to being the class outcast. I came from Small Town, USA. In fifth grade, the girls were all about fashion, popularity contests and playing sports. I had no clue about any of these. I dressed differently and wore thick coke-bottle-lens glasses. I made friends with our neighborhood kids who all went to private Catholic schools, so in my class I had no friends. Waiting and watching for the helicopter on recess was my past time. The airpark was nearby and I saw and heard the helicopter all day long. We always ate dinner together as a family and on the nights that my father wasn't working, we listened to him share the stories of his recent flight adventures. It sounded so exciting and I couldn't seem to get enough. I would beg to go up in the helicopter every chance I got.

I hated school. The kids were so mean to me. I was everyone's punching bag, scapegoat, and was tormented daily. During the sixth grade, I learned that we were to go to the Shasta County Environmental School, aka camp for an entire week. I was horrified that I had to go live with these bullies in the woods. Camp seemed like punishment. I hated it there.

One day walking back from lunch to my cabin, I noticed the grassy area in the center of the camp was all roped off. I didn't pay much attention other than thinking it was likely another game of red rover, flag football, or some sort of brutal sport for me to be targeted for easy take down. I went back to my cabin and sat alone on my bunk, drawing.

Soon I heard the familiar sound of rotor blades chopping through the air. Rotor blades with pitch on them; rotor blades of a helicopter landing! I was so excited I ran out the door to the deck of my cabin to see. There, making a landing in the center of my camp was H-12. I was so excited! I ran to the rope and the counselors all began yelling at me to "stay back" as if I didn't know what I was doing. As they powered down H-12 and the door popped open, my father stepped out and removed his helmet. He waved and then motioned for me to come over. As I ducked under the rope and ran towards him and my beloved H-12, so did all the other campers. My father quickly gave them the 'STOP' hand. I was the only one al-

lowed to approach. Suddenly I was in a position of power, and I loved it. The pilot stepped out and greeted me with a hug as well. I turned around to see hundreds of sixth graders all watching me! I could only hope that some of them felt fear as they wondered if these officers were here to deal with them for their mistreatment of me. My father handed me a bouquet of flowers and asked if I would like to show my friends the bird.

As a matter of fact I did. I knew that bird inside and out. As I pointed out the features and explained them, my father and his pilot opened hatches and laid out equipment. It was a team effort and I was in charge. We showed the medical equipment, the expansion bubble when transporting a medical, the radios and spotlights. The students began a question and answer session and most of the questions were for me and why I knew so much about this helicopter.

I remember smiling and pointing as I answered, "Because that's my Dad."

· ·

Think: What are some things I've done well as a parent? Where can I improve?

Debrief: What age span are your kids in currently? Do you see some similarities in their stage of life in this chapter? Brainstorm some ways as a couple on how to build into your kids more efficiently.

Strategic Action: Think of one trait of each child that you love. Take each kid on a one-on-one outing. Tell him/her about the quality you see in them. Don't bring up anything they need to improve on during this date. This will bring much encouragement and boost the trust and relationship between you.

> *"I love that my dad protects people so that all the other moms and dads can tuck their kids into bed every night."*
> Lauren B. Wade, *My Dad is my Hero*

CHAPTER FIVE

SERVE AND PROTECT YOUR MARRIAGE

"Every worthwhile accomplishment has a price attached to it. The question is always whether you are willing to pay the price to attain it—in hard work, sacrifice, patience, faith and endurance."
John C. Maxwell

There are many assaults on marriages—outside pressures, inward hurts, past baggage, unhealthy relationships and a lack of marital knowhow. They threaten the well-being of two people who have joined their lives to one another, as well as the children involved.

Our marriages are worth fighting for.

As a peace officer, you took an oath to protect and serve the people of your jurisdiction. Circumstances are not to deter you from honoring this promise. You swore to lay down your life rather than swerve from the path of duty. You knew the costs, the sacrifices, and yet you made a promise.

Have you made a commitment like this to your life partner?

There is honor in the oath you take as a peace officer. There is honor in marital vows, too. Perhaps even more, as marital vows are for life. Unfortunately, honor of this kind is becoming more and more rare.

The following is an adaptation from a Texas police officer's oath. What if we accepted the honor and responsibility of this oath in our marriages:

"As a partner in this marriage, my fundamental duty is to serve my spouse; to safeguard our union; to protect our commitment against those who would seek to destroy it, and to respect the person to whom I'm bound in liberty, equality, and love.

"I will keep myself unsullied as an example to my children; maintain courageous calm in the face of conflict and difficult circumstances; develop self-restraint; and be constantly mindful of the welfare of my family. Honest in thought and deed within my marriage, I will be exemplary in keeping myself only to my spouse. Whatever I see or hear in a confidential nature or that my spouse confides in me will be kept ever secret unless given permission to share with others.

"I will never act unbecomingly or permit feelings of animosity and unforgiveness to influence my decisions in this marriage. With no compromise and relentless tenacity, I will devote myself to my spouse courteously and appropriately without fear, malice or ill will, never employing unnecessary force or violence.

"I recognize the ring on my finger as a symbol of commitment, and I accept it as a sacred trust to be held so long as I live. I will constantly strive to achieve these objectives and ideals, dedicating myself before God to my chosen partner... my spouse."

It takes consistent courage, determination, and unselfishness to see this kind of commitment through. We must serve and protect our marriages, just like you serve and protect the community.

Pledging loyalty for life lays a framework and foundation for your relationship. It dictates intention of both parties to begin building a life together. Once the vows are pledged to each other in the presence of God and loved ones, there is a sure place from which to operate.

It's a choice to serve and protect your marriage. It's a resolution. It is unwavering resolve that starts in the heart, flows through the mind, and results in honorable behavior. It's a series of choices through each season of marriage, and each season of your career.

Commitment also dictates boundaries for our conduct. There is a declaration of safety in which to build trust, enjoy fidelity, and grow as a family.

It's much like a seatbelt. We get in the car and buckle up. We do this to keep us in place should the car run into an unplanned obstacle. If the car is thrown into a rollover, the only thing to keep us in place is the seatbelt. Should the car spin out of control for some reason, again, the seatbelt will keep us safely in place.

Like buckling the seatbelt, commitments need to be made ahead of time, when it seems there's no danger. Trying to fasten a seatbelt in the middle of an accident just doesn't happen, as you well know. Like seatbelts, commitment keeps us in place when circumstances spin out of control.

You've made a commitment to the job. You've made a commitment to your spouse. Now how are you going to succeed at BOTH?

> *"Commitment strengthens. Lack of commitment weakens."*
> Ray Johnston

Serve Your Marriage Through Investment

As a young mom I was involved in a community group consisting of moms of preschoolers. One thing most of us had in common was that our husbands were very focused on their careers. After the early years as couples, we naturally began to grow our families. But adding kids also increased responsibility and the necessity of paying for those little additions. As moms were tending to the needs of children, husbands were becoming more focused on their careers. It was the natural season to do so.

Children change relationship dynamics in the home. More demands. More opportunity. More responsibility. For those who work outside the home, it's easy to get caught up at work. Add to that the excitement of policing, and there is huge potential to become imbalanced.

This is why the best investment you can make in your family is to be present, accessible and engaged.

Think about the hypervigilance rollercoaster described in chapter two. Work produces an adrenaline-induced high. After work, you chemically counter that high with a depression-like low, which naturally occurs at home. There are many police households where night after night the officer is vegging in front of the TV or computer—unengaged in the relationships around him.

There have been many nights that Brent and I had conversations that he didn't remember later. I think he actually was listening at the time, but because he was zoned out or distracted, those conversations didn't enter into long-term memory. He forgot we even talked about things. On my end, I trusted in the fact that he responded, and expected him to recall our conversations. It got frustrating reminding him of things, or even worse, he'd get angry with me for not giving him a heads up beforehand. Feel an argument coming on?

You are able to multi-task on duty. You drive, look for crime, communicate by radio, and monitor the computer, all at the same time. Unfortunately, that multi-tasking ability doesn't translate well at home without that adrenaline push. When you need to talk or spend some time together or with the kids, you've got to turn off the TV, computer and phone. Decompressing after work and then finding the energy and motivation to be fully present takes an intentional deep breath and a deliberate switch to off-duty mode in your mind and heart.

Serve Your Marriage Through Love and Respect

Love is a word that is often used, but has many different meanings. In the Greek language, there are at least four words that describe love. One is eros, which refers to an intimate, sexual love. A second is philia, which refers to a friendship between equals. Philadelphia, "the city of brotherly love," is derived from this word. A third is storge, which describes the affection between a parent and child. The fourth is what I want to talk about here—agape, which is described as a selfless and unconditional love. Agape could be likened to the police definition of duty.

It is your duty to serve and protect, regardless of how you feel at any given moment. You take the good with the bad each shift. Some things tire you out; other things energize you. At all times, even when provoked, you are expected to maintain a professional demeanor.

How about your duty to your spouse? Consider these questions:

- Do you treat your spouse with kindness and tact like you would handle things professionally on the job? Do you give her the courtesy of communication as you would someone you pulled over for speed?
- Do you respect your spouse? Or do you downplay her thoughts, feelings, and actions? Do you listen to try to understand what the problem is—perhaps something she's not even aware of yet?
- Are you rude to him because it seems he doesn't understand where you're coming from, and you're too tired to explain?
- Are you patient with your spouse? Your children?
- If a member of your family is fearful, do you take the time to put her mind at ease? Follow through on a little investigative work on her behalf?

It is very disconcerting when I hear from spouses that their officers treat total strangers with more respect than they do their own family. If you are in this category, why is that? Give this some thought.

> *"Real love has little to do with falling.*
> *It's a climb up the rocky face of a mountain, hard work,*
> *and most people are too selfish or too scared to bother."*
> Stacey Jay

The best way to love and respect is to approach love not as a feeling that comes and goes based on circumstances, but as duty to the vows we pledged. I asked a group of officers how they can work long hours without proper sleep, and effectively deal with stressors from the streets and in the office. Jonathan answered with a grim, determined expression: "We just do it."

When it comes to love and respecting one another, sometimes duty calls. Those that stay married and reap the benefits from it know that it is important to love and respect—a choice, an action—whether you're feeling it or not. Romantic feelings and intimacy are the byproducts of such commitment.

Serve Your Marriage By Building Trust

Your job is cutting edge. You make decisions throughout your shift that affect the lives of many, directly and indirectly. The stakes are high, and you are under constant scrutiny—now more than ever.

Trust is crucial.

You can't trust the people you come into contact with on the streets. Sometimes you can't trust management. There are officers you work with that you don't trust.

But there are other officers that you've built rapport with and trust in their loyalty and abilities. You may have some in leadership that have proven they have your back. There are those who you know without a doubt they'd take a bullet for you. It took time to build that trust.

It's the same with those closest to you off duty.

Deposits into the Trust Account

Building trust into our relationships is a lifelong endeavor. As the years progress, there will be deposits and withdrawals as we exceed and fall short of each other's expectations. Much like a bank account, we give and take from our relationships. Here are some ways to build trust into our marriages.

Intentional Time Together

We must spend time together. When relationships are new, the thought of not spending time together is ludicrous. Being together is exhilarating. As the relationship ages, for some there is a tendency to allow other priorities to take that time. Then when kids are added to the mix, careers take time and effort, and responsibilities pile up, spending time together can seem like a luxury. But it isn't a luxury. It's a need—and as all these other things crowd our lives, we need time together all the more. This is when we have to get creative—and intentional.

When the kids were small and we didn't have much money, Brent and I didn't get out much as a couple. One thing we did was date nights at home after the kids went to bed. At one point in our lives, we watched an hour of X-Files every Friday night (except when he worked) then followed with a relaxing beverage or dinner, cuddling on the couch with the fire going. Didn't cost much at all, and some of our best discussions happened during those home dates. Other times we just enjoyed the silence of kids sleeping upstairs.

We must have time to get in sync with one another. As we grow older, we change. We need to dream together about the future, no matter how long we've been married. We need to talk about things we enjoy individually and together. We need to laugh together. We need to set financial goals and talk about how we're doing. We need to share a vision for our kids. All of this requires time to talk together. Whether we've been married three years or thirty, these conversations are crucial to us as individuals and as couples.

Keep Your Word

We build trust when we keep our word. This can be difficult for law enforcement lives. Not that we lie, for we generally place great value on truth. It's more about integrity. Off-duty life in law enforcement can be one promise unkept after another. With a crisis-driven career and a sincere love for it, sometimes an officer can't (or won't) always live up to what he promises. Many officers' wives harden because too many promises go unmet and wound her. After awhile she will develop protections against getting hurt again, and that will show up as frustration, sarcasm, and disrespect. She doesn't trust anymore.

If you say you'll take your son to a ballgame, take him. If you say you'll pay the water bill, pay it on time. If you resolve to go on a vacation for the first time in two years, make it a priority and make choices that will allow it to happen. If something comes up as it inevitably does, apologize and then double down the next time. Focused follow up is important to build trust.

Build Each Other Up

Another deposit in the trust account is to build each other up. We all need encouragement. As we grow closer to our spouses, we will learn the most effective ways of building each other up, and unfortunately, tearing down. With some, encouragement comes through words. With others, it's demonstrating respect. For others, it's a good meal. So often it's easy to forget to give a little encouragement. It may be small, but it goes a long way.

Nothing makes us more unsafe than when we tear down other people with our actions and words. Words or actions, sometimes unintentional, can spark anger. If you find your spouse angry or withdrawn after a discussion, it could be that you are unaware that you're tearing her down. Ask the question—what'd I say? What do you think I meant by what I said? When you're building trust within your communication, don't allow misinterpretation to sabotage your efforts.

Recognition of Value & Appreciation

This is a big one. When you are working long hours, putting in time and effort, and you don't get feedback from your supervisor, it is a natural inclination to put yourself at odds. You feel underappreciated and devalued. And that creates distrust. Worse yet, if your efforts are met with criticism or harsh words, anger and resentment naturally follow.

Everyone wants to feel that the work they do is making a difference and has value. It is the same for your efforts at home. If your spouse were struggling to get dinner on the table night after night, a simple kiss and acknowledgement of her efforts (even if they're not perfect) would communicate value and encourage her to make even more effort. Same with the house, the kids, sex, and other areas of your relationship. Focus on what is good and let your thoughts and words reflect that perspective.

Withdrawals from the Trust Account

None of us married a perfect person. Inevitably we will let each other down at some point. Expecting this from the get-go, we may be able to let things slide here and there. But there are some things that negatively affect trust.

Comparisons

Comparing ourselves to one another separates. Perhaps in wanting understanding or justification, we inadvertently alienate the other spouse. Someone comes away feeling devalued because the comparison ends in a place where one of you has it better (or worse). More often than not, someone comes away with the feeling that their issue doesn't matter because it's not as bad as their spouse's issue. In some cases, it shuts down communication altogether, and breaks down trust.

Comparing one another with other men or women is equally destructive. Every individual has his or her own strengths and weaknesses. To compare with others or tell your spouse that they should be more like so-and-so introduces resentment, and insecurity. Forbid any thoughts and comments like this to exist in your relationship.

Control

A second withdrawal from the trust account is trying to control each other. Usually the person who is trying to control the other doesn't mean to hurt anyone. It tends to be a reflection of selfishness or fear. Fear of the what-if. Fear of my inability to handle whatever the situation is. Fear of trusting. Yes, that's right. When we try to control another human being, we are in essence saying that we don't trust them. I need to take control because you are inadequate. Ouch. Selfishness comes in when we assume that we have to take control because we feel we are superior in our ability— I'm better equipped than you. Manipulation can be a result of this as well. I want something and I don't trust you enough to just ask for it. I need to get it by fooling you or wearing you down by making you angry.

Do you understand how this can break down trust?

Lies

The third withdrawal is the most obvious: lying. When we intentionally lead others to believe something other than what is the truth, we lie. There are big lies and small lies, in regards to the impact that the lie will have. But they are still lies, and they break down trust.

On duty, you are used to people lying to you. You have ways of exposing it, and you come to believe that most you talk to are in some way lying. It's why you don't trust your customers.

Most of them are lying to get out of the consequences they deserve. Others lie to protect themselves from retaliation for being a snitch or guilty by association. You have to seek other ways of bringing out the truth, like evidence. Evidence doesn't lie. You can trust it.

> *"You know a murderer will kill and you know a thief will steal, but you never really know what a liar will do."*
> Unknown

In our relationships, most of us lie because we have fallen short in some way and are too embarrassed to own up to it. We are protecting our pride. Some of us lie to keep from getting caught in something we've done wrong. We are protecting our deceit. Some of us lie because we just don't like the truth. But like you can't build a case on lies, you can't build trust in a relationship on lies.

Affairs

The last withdrawal is the big one—having an extramarital affair. This is the ultimate breech of trust in a marriage and more often than not will break the marriage apart. Someone invites another person into your union, and that person isn't welcome by the spouse. In my online survey taken by law enforcement families, the number one cause of those who'd been through a divorce was because of at least one affair. This happens, but we can safeguard our marriages against it. More on this in the next section.

> *"I've seen officers with Meg Ryan or Beyonce at home,*
> *but they're buying Rosanne a beer. I've seen officers with*
> *Denzel Washington and Hugh Jackman at home,*
> *but they're buying Danny DeVito a beer."*
> Kevin Gilmartin

Serve Your Marriage Through Sex

Sex is a beautiful experience that creates intimacy within committed love. It literally brings two people together and makes them one. There is no other act that is as binding, no other act that is as pleasurable, and no other act that is so vulnerable. When we have sex, we are inviting our spouse into our most private places, giving and taking of ourselves in an incredibly intimate way. At that point, there is nothing in between us. Healthy sex between a married couple builds trust.

But your job again complicates things. If you and your spouse work different hours and kids to juggle in between, good luck! Unless you want to take cold showers all the time, you may want to set the alarm for the middle of the night. In this season of life, both of you have to be creative, otherwise resentment builds (on both sides). If it's been awhile, put on a movie for the kids, lock your bedroom door and enjoy!

Job stress is an inhibitor to sex. When on-duty problems disturb your off-duty thoughts and you pull away because of it, the last thing you're thinking of is sex. But perhaps it's what you most need.

For those of you who are working crimes against persons, this could disrupt your sex life as well. Dr. Gary Lowe, a criminal justice professor at Sacramento State University, has done much research on this phenomenon. "For women who are investigating personal crimes, sometimes rape scenes will come to mind while having sex," he says. "For men, it's more of sexual dysfunction." Talk about a mood killer! If this is an issue for you, you may want to keep your eyes open to keep yourself in the moment, or mentally shut the door on those thoughts. You may need to give yourself more down time beforehand, totally disengaging from work first. If these thoughts persist, you might want to talk with a therapist. It's a normal reaction to being exposed to evil.

Fatigue is a big problem, too. That's a little easier. Set the alarm for a half hour earlier and have sex after you've slept. Dehydration can limit sex, so if possible, drink a bottle of water an hour beforehand (or before you go to sleep).

Perhaps the problem isn't you, it's your partner. He/she doesn't seem interested. There could be any number of reasons for this—a trust issue, baggage from past relationships, past (or present) abuse, health related inhibitors, infidelity, fatigue, or unresolved anger. Sometimes it's as simple as you just have gone too long without real connection and there's a wall built up between you. Most of these problems can be worked out with uncomfortable yet needed conversations or intentional effort. Others require help from a counselor.

> *"Romance is like the tide; it ebbs and flows with time."*
> Bob Sprague

Sex can be a barometer for the connection between you. Kory and Tom weren't connecting after a difficult situation with their son. The problem had driven a wedge between them as they both were hurt, but saw the cause and its solution differently. Unable to come to terms with it, they grew further apart, and Kory wanted nothing to do with Tom sexually. "I feel like a prostitute when we have sex. My mind and heart are not into it at all, so it's just my body. I don't feel comfortable with that," she confided. It wasn't until a little time went by and they were able to resolve their differences that her desire for sex returned. But it did return. For women, our minds are the greatest inhibitor to good sex.

If you're in a season where your sex life isn't the greatest, don't pull away. Have a conversation (bring gentleness, charisma, and humor). Learn what your partner needs, whether its romance, a night in a hotel (away from kids), a little more build-up of anticipation through the day, perhaps a hot shower or back rub before you get to it, a new nightie, or some creativity. A little extra effort can go a long way.

Serving your marriage is one aspect of your life together. But there are also ways to protect your marriage. This goes right along with who you are as a police officer.

You exert a lot of energy and time keeping yourself safe on the job. You've been trained to protect yourself by putting strategic boundaries in place, and ways to react should something go wrong. Your marriage and family need protection too.

Protect Your Marriage Through Provision

Planning for the what-if is a necessity in your line of work. If something happens to you, you need to know that your family will be taken care of.

Departments differ widely as to what they offer as far as benefits and programs that offer assistance for LODDs or disability on the job. Educate yourself in what you have available and what you don't have. Then make it a priority to make up the difference.

Here's a checklist for every law enforcement family to make sure that you have your bases covered:

- Life Insurance: How much do you need? How much can you afford? Do some shopping around. Dave Ramsey, author of The Total Money Makeover, has a program on his website that compares different companies and what they offer. Check the Resource Guide at the back of this book.
- Do you have disability insurance? See the Appendix to make sure that you are covered in case of injury on the job.
- Do you have a will or living trust? If not, get one.
- Have you written down preferences for burial and funeral?
- Who is your current beneficiary? Be sure to update this information regularly. I've heard many stories of ex-wives or es-

tranged families that get the insurance money and Line of Duty Death (LODD) benefits, leaving children penniless.

- Do you have an emergency fund of a minimum of $1000?
- Do you have an emergency plan in case of fire, earthquakes, tornadoes, or other disasters? Have you trained your spouse and kids on what to do?
- Do you have extra food, water, candles, and batteries in your home?
- Do you have a master list of passwords for all of your accounts?
- Where is all of your information kept? Do you have it organized and accessible should your family have to evacuate in a hurry?
- Are the weapons in your home in a safe? Do you have the combinations accessible for your spouse?

Because your job puts you at risk, having these provisions in place will alleviate some fear and keep you ready for the unexpected. You hope to never have to implement any of it, but if you do, you protect you and your family.

Protect Your Marriage: Set Boundaries

Because your family deals with many complications that chip away at time together, you and your family need to set boundaries.

Your time is valuable. You need to take care of yourself physically, which includes healthy food, exercise, and sleep. That takes time and effort, and can be interwoven with time spent with your spouse and children. You work long hours, and there are times where overtime is mandatory. But when overtime is a choice, think twice about the cost of being away from your family.

In preparation for this book, I put together four focus group dinners of officers in the area. I was very pleased to hear the reasons for those who couldn't make it—it wasn't necessarily work that kept them away; it was time with their families. One officer elected to attend his son's soccer game. Another took his daughter to a father-daughter dance. Another couple became grandparents the very week of the dinner, and made their family a priority. And the dinner I tried to put together with female officers didn't actually happen because the majority of the gals couldn't get away because of their children. For the officers that did make the dinners without their wives, I sent flowers home to their spouses—because I know and understand the sacrifice they made by giving me the evening.

Your uniform attracts attention that could be dangerous to your marriage. There's a name for women who are turned on by the officer image—badge bunnies. This is a humorous and seemingly harmless label, but there are many who've brought an officer to ruin relationally, financially, and for some, their very job.

A retired CHP officer told me that as a rookie he was having coffee with his supervisor and a shapely waitress sauntered by with an alluring smile. His sergeant noticed the exchange and warned, "That badge will get you ass; but that ass will get your badge." I personally have witnessed several officers over the years that "fished from the company pier" and brought on a divorce and negative career consequences.

With these all-too-common realities, placing boundaries in three areas will protect you from having an affair. They are our minds, our bodies, and our unions.

Guard Your Mind

Actions come from choices. Choices come from thoughts. Therefore, we have to start with our minds.

Most extramarital affairs begin with some kind of emotional attraction. Emotional affairs can and do lead to sexual affairs. It usually starts out innocent. There's a mutual respect that leads to more time together. The respect can lead to trust and if not checked, vulnerability and dependence develops. This is an emotional affair. We begin to depend on someone other than our spouse for emotional support, and this is dangerous.

This type of thing happened in the aftermath of 9/11. Because so many policemen and firemen were lost, those who survived decided that they would take care of the surviving families. In many cases, emotional affairs began as the widows depended emotionally upon these men. The emotional affairs developed into sexual relationships, and some of these men divorced their wives and married the widows. It was devastating on many levels as wives and children of surviving rescuers eventually lost them to the widows of those who had died. They, too, became victims of 9/11.

So how do we protect ourselves from emotional affairs? First of all, awareness helps. Beware the person who claims that you are the only one who they can talk to. This is a red flag, and it isn't true. What is true is that this person has chosen you as their confidant and is already becoming emotionally attached. Guard yourself against this situation.

Create boundaries with others in this regard. Learn to keep an eye out for those who would seek to attach themselves emotionally to you. Brent refers to his "spidey-sense"—a feeling that something isn't quite right that puts his guard up, even if he can't identify it at a conscious level.

Many years ago, Brent was working on a project with a co-worker. Their interaction was easy and comfortable. Then one day Brent felt a slight change in her demeanor, and soon after she suggested they meet for lunch to discuss an aspect of the project. He agreed, but then something didn't sit right. Because he had that "spidey-sense," he asked a couple of guys about it the next day. "Run," they told him, "and don't look back." He took their advice. He called the woman, told her something came up, and didn't reschedule.

Guard yourself on social media and email, and especially texting. Oh the sordid tales that began with innocent texting, developed into sexting, and then full-blown affairs blew up in their faces. Where is the appropriate boundary? Draw a line and step far from it. Stay out of the gray area.

Another pitfall of the mind to guard against is pornography. Billions of dollars are spent in the shadows of time spent alone drawn toward these images. Many people think it is harmless, a cheap thrill. Problem is, porn is addictive and warps your perspective.

Years ago I met with a friend every few weeks for coffee. One morning I overslept, so texted her to cancel. She chased me down, as her entire family was in distress. Her daughter caught her husband in an awkward porn moment, and the secret was out. The humiliation was overwhelming, not only for the dad, but for his wife and kids. They ended up having a family meeting with all their kids, exposing the problem, and then sought help and accountability to begin the healing process within their marriage and family. Bringing this issue out into the open was actually very positive; there were no secrets anymore, and their trust as a family grew. The couple is still together today, growing together as they grow old.

Pornography is not a victimless crime. Many women are shamed when they learn what they compete with, or are subjected to in response to ideas that cross their comfort zones in the bedroom. For one officer, getting caught in a porn moment by his wife escalated into domestic violence, and ultimately a broken marriage. At the very least, pornography fills your mind with sex that doesn't include your committed partner, and that separates and isolates you, threatening the bond you share with your spouse.

Guard Your Body

Every affair begins with a choice to entertain temptations. Our bodies have strong biological needs. Somehow, those needs have to be met. So, the first way to safeguard you from extramarital affairs is to have frequent sex together. Like I said earlier, sometimes this will take an act of the will, depending on circumstances. But if you are investing in your sex life, temptations toward someone else will naturally decrease.

But what if one of you is in a season of boredom in this area? What if you aren't getting along like you used to? What if our eyes wander toward someone who is attractive, or that badge bunny comes onto you? How can we abstain from those temptations when there are problems at home?

We have to be all the more vigilant. Recognize the enemies that want to destroy your marriage and be wise to your own vulnerabilities. You do this on duty—you listen to your sixth sense that is keen to something that isn't right, and you put yourself on alert. In this sense, you must remain vigilant at all times.

Another way to safeguard from affairs is to keep away from the wrong places and the wrong people. If someone is coming on to you, cut off contact or distance yourself, no matter how tempting or non-tempting they are. Both Brent and I over the years have had to put this into play a couple of times. We also talk about it. Many times I can tell if a woman is dangerous—someone not to be trusted because she's attracted and available to my husband. She won't look me in the eye. Or she ignores me completely. Or she acts overtly fake. I will warn Brent if I sense something, and I'm usually accurate. He's learned to trust this, and will take appropriate action, whether he senses it or not.

If you are attracted to someone else, make yourself accountable to someone you trust. And that could include your own spouse.

The Partner/Spouse Dynamic

I had a conversation about police wives with Angel and Cathy, officers with the California Highway Patrol.

"Spouses hate us," said Angel.

"Oh yeah, we get dirty looks, comments, and spouses who fight with their officers about working with us," agreed Cathy.

"I don't get it, because we are both happily married. Just because we work with men, doesn't mean we want to sleep with them," added Angel.

This conversation gave me new appreciation. I would've been a little worried if one of them were my husband's partner. There's something threatening about a beautiful woman or handsome man in uniform that spends many hours with your spouse.

"I get it," says Kim, "There are wives who don't like their husbands being in a car with a woman all night. They see an empty pillow when they're sleeping, and wonder and worry. I'm spending all night with their husband and the imagination can run wild. You spend more time with your partner than your spouse."

Early on in Brent's career he had a female rookie he was training. He told me she was pretty and very sharp. I was tempted to be jealous, so I invited her and another officer over for dinner. Yes, she was beautiful. And she was in shape. At dinner they shared details of some of the incidents they handled.

Intimidating? A bit. But I allowed myself to like her. She was funny and tough as nails. She had a twinkle in her eye and a great smile. We are friends to this day.

Women sometimes feel threatened by each other. We are jealous of what the other has that we don't have. We can be fearful that someone more beautiful, more clever, or with bigger breasts will interfere with the relationship we're building. When a spouse is eight months pregnant and irritable and her husband is partnered with a female hard body, that messes with the insecurities of being unattractive, even if temporary. If a spouse and her husband are having difficulties in their relationship, the fears grow. It isn't fair to cops who have no interest in their partner as a lover, but it is the reality of this adversarial jealousy thing.

There are, however, some things you can do to alleviate a spouse's fear. The number one thing is to meet each other. Kim and her male partner became best friends over years of working together. Early on she said to her partner David, "Tell your wife we're coming over. Introduce us. Let her see me."

When you as the partner meet the spouse, look her in the eye. Talk to her. Find some common ground. Show her that you're friendly, in love with your own spouse (if applicable), and that this is a professional relationship.

Then follow up on that professionalism. It's important to keep your boundaries on and off the job. If your partner is married and you're not, you may want to step up the boundaries even more. Physical affection should be seldom or non-existent. Texting off-duty unless work-related is a red flag. Sexting is taboo.

One way I keep myself in check as far as other men is linking the married couple as one in my mind. When I see Scott, I see Heidi, and vice versa. They are one. If I say something to a guy that I wouldn't want his spouse to hear, I've crossed the line.

Spending time with your partner and his family is a good thing, too. Male partners do this all the time, why not you, too?

April is a dispatcher and a valued member of the peer support team. Officers in her department were involved in a shootout that affected many. The last of six critical incident debriefs included spouses. One spouse was extremely agitated, exhibiting horrible behavior towards April. April recognized that this gal was fearful and putting up a fuss to cover her inner turmoil. April decided to be overly kind to her. This allowed the gal to lower her guard and eventually talk about her fears.

"These ladies don't know their husbands on a work level," April explained. "They don't get it, they don't know the jokes, the language. They don't see it on a regular basis. They do a lot of guessing. When this lady broke down, it was built-up yuck from years and years of being in the dark."

Lastly, if the spouse is unable to come to terms with insecurity, let it go. Mary says, "If something goes sour and you're innocent, you can't do anything about it. Don't own it. That's their problem. You do what you can do to better it, but it's something they need to work out."

Guard Your Union

I once heard a speaker refer to sex as fire. He said, "A fire in the fireplace will warm a home. Fire outside of the fireplace will burn the house down." In other words, sex has great rewards if it has boundaries. Sex without boundaries can ruin everything.

Sex is an intimate, trust-building uniting of two bodies, hearts, and souls. The boundary here is that we keep it just between husband and wife. We have to safeguard our union by not letting anything or anyone join us in the bedroom or come between us during sex. This includes other people. This includes pornography. This includes letting our minds wander during sex. Any inclusion of others into our sexual relationship will break down the uniting factor in our relationship. And it will introduce mistrust.

The following section is tough talk for those of you who are choosing to break up your family for someone else.

An Appeal to the One Who Wants Out

This section is for the one who serves and protects. You stand up for our communities and say, "I will not let you" because the act is destructive. It hurts others, causes chaos, and even though what the criminal wants to do may seem good to him at the time, it will ultimately lead to destruction of his own life. Thank you for putting on your uniform day after day and going out on the streets, protecting and serving those of us who appreciate you, and those who don't appreciate you.

You want out of your marriage. You are tired of the life that you have made with your spouse and you are daring to think that a life without him/her would be better. You have walked away, shut down the love, and have been looking elsewhere.

You work long hours. The job takes its toll. You see things that people do to each other that are inexcusable. You've seen that life isn't fair. You've seen who people are at their worst. Your job as a peacekeeper is difficult and lonely.

I've heard that almost three out of four police officers experience divorce. It's become a common thing—an expectation even—something other cops will tell you up front you're headed for. So don't even try. Lower your expectations, get what you can out of each relationship, and then when it gets tough, just cut bait and leave. Move onto wife number two. It's what cops do.

I acknowledge the person you married is difficult to live with. She doesn't understand. She complains. She doesn't seem happy. You're not getting enough sex. She doesn't look like she did when she walked down the aisle to pledge her life to you.

Your life may not be what you imagined it would be. It isn't what you want anymore. It's been this way for so long that there's no point in trying because you're so tired and worn out and it's just not worth the work to try.

There are others who look at you in your beautiful uniform and desire you. They are ready, willing and able to please you. They seem to understand, especially if they are wearing the same uniform. You're beautiful. You're desired. You feel things you haven't felt in a long time.

But it's a lie.

Being a cop does not mean that you have to be alone. It does not mean that you will get a divorce. This is, pardon the pun, a cop out.

I appeal to you as a warrior. You are willing to stand up and say NO! To fight for what's right. You're willing to lay your life down for this. Why, as a warrior, are you so unwilling to fight for your own marriage? For your family?

Your spouse is a human being. Complex. Difficult. Hard to understand. So are you. Complex. Difficult. Hard to understand. And your job makes things even more complex, difficult, and hard to understand. You put your life on the line, and you know what? So does she. She puts her sense of security on the line. She puts her heart on the line. She says if something happens, I will make up the slack. I will carry on the family in your stead. And while your crisis-driven career makes your lives tumultuous, she says I will support, I will flex, I will go to things alone, I will let go of my expectations, I will do what is needed to make us work.

Who does that? Who puts up with that? Someone who fiercely loves. Someone strong. Someone who has character. Someone who deserves that fierce love back. Someone who will serve and protect the life that she herself is willing to sacrifice for. She doesn't deserve to be walked away from.

A long life together is a progression of seasons. There will be winter seasons—when life is colorless and there isn't much sex and you're bored. But if you stick with it, and make choices to invest in your relationship, the spring will come, the summer will come, and it is continually a life of adventure, and pain, and happiness, and history, and goodness.

I appeal to you as a discerner. When your gut is telling you that something isn't quite right, you put yourself on alert. You get in defensive posture, ready to take on the threat that you sense. But why do you allow yourself to be lulled in by a beautiful woman or sweet-talking man? A person who is willing to enter into a relationship with a married cop is nothing but a thief. That person is willing to take something that isn't theirs because they WANT it. Don't you arrest thieves?

She may be hot, but she's selfish. He may seem to understand, but it really is all about him. And she may be willing to have sex, but she'll dig her claws into you and destroy your marriage, your kids, your wallet, and your soul. And when he's drained you dry, he'll move on.

I appeal to you as a peace officer. Why have you stopped protecting your marriage? Why have you stopped serving your marriage? Because it was too hard? Because you're too tired? Those cops who turn and run in the face of difficulty are called cowards. Stand up and be the brave officer that you are.

You took an oath. To love, honor and cherish till death do you part. When did you stop loving? When did you stop honoring? When did you stop cherishing? Go back there. Start again. You have a choice to stand in the gap and say, NO! No divorce. No bad marriage.

As one who has put her heart on the line, she deserves it. As one who has put your life on the line, you deserve it.

This is for the one who serves and protects. I'm appealing to you to stand up for your marriage and put your choice on the line and say, "I will not give up." Because leaving for someone else is destructive. It hurts others, causes chaos, and even though it may seem good to you now, it will ultimately lead to destruction of your own life.

When the Worst Happens: Kyle's Story

Kyle never dreamed his wife was having an affair. They'd been through a lot together over the years and had come through it. Things were good. Until he walked in and caught his wife in bed with another man.

"You'd be proud of me, Vick, I didn't kill him," he confided. "I wanted to, but frankly, God stopped me." What followed was a long road to reconciliation, after the investigation into her claims of when it started, of course. "I stopped investigating at five months prior to finding out. That was enough. I couldn't believe she would do this and I didn't have a clue."

Kyle talked about the fallout. "Adultery opens the exit door in marriage," he said. "I was in it for forever. But after that, I realized she had introduced mistrust at its core. And it was the darkest, most painful time in my life. I was a former fighter and have had broken bones all through my body. But nothing compares to the pain of that night."

Once someone steps out of the marriage to sleep with someone else, that person becomes a cheater—someone who has proven they can't be trusted. For many couples, that's it. The marriage is over. To trust again is very difficult; and if the relationship is to continue, it takes years to rebuild that trust.

If you've decided as a couple that you're going to try to work it out (see Kathy and Adam's success story in chapter seven), there are realities that apply to this situation:

- The cheater must be repentant. Repentant actually means, "to return." It's not just about being sorry that you made a mistake. The cheater has to make a choice to leave the affair, end it completely (all contact), and return to the spouse. There is no other way to make it work.
- There has been a wounding, so there must be time allowed to heal. This probably means the cheater may be taking cold showers for a while while trust is built back up.

- When trust has been taken, it has to be earned back. The cheater should be completely transparent for however long it takes (emails, phone records, texts, and time accounted for).
- Because affairs are symptoms of other issues, go back and look at the problems you had in your marriage before the affair. Go back and talk, make choices to improve together, and work at making things better than they were.
- For the one who's been cheated on, there is usually some kind of traumatization or devastation involved. Kyle said that he was exhibiting some of the symptoms of post-traumatic stress—so went to counseling not only with his wife, and also alone to deal with these symptoms. "It's like a videotape that replays in my mind over and over," he described. "I'm dealing with the trauma of the cheating."
- The last thing I'll mention is that at some point, there needs to be forgiveness. Forgiveness is not cheap, and it isn't a free pass. "Grieving begins with denial—believing this can't be true—and ends with acceptance of the reality that exists," says Dr. David Stoop in his book, Forgiving the Unforgiveable. "In between these two stages of denial and acceptance are the two basic facets of grieving: anger and sadness. In order to process our grief, we must experience both anger and sadness, and in order to forgive, we must grieve." Forgiveness is a process. Once the grieving is done, there is a decision to let go of anger and sadness, then to move on. In Kathy and Adam's case, this was key—even though he had hurt her deeply, she grieved for months but chose to stand by him, forgiving him. Then over time they rebuilt trust.

Protect Your Marriage Through Gratitude

The last thing that can protect and bless your marriage is gratitude. When years run together and your marriage seems to take more work, it is easy to lose perspective. We get tired. We get grumpy. And we can concentrate on each other's negative qualities and be tempted to look elsewhere. Choosing to be grateful for each other can turn this around. We all have weaknesses and things in our character that could use improvement. But that's only half of the story. We all have good qualities, too. When we choose an attitude of thankfulness for positive things in our spouse, we reinstate value to each other and our relationships. Gratitude protects.

• •

Think: What area do I serve my marriage well? What area do I protect my marriage well?

Debrief: Is there an area in this chapter that deserves some special attention in your marriage?

Strategic Action: Take a look at the provision list. Work on one or two items with your spouse and children. Make it a project to work on together.

"My heroes are those who risk their lives every day to protect our world and make it a better place—police, firefighters, and members of our armed forces."
Sidney Sheldon

CHAPTER SIX

COMMUNICATION

"Effective communication solidifies relationships,
while poor communication can destroy them."
Jim Glennon, Arresting Communication

It had been a long and stressful day dealing with the death of a five-year-old girl for Robert, who was a new detective. He checked his phone and sighed. His wife had called several times. He'd not had a chance to text or call to let her know he would be late. No doubt she was upset.

He walked into the silent house and called her name. Nothing. He made his way to the bedroom, where she lay bundled in the covers. "Hey," he whispered, not sure if it was better to just let her sleep.

She wasn't asleep. What followed was a barrage of verbal ammunition, two to the body, and one to the head. She unloaded, reloaded, and went on to complain that she was very sick, worried, angry, and dinner was thrown out hours before.

Robert took it, reluctantly. She had no idea what he had dealt with all day. The images burned deep, and his compassion was a vice that tightened its grip on his mind. He didn't want to explain. He was too tired to fight back. So he said nothing.

Sometimes there are so many words that you just can't find one.

Communication is the most important aspect of your job. Information in and information out provides direction, shapes each shift, and helps meet expectations of brass, colleagues, dispatchers, and customers. Clear communication keeps you safe. You're dealing with all kinds and interaction with each person is a bit different. You will talk differently with a suspect than with your supervisor. Communicating with an accident witness is very different than when booking a drug addict into jail. You ebb and flow with the situations, as do your words and tone.

Communication is also the most important aspect of your marriage. It gives direction, enhances or detracts from intimacy, and educates you both on expectations. Clear communication keeps you thriving. Through the years, as you learn to communicate with your spouse, you ebb and flow with the changes. Somehow along the way you begin to really understand each other. Your relationship is a work in progress—learning and growing as you communicate.

But somehow communication is also the greatest problem in marriages. It's the basis for everything, from what to have for dinner to sharing your most intimate thoughts. There are many hurdles to good communication.

Words come from deep within a person's soul. They originate from a set of values, experiences and personality. But those same words, when heard by someone else, are received into a whole new set of values, experiences and personality. The same word can mean something completely different to two people and changes based on tone, inflection, and context. We speak different languages based on the filters of growing up, personal beliefs, memories, even your training as a police officer.

It's in this moment between mouth and ears that miscommunication happens. The words are lost in translation. Since good communication is so critical for a lasting relationship, we must learn to speak each other's language.

When you're part of a team, whether a patrol team or SWAT, or even a K-9 handler, you agree on the terms of communication. Hand motions, codes, or commands in German become second nature as you learn and train together.

The same goes for you and your spouse.

Two individuals. Common direction. You've got to learn and practice how you talk with each other. It's not me, it's we. As you work through the day to day living together, you develop communication that is unique to you as a couple. But like team training, you both have to listen to each other and talk to each other, agreeing on the common goal. Healthy couples are deliberate in their communication.

Tactical teams spend time learning to communicate—hours and hours of repetitive drills so that everyone knows what each other's roles are and how to work alongside each other in high stakes situations. Although you and your spouse are not conducting a search warrant or dealing with a hostage situation, you are maneuvering through years of challenges, child-rearing, financial pressure, health issues, and each other's careers.

Let's take a brief look at four of the challenges of learning to speak each other's language—personality differences, gender differences, the ways we give and receive love, and the filters that we place in between each other. Gaining knowledge and wisdom in each will go a long way toward improving communication with your spouse.

> *"Never be afraid to say, 'I love you.'*
> *Those are three powerful words*
> *that should be spoken often."*
> Chuck Norris

Communicating Amidst Personality Differences

No matter how intentional you are about finding someone to share your life with who is like you, chances are you are married to your complete opposite. It is true that opposites attract. Extroverts pair up well with introverts. Artistic people pair well with intellectuals. There seems to be something about our differences that fit together—almost like we need each other to fill in the blank spaces where we are lacking. Communication is key to your marriage, whether you allow those differences to completely separate you, or to embrace the differences between you and learn from each other.

Several years ago, Brent and I had reached a point in our marriage where we were in a rut, struggling to understand each other. We were clashing—not in sync—and we were both frustrated. We are naturally very different in our personalities, and we weren't getting along. Then Brent brought home a book called, The Delicate Art of Dancing with Porcupines, by Bob Phillips. This book describes four types of people—the Analytical, the Driver, the Expressive, and the Amiable—and explores how each interacts and communicates. We answered the questions in the book and were amazed at the results.

Once I understood the natural tendencies of my husband, it was a huge aha! moment, and vice versa. We spent a couple of hours laughing at each other's tendencies, and how we differ. It gave us freedom to be ourselves, and a non-threatening way to give each other the freedom to discover who we are. It was a huge step toward understanding each other, and our relationship has improved because of it. When we come to a situation from two different sides, we are able to see where each other is coming from, and then come to a better solution for both.

This practice has actually mellowed us both out over time. I've learned so much from Brent's "just the facts" demeanor, and he has learned from my relational insight. We've worked hard at it, and the payoff is healthy communication.

"Communication leads to community, that is,
to understanding, intimacy and mutual valuing."
Rollo May

Gender Tendencies

Many people get irritated with the obvious differences between males and females. I've seen women try to make an attempt to get their husbands in touch with their feminine side. Men seem to either joke or just shake their heads at female tendencies. It is almost impossible to truly understand the inner workings of the opposite sex, especially in a relationship.

But if we accept the differences and learn to appreciate them rather than try to change each other, we'll save ourselves the frustration. Be who you are as a woman or man, and let your spouse be the same. Accept the fact that she has a lot more words to say in a day, and make your fewer words count. Celebrate your ability to be firm with the kids when your spouse wavers. Understand the way you like to have a conversation—women generally like to talk face-to-face, while men talk best side-by-side while occupied.

Our personality traits, strengths, and natural tendencies are so different, it seems that we could never be compatible. But with the right attitude and enough time, you and your spouse can learn to respect each other's strengths and weaknesses. It is beautiful to behold a couple with this kind of balance.

I had to laugh when I heard a guy talk about the ways men and women communicate. He said that when women describe a situation, they speak to inspire first. Men tend to identify first. This describes Brent and I to a tee. I like to tell stories—to make you feel like you're there, what the context is, and then I'll give you the blow-by-blow. Brent has asked me to "go in the barn" on more than one occasion. I'll be sharing my story—describing the barn in detail, how I feel about the barn, and how I walk into the barn. He wants me to just go in the barn. In other words, get to the point.

In our early years, I took offense at this. But then I realized he listens better when he knows where we're going. The details take on more meaning to him when he knows what the point is. He does care and he does want to listen and understand. Going in the barn right away and then adding the details later is good communication, for him and yes, for me as well. I've since adapted this practice in professional interviews and when dealing with my kids.

The key is to understand the effect that gender difference has on your marital communication. Talk this over with your spouse and purpose to get better at communicating by appreciating the differences. The things that cause friction now are sometimes related to traits that attracted you in the beginning.

Love Languages

Depending on our personalities, we feel loved and show love in our own language. In Gary Chapman's book, The 5 Love Languages: The Secret to Love that Lasts, he describes five ways in which people feel loved. They are:

- Quality Time
- Gifts
- Words of Affirmation
- Physical Touch
- Acts of Service

Each person has at least one of these ways they feel loved, and they tend to show love this way as well. But when spouses have different love languages, it may be that neither actually feels the love that's communicated. More often than not, this is the case.

Brent shows his love most naturally by taking care of things around the house, ordering for me online, solving my computer problems, or shuttling the kids so I have a break here and there. This is Acts of Service. I am a word gal—I like to tell him how much I appreciate him, send him notes, and say, "love you" often, which is Words of Affirmation.

Before we understood each other's love language, his Acts of Service ways of telling me he loved me fell short. I didn't recognize these acts as his way of loving me. I also couldn't understand why he'd get so amped when I didn't pick up his uniforms from the dry cleaners. In his mind, I didn't care. But I certainly did—I told him so over and over!

When we identify our spouse's love language, we teach ourselves to speak it. When I want to really show Brent that I love him, I clean the house from top to bottom. I get groceries, and have supplies on hand for him when he runs out of something. This is more important to him than my verbal encouragement (although I naturally do this, too). Brent speaks my love language by buying me cards, speaking words of gratitude, and making it a point to affirm my good points on a regular basis, in addition to washing my car. This way we are both feeling loved in our own languages.

Just knowing how to speak each other's love language can improve your communication dramatically. It takes a choice on two fronts: Choose to show love in her language, and recognize her love language towards you and appreciate it. If you want to be proactive—talk about love languages together and use the knowledge to love each other more effectively.

The Sixth Love Language—Verbal Spar

I mentioned five love languages. About 98% of the population give and show love through these five practices. To my knowledge, nobody had ever come up with another, until a conversation I had with some friends.

"I don't think my husband shows or feels love in these ways. There is a sixth love language."

I don't remember what she called it, but she went on to describe a sort of sarcasm that isn't designed to wound. It's a way of communicating with a smirk and a twinkle that is affectionate. It's a challenge to step into the ring and tease each other because we're friends. Similar, yet opposite of Words of Affirmation, there are words that communicate love, but on their face are anything but affirming. It's a different level of sophistication—entering into an arena that is insulting yet playful. Unsafe and safe at the same time. But it still communicates love.

My father-in-law communicates this way (he's a former deputy sheriff). If you can't handle the verbal spar, he doesn't respect you. My thoughts went to several co-workers of my husband, and a Vietnam Vet whom I dabbled in the ring with at a book function, and especially my co-author of Selfish Prayer—he is the champion of Verbal Spar.

I thought of the time I presented to 30 middle management police officers in Oakland. It was slightly uncomfortable talking to this group of mostly men who sat in a U-shape, dressed in their uniforms with bars gleaming from the fluorescent lights above. They sat stone-faced, wheels turning, some making a few notes as I shared what I offer police marriages. I spoke in my normal way, speaking passionately about my cause. And then, one poked at me by asking, "Got anything in that book of yours that deals with cops that want to sleep with married cops? Cause that's what I'm dealing with right now."

Here we go, I thought, and went on to mention that yes, I do mention this briefly in my book, and then said something like, "That's why I do what I do. It may be kind of Pollyanna, but perhaps if we can strengthen marriages, you won't have to deal with it on duty."

Non-verbal cues told me they weren't convinced. So I switched to

Verbal Spar—the sixth love language. "Look, we do what we can, but shit happens!"

The entire room erupted into laughter. I was suddenly one of the club. Believe it or not, I felt trusted. I'd made the connection. Not by speaking my language, but theirs.

I'm declaring that there is a sixth love language. It is a language of love and trust spoken by men and women who deal with painful realities of the world—cops, military, search and rescue, firemen, and medical personnel. Probably others, too.

Verbal Sparring is a tough language to speak because it dances close to uncomfortable. And sometimes Verbal Sparring draws blood. It is a different way of loving and communicating love that is safe within the life that demands we toughen up and deal with the crap flying around.

Filters

In my seminar I bring up volunteers and have them play a couple rounds of Catch Phrase. Catch Phrase is this little machine that gives you a specific name or phrase and the user tries to describe it in a way that helps your team guess the answer. Afterwards we debrief the different communication tactics used.

One police officer made a really great observation. "Beware, I'm goin' deep," she said. "When I got my phrase, I clicked it forward—I didn't like it and felt I wouldn't be able to describe it. I didn't like the second phrase either, so I pushed the forward button again. Finally, a phrase I could describe. When I talk to my spouse, I put a filter on the things I say—for his protection, or sometimes my own. There are things I don't want to say, so I move on to something else."

She touched on something we deal with more than we'd like to admit. There are definitely things you don't want to tell your spouse—perhaps things you've seen and dealt with on duty, or something you did you know she hates. It's to protect her in the first, and protect you in the latter. Some of these filters are necessary. But what if it's something you really need to talk about but your spouse isn't willing—like problems with the kids, or sex, or overspending? If we push the forward button again and again on a sore subject because we are avoiding a difficult conversation, we sabotage intimacy and trust. Eventually the problem will grow so big it becomes a crisis. Have the conversation. Use filters only when absolutely necessary. Seek understanding on both sides, and then work towards a solution.

Communication Killers and Keepers

Learning to speak each other's language is a lifelong pursuit. It's the big picture—a little something to keep in the back of your mind year to year. But what about day to day? That's where the bulk of our communication lies.

There are behaviors and mindsets that will kill the ability to communicate and there are attitudes and boundaries that will keep the communication flowing—communication killers and keepers. In the following pages, I explain each killer, and it's opposing keeper.

Unspoken Expectations vs. No Assumptions

If you want to learn each other's language, you have to speak. Much of miscommunication is unspoken. We develop assumptions based on our own personal views and values. We have assumptions about how relationships operate, how they should be, and then these assumptions turn into expectations. But when those expectations are not talked about, they inevitably are unmet.

When Robert's wife unloaded on him because he was late, the root problem was unspoken expectations. Job changes brought on the expectation from work that he stay and deal with the investigation until he was done. Robert and his wife hadn't discussed this new way of doing things. She also had not voiced her expectation that he call, or that when she was sick it was even more important that he be home. He did not meet these expectations because he didn't know about them. A 30-second text that says, "I'm safe, on a case, no dinner. See you late tonight," would've holstered her weapon. She wouldn't have been happy, but at least she could've slept while he worked his case instead of fixing dinner and then seething when it went untouched.

Expectations do not kill communication; failing to express them does.

"Assumptions are the termites of relationships."
Henry Winkler

Take the time to talk about expectations for events, the what ifs, your job, even how you wish to be comforted or loved. Then negotiate realistic solutions to those expectations. There are no assumptions!

Unforgiveness vs. Keeping Short Account

Unforgiveness will not only kill communication, it will kill your relationship, and could eventually kill your soul. No matter how you look at it, you lose. The thing that keeps communication flowing is to keep a short account. Let the anger go.

Brent refers to this as the emotional bank account. When we spend time together, speak each other's language, have good sex, etc., we are making deposits into our relationship. Chronic arguments about the same thing, harsh words, unspoken or impossible expectations, slamming doors, etc., are withdrawals from your relationship. Just like money, you look at your account at the end of each month and hopefully your account is in the black. But too many withdrawals will cause your account to be overdrawn.

The currency of your relationship isn't cash, it's trust. When there isn't enough give for the take, you run into problems.

The overdraft protection is forgiveness. Forgiveness doesn't condone or make excuses for the wrong, but rather sets the anger free so that it doesn't cause long term damage.

The fact is we are human, and humans are flawed. You married a flawed human being. Your spouse married a flawed human being. He will make mistakes, he will hurt you, and he will handle things with selfish motives. You, too, will make mistakes, hurt others, and handle situations poorly. Knowing that your spouse and your children will let you down from time to time, resolve to talk it through and then respond with forgiveness.

Unkindness vs. Setting Speech Boundaries

"We have a rule in our marriage. No name calling.
My husband's first marriage was an abusive one, both
mentally and physically. I don't fight or argue that way,
and I never have. My husband doesn't either.
As far as both of us are concerned, there's never a reason
enough to resort to tearing each other apart that way.
And it does. No. Good. Ever."
Bethany, Michigan

As a law enforcement family, there will always be pressures. Unfortunately, the easiest place to release that pressure is on those closest to us. The closer you get, the worse it can be. Because we are so entwined, when our spouses go through stuff, it affects us and vice versa.

Add to that the reality of moods. Everyone gets irritated with each other, and the kids. You or your spouse could be pushing aside bothersome thoughts, and it comes out in rudeness. Unkindness has a way of creeping in and we treat each other poorly. Little digs here and there, our voices raise a bit, our patience wears thin.

Our first Christmas together, Brent and I got into a huge argument. I was so angry I threw a hairbrush at him, which further inflamed the situation. After we calmed down and talked through the issue, we also decided that we needed to implement some ground rules for the way we speak to each other.

We never use divorce as a threat. We decided that this was too big of a withdrawal for us both. Brent's parents divorced when he was young, so divorce is a painful subject. I came into our relationship with trust issues brought on by philandering ex-boyfriends. We chose to treat this topic as taboo. The commitment that we made has taken away from this temptation. We never go there.

Second, we don't use sarcasm (different from verbal sparring).

When there are unresolved conflicts in a relationship, sarcasm is so tempting. But it is also a cowardly way to throw insults. Someone says something mean and then laughs it off as a joke. It's not a joke. It hurts just as much. And usually, sarcasm is used when other people are around. Let me just say, if you use sarcasm against your spouse in front of other people, you just created an embarrassing situation, and cast a shadow on your own character.

> *"The Bible gives a list of what love looks like. It begins with love is patient; love is kind. In my relationship with my wife, I can't even get past the first two..."*
> Highway Patrolman, California

The third boundary we set is that we will never insult each other's character. This includes name-calling, comparisons with other people, and just being mean.

This doesn't mean that we don't joke or tease. But jokes and teasing are not meant to cut someone down, but rather to lighten up. In fact, humor is an excellent way to release some pressure.

Selfishness is a Barrier

Selfishness is both a part of our culture, and very destructive to our relationships. Culture encourages us to look out for ourselves, to be self-focused. We're also naturally inclined to respond to our own desires, feelings, and whims. It's so ingrained in culture and our being that it can be difficult to identify this in ourselves.

The problem with being self-focused is decisions and actions don't take into consideration others, and this can lead to mistreatment and hurt. Selfishness tends to blind a person to what is best for everyone involved.

You have sworn to your department that you will set selfishness aside—to lay down your life to save another. This is unselfishness at its finest—a quality hard to find when everything goes sideways.

But in our personal relationships, we each have wants and needs that call to be met. There will be times where you don't really care what your spouse needs. You're the one who's worked 12 hours and are so tired you can't see straight. You are so distracted by what you need, it's a stretch to even consider what she wants.

"The biggest communication problem is
we do not listen to understand. We listen to apply."
Unknown

It is then we have to make a choice to listen with a desire to understand what would be best for each other. Think we, not me. Close our mouths and let the other talk. Engage. It requires character—humility, even—to set ourselves aside for a time to carefully listen.

You've probably heard that marriage is a 50-50 endeavor. Each partner gives 50% and meets the other in the middle, so no one is giving or taking too much. Great theory, but doesn't work. When both spouses are striving towards giving 100% of themselves, you've got a surplus to work with. As life moves on, one spouse gives what they can give, and the other can make up the difference for a time. And then vice-versa.

What are you willing to give to make your relationship thrive? How relationally giving are you? Are you relationally stingy much of the time, not giving of yourself in ways that your spouse would really appreciate? Or do you love as if it were your duty, counting it as joy?

Self-centeredness in a relationship complicates the difficulty of meshing and growing and creating a life together. Being relationally generous—giving of yourself, thinking we not me, and working hard to understand—this is the formula for a great marriage.

Fixing vs. Listening

> *"Men listen for one reason: the point… There usually has to be a logical reason for any conversation–a point, and at least a chance for a conclusion… For women, the situation is totally different. Conversations don't need a reason to exist. Rather, they're part of a bonding process."*
> Jim Glennon, Arresting Communication

This is really great insight. One of the most frustrating things for men and women and their approaches to relationships is this piece right here. If you are a man, you tend to want to solve your wife's problem. It's natural. It's logical. She's got a problem; she's coming to you to fix it.

In truth, that's not why she's discussing her problem with you. She just wants you to listen. Be present. Listen with your eyes. Give her the space to process things for herself as she talks it out. It'll take a little more time and attention. It'll require some patience, and the resistance to rush in with the solution. But in that careful listening, you build trust.

You also prefer to be listened to.

Mark responded to a nightmarish call. A deputy's little girl found his gun and accidentally shot herself with it. He didn't know the deputy, but didn't have to—this is a cop's worst nightmare. After several hours on scene, Mark headed home. There was one person he needed to talk to.

April, a dispatcher with the same department, was having dinner with the kids when Mark walked in. She immediately sensed something wasn't right. He stormed into the bedroom as she followed after telling the kids to stay at the table and eat.

He paced, blurting out what happened. She listened intently, stomach tightened, shoulders square. She didn't have to say much; maybe a couple questions at most.

He fought back tears as he recounted the horrific incident. After all, he was still in uniform. Still on duty.

He got it out and stood shaking for a moment. April watched as he squared his back, stood up tall, took a breath and steeled himself. It was time to go back to work.

She hugged him, walked him to the door, and then sat back down with the kids. She had said maybe a few sentences the entire time. There just weren't appropriate words—just the comfort and trust of a safe listener.

As Trust Grows...

Mark and April had built trust between them. They also have spent time understanding what works for their communication. They'd received training on how to listen to each other (peer support training from their department and relational information through their church), and over time the trust has deepened.

It took practice. Time. Patience. Love.

• •

Think: Which communication keeper are you best at? Which communication killer do you find is easy to slip into?

Debrief: How are you doing at learning each other's language? Give an example of something you've learned that is different from your own way of communicating. Keep it positive!

Strategic Action: Spend some time looking at each other's personalities. Either pick up Dancing with Porcupines or take a test online. Talk about the results. Give each other permission to laugh about each other and your own tendencies.

"While I slept last night, I actually have no idea how many drug dealers you tackled to the ground, how many doors you kicked in to rescue women and children being abused. To be honest, I didn't give it much thought. I am so confident in you and your fellow officers; I slept quite soundly knowing you were up all night patrolling the neighborhoods and the streets."

Troy Dunn, Open Letter to Law Enforcement

CHAPTER SEVEN

RULES OF ENGAGEMENT

"Great marriages aren't trouble-free; they just do trouble well."
Chris Brown

"We fight all the time," said Barry, a policeman from Virginia. His wife, Marie, nodded nervously. We stood together in the middle of a sea of peace officers, survivors, spouses, strollers, and others, waiting for the Candlelight Vigil to begin. We were at the National Law Enforcement Memorial.

In the heart of Police Week, many groups of officers descended upon Washington D.C., paying tribute to their fallen comrades in their own way. Some spent the week tipping back red Solo cups. Others biked, ran, and drove to honor specific heroes. Some brought their spouses, eager to share the experience with their backup at home. This is why Barry and Marie were present.

We began to talk about their conflicts, giving them a different perspective of their arguments. Soon, Barry declared, "We need your book."

They looked at their disagreements as something negative. It scared them; made them wonder if they'd made a mistake in getting married. Understandable. But not true.

Marital Disillusionment

You meet someone who is a little different than everyone else. There's chemistry. Attraction. Camaraderie. You take the plunge.

Your marriage begins with great joy. You are starting a life together in deep love that you are confident will never wane.

Until disillusionment creeps in. The time of arrival of this unwelcome visitor varies. But at some point, you realize that things aren't exactly what you thought they'd be.

There was a shift. A difference. Unmet expectations. Arguments. And suddenly, marriage is hard. Disillusionment gives way to doubt. You find yourselves questioning yourself, your spouse, and your future together.

A lot of marriages will hit this stage hard. They're surprised. There was no plan for what life would be like after the wedding. Little vision for the years to come. The engagement was about the wedding, the honeymoon, and then where to put all of the really awesome stuff you got. The excitement dies down, life goes back to normal, and then what?

"Incompatibility is grounds for a very rich marriage.
If you're identical, one of you is not necessary."
Ray Johnston

Skate off into happily ever after, right? Not exactly. This is where the work starts. This is where the process of integrating two lives into one begins. And it isn't easy.

To get through the disillusionment stage, deeper understanding is needed. Whom did I marry? How are we going to live together amidst these conflicts? What do we want in our lives? What has changed? Why are we having so much trouble?

If you seek out the answers to some of these questions, you will find understanding. Understanding your spouse. Understanding you more completely. Understanding how to live together, resolve differences, make compromises, and make changes that benefit you both. You then find yourselves knowing how to love each other just a little bit better. Your love begins to mature and grow.

Falling In and Out of Love

When some couples hit the disillusionment stage, they assume that they've fallen out of love. We say that we fall in love with someone, as we find ourselves primarily intensely attracted to that person. This emotion is only one aspect of what committed, lifelong marital love is about. Love is an action, not a feeling. Feelings flow from actions. You can't fall out of love.

You can, however, choose to stop loving. And when you're struggling, or even miserable, that's what many people decide to do.

Love is about choices. We choose to move forward in our relationships. We choose to learn more about our spouses, and through what we learn, we gain the understanding to be a better lover.

> *"We are creatures of choice. That means that we have the
> capacity to make poor choices, which all of us have done.
> We have spoken critical words, and we have done hurtful things.
> We are not proud of those choices, although they may have seemed
> justified at the moment. Poor choices in the past don't mean we
> must make them in the future. I have seen marriages rescued from
> the brink of divorce when couples make the choice to love."*
> Dr. Gary Chapman, The Five Love Languages, Military Edition

The emotions that drew us together in the beginning may disappear for a time. But those emotions will return once you make a choice to actively understand, actively love.

A New Attitude About Conflict

Conflicts occur when my motivations or ideas are at odds with my spouse's. Essentially, the two of us come from different places, and we've met at the point where we're at an impasse. Marriage brings together two individuals into one life together, and many of the goals, values, and ideas will not mesh immediately. We have two independent personalities that need to work together, depend upon one another, live and love together. This is interdependence.

Arguments are the hashing out of these differences. Conflicts are either barriers to interdependence, or bridges to intimacy. Our attitudes and choices determine which one it will be.

"Once I realized arguments were to move towards resolution instead of to be won, we started moving towards that goal," said Randy. "A cop will win every argument...we're trained to."

We have to ask ourselves, "Am I seeking to understand my partner, or just standing my ground to get my own way?"

> *"What you need when you're angry is empathy. You need somebody to listen and to say, 'I care about what you're going through, and I want to understand.' Having a receptive listener help you to accept your angry feelings, work through them, and calm down."*
> Dr. John Gottman and Dr. Julie Schwartz Gottman,
> Ten Lessons to Transform Your Marriage

Before we were married, Brent and I had an argument. His perspective made sense, and I couldn't get my thoughts together to make a rebuttal. So I reverted to withdrawal and pouting. "OK, you're right. I'm wrong!" It was a move I'd done my whole life to avoid conflict, which was extremely uncomfortable for me. He wasn't buying it.

"How do I know that you're wrong? You're not talking to me," he reasoned. "I may not be right! You have to talk to me, so we can figure this out!"

Well, there's a concept! Squashing my opinions to avert an argument would not have resulted in peaceful resolution. I wanted the uncomfortable feelings between us to go away, but just because the argument ended didn't mean I had peace. I just replaced the argument with self-pity. I became a victim in my mind, and this is not peaceful by any stretch of the imagination.

I took him up on his challenge. We had the most mature conversation of my life to that point.

My way separated us—shut down communication and put up a wall of anger and bitterness. His way unified us—both have a say and thus arrive at a solution that benefits us both.

"People are lonely because they build walls instead of bridges."
Joseph F. Newton

Growing up, I used to think that conflict was bad. I created a habit of shutting down my feelings to avoid conflict. Eventually I lost my ability to communicate, and then pity set in—I made myself a victim. When Brent gave me permission—a safe place—to argue my point, this empowered me to believe what I had to say was both valid and valuable. In the process I found my voice.

Now I look at conflict as a way to work towards a deeper layer of trust and intimacy. We have the opportunity to discover more about our spouses and ourselves as we dissect the motivations and ideas we each have to offer. We have the opportunity to move past something together—to learn to cooperate. When we approach our conflicts this way, we build trust and understanding. The ingredients needed for mature, thriving relationships.

There's another benefit to conflict. When two minds tackle a problem, a different solution altogether has the chance to emerge. Not his way or her way, but our way. The discussion that two individuals contribute to has the potential to break through, change thinking in a positive way, and then something beautiful happens—clarity.

Resolving Problems: Rules and Tools

On the job, you constantly are solving problems that you come upon or are called to. You're given tools on your duty belt to take care of these problems should they escalate. In the spirit of what you do, I thought it would be fun to point out that some of those tools can be reminders of how to resolve our relational conflicts.

- Flashlight. Whether it's searching the interior of a house or looking at a suspect's eyes for signs of intoxication, the flashlight is indispensible. When you are in the midst of a conflict with your spouse, you need more information. You need more understanding so you can pinpoint the issue and then resolve it. Most conflict is caused by misunderstanding or unmet expectations. Get out your flashlight, so to speak, by asking questions that will bring light to the conflict.

- Handcuffs. When a suspect is taken into custody, you cuff him to keep him and you safe. When you and your spouse are in a disagreement, resolve to keep you both safe by remembering you are on each other's team. You are not adversaries, even if you're both passionate about your views. Use restraint and turn toward, not against; listen to understand.

- Taser. This tool stops a person in his tracks so you can get him under control. When anger is out of control, stop it in its tracks by a soft answer. Acknowledge the anger, investigate why the anger is there, and then understand it.

- Radio. When using the radio, dispatch speaks; you listen. You can't talk over her otherwise you'll miss what she's saying. You respond and vice-versa until both of you understand what needs to be done. When you are in the midst of an argument, do the same. You'll solve a lot more than speaking or yelling over one another.

  Matt and Laura take walks together when they have disagreements. They used to fight the entire time and come home angry. Then Matt suggested they argue to the halfway point and resolve to come to resolution the rest of the way. The walk they took was four miles long. At two miles, there is a stop sign that they touch—a symbolic signal that it is time to stop arguing and come to a solution. This approach has been very helpful.

- Ticket Book. Although not carried on the duty belt, the ticket book is a reminder of a crucial ingredient to resolving conflict. You issue citations to record what the violation was. We have to own our trash, and apologize to our spouse. A little humility can cover a multitude of mistakes.

  Somewhere in the course of our culture's evolving relational intelligence, we think that admitting our shortcomings will have a negative effect on our self-esteems and the respect others have for us. I've got news for you—those you live with already know you aren't perfect. Understanding and acknowledging the stupid things we do makes us authentic and engenders respect.

  When we admit our shortcomings, we take away their power over us. Rather than expend the energy to hide, deflect, and lie about the things we don't do well, or the wrong things we say, the mistakes we make, or whatever the case may be, we can use the energy to come clean. It's much less exhausting to be authentic than to keep up the lie.

  There's an added bonus. When we give ourselves freedom to make peace with our weaknesses, we're much more willing to forgive others for their shortcomings. A willingness to come closer and connect emerges because there is permission to fail. I can be who I am—good, bad, and ugly—if there is mercy, forgiveness and restoration. (This doesn't extend to abuse, and it doesn't give license to chronic bad behaviors. Although, admitting a problem is the first step to restoration in such cases.)

Expectations: Reasonable or Unreasonable?

If there is discord, misunderstanding or conflict, often it is because others failed to meet our expectations. They didn't make it on time, they didn't have the right response, they were insensitive, or they didn't do what was asked. We are disappointed, even angry. We want to lash out, and sometimes we even want to give up. So much of failed expectations are based on assumptions. Is it possible your spouse is failing to meet your expectations because they are not understood? Could this be the case for your spouse?

Here are some questions that will help to expose expectations:

- What am I expecting of my spouse? My kids?
- People at work, school?
- What am I expecting of friends, family?
- What am I expecting of God?
- What do others expect of me?
- Are these expectations fair? If not, we adjust.
- Have I communicated them clearly? If not, start today.

We can't control the unexpected happenings of life, and obviously we won't always get what we expect. But we can take honest inventory of what we expect from those we love, and communicate clearly, improving our relationships, and making life just a little bit better.

Sandcastles

Brent and I have gone through many ups and downs through his career and our life together. One of the most difficult seasons was when he was the Academy commander for three and a half years. He loved the work, and so did I. The opportunity to build into a staff that trained over two thousand new officers was something he took seriously, and rose to the occasion under incredibly stressful demands.

But it was a sacrifice for our family. We did well for a couple of years. I got on board with the vision and took it as a personal mission to support him under every circumstance, including getting involved with cadet families, Employee Assistance, and survivors of our fallen (there were several during those years).

After awhile, the stress was getting to be overwhelming. He was angry, distracted, and in some ways became victim-like. This wasn't his normal mode of operation.

I was frustrated and losing hope. I thought this would be how our marriage was going to be from then on, and at that point, I gave up. It was the first time in our marriage I thought we were over.

We went to Southern California on vacation with the kids. He was there physically, but not mentally or emotionally. He was distracted the entire time with an upcoming promotional exam. We took the kids to the zoo, and he was on the phone a lot of the time. As we were leaving, we got into an argument about something really stupid. I was done.

After an uncomfortable dinner I stole away for a walk on the beach. I noticed an elaborate sandcastle on the beach someone had built that day. The tide was coming in, and splashed into the moat that surrounded it. I sat down, riveted by the slow disappearance of this work of art. At one point, a wave came washing in, causing the whole thing to split. I began to cry, thinking this was not just a sandcastle—in my mind, it was my home.

I heard a voice in my head, "Are you going to do this to your family?" Pain shot through me as I thought about the consequences of leaving. I didn't want that. I watched the last bits of the sandcastle wash away. All that was left were the rocks that surrounded it.

"No, I'm not going to do this to the kids, to Brent," I thought. I sat for a long time, praying, arguing with myself, and realizing that there were no guarantees. But I gathered strength as I remembered the good things from the past, and then resolved to commit to our relationship even more.

It wasn't easy, and nothing changed for a week or so. We argued some more, yet I remained steadfast in my mind.

One day he shared with me some of what he was going through. I realized that this was an inner battle about work and himself. He didn't need me to leave him now. More than ever, he needed me to walk through it with him.

That's just what I did, and I'm so glad. We grew closer. We built trust. We learned some lessons about life and suffering and who we are. And it strengthened us for troubles to come. Tremendous blessings. I almost missed it all.

When You're Miserable

If you and your spouse are in one of these seasons, there are some things to try before you file the papers. If there's anything in you that wants to fulfill the vow you made on your wedding day, you must recommit to the health and future of your marriage.

The first place you start is in your mind. Are you still in? If not, recommit yourself to your spouse one more time.

Second, look at your relationship objectively. You may not understand where your spouse is coming from, so start with you. What is it about the relationship that you can change?

I sat with Brendan as he told me his marriage was over. "I just need a reset. I don't like who we've become. I just want to start over."

"Obviously you don't want the marriage you've had up to this point," I countered. "But what if you could have a different marriage with the same person? A fresh start doesn't mean everything has to change—maybe just some things."

We have the ability to choose to do things differently. Brendan went back to his wife and they talked about the areas of their life together that they didn't like. They realized that a lot of it were things they could change, like where they lived, and habits they'd formed.

Third, choose to love as your duty. Go through the motions of acting like you love your spouse. The feelings will follow later.

"...Ultimately comfort is not the issue. We are talking about love,
and love is something you do for someone else, not something
you do for yourself. Most of us do many things each day that do
not come 'naturally' for us...Our actions precede our emotions."
Dr. Gary Chapman, The Five Love Languages, Military Edition

Let time give you clarity. When you're in crisis and there is hurt between you, there is a tendency to get caught up in the drama and make rash decisions. Slow down. Take a break. Let things ride for a while, giving you both a chance to listen, understand, and make reasonable decisions.

Lastly, invest time and attention into your relationship. Attend a marriage retreat. See a therapist who understands law enforcement. Date once a week, or as often as you can. Ask questions with the intent to understand. Flirt with your spouse like you did when you first met. Renew your vision of who you want to be as a couple.

Forgiveness

In this season, there is something else critically needed—forgiveness. Forgiveness is not about condoning poor behavior. It's about accepting our faults, embracing reality, and choosing to move past wrongs so that we are no longer victims. Brent likes to say that anyone can be victimized, but becoming a victim is a choice. Don't be a victim.

Making a choice to lay aside intense feelings of resentment is necessary to grow closer. It is a choice that benefits peace of mind.

One night Brent and I had a serious discussion. I wasn't happy, so left the dinner table and slammed the door behind me. He let me cool off a bit and came in, gently. And then I let him have it.

I had piled up his offenses from that day. I piled up his offenses from last week. And last month. Last year. Even ten years ago. He didn't stand a chance.

Never mind that I had wronged him. Never mind that we misunderstood each other's motives and actions. Never mind that my responses were loaded and undergirded by unresolved anger. I found my voice, and said what I wanted to say. He had been indicted, underwent a trial in my mind, and deserved a harsh sentence.

So, why did I feel crappy? The self-pity that motivated me felt empty. The hurt I saw on his face and the angst I heard in his voice reverberated in my mind and made my heart burn. Tears of a different kind stained my cheeks. Then in my silent prayers, I thought, "Perhaps it's time to forgive him—for what he hasn't done." And suddenly, I knew that was the problem.

Brent is a good man. He loves his kids, and he loves me. He works hard at this, and tries to do what's right, even when it isn't popular. He's provided for us, he's been loyal, hardworking, and a great husband and father. He's a successful man who is dedicated to his work. But when it comes down to his motivation, he does it all for us.

Sometimes I want the fairy tale. To be adored. Swept off my feet. To be number one. To be known to the point that he would know exactly how I feel and know exactly what to do or say to comfort/inspire me. That kind of love takes a lot of time and effort. A constant and habitual focus. Looking beyond many things that happen day to day. Kind of like when we were dating!

But in real life, this is entirely unrealistic. When it doesn't happen, I sometimes throw my pity party and complain that he doesn't do x, y and z, completely ignoring the fact that he does a, b, and c. Regularly. Faithfully. And well.

I know deep down these expectations aren't fair. I can't expect this from him or anyone else. It isn't right to judge him for the way he loves me, nor for how he doesn't. I choose to accept the love he gives, and then return it tenfold the best I know how.

Forgiving is the first step. Sometimes we have to forgive for something each other does that hurts. But in this case, I was angry at the absence of something, and I needed to forgive Brent for not meeting my expectations. Subtle anger had crept in and sabotaged our relationship. I was looking for something—anything to justify that anger. Once I forgave and then shut the door on those toxic thoughts, my anger subsided, the sun came out, and it was a beautiful life!

Attitude

If conflicts are to be resolved in a marriage, two ingredients are required: humility and respect. If both people in the relationship are to have equal value, we have to understand that there are two sides to every story. When you investigate an accident, you don't just get one side. You talk to both drivers to get their perspective, interview witnesses, and then you look at the evidence to determine what really occurred. When you've got a disagreement, be open to the possibility that you may be wrong. Humility takes us there. To take on an attitude of humility, we choose to ask questions first instead of demanding our position. Humility teaches that our perspective is never perfect and acknowledges when we make a mistake. Humility also softens the tone and slows down the disagreement, allowing for understanding.

> *"...We own our attitudes: We are responsible for them;*
> *we developed them; they are who we are; and they are*
> *under our control. To believe anything else is crippling,*
> *because not taking control of and accepting responsibility*
> *for your attitude means that you are failing to take control*
> *of and accept responsibility for your life."*
> Jim Glennon, Arresting Communication

Mutual respect is also crucial to conflict resolution. Much conflict is due to misunderstanding or miscommunication. When we respect each other, our thoughts are not poisoned by mistrust—we believe the best of each other. I value my spouse—therefore I want resolution.

A Word About Getting Help

There may be problems in your marriage or at work (that affect you at home) that you won't be able to solve without getting help. You may be surprised to hear that there are many avenues of assistance available for you as an officer. There are organizations all over the country that come alongside our Blue Line Family in times of need. Foundations, ministries, churches, treatment programs designed for first responders, therapists who are trained to deal with officers and military, spousal abuse programs, hotlines, chaplaincies, and more have been put into place by people (many times former officers or relatives of officers) who care deeply about you.

Many departmental programs are considered taboo by officers because of the potential repercussions should someone learn of their struggle. Because the police culture has not yet been changed in many areas, and in many of the minds of officers, there is a risk involved in getting help. Melissa Littles comments on the stigma of getting help.

> *"Police officers do not seek help for several reasons, which include but are not limited to:*
>
> • ***FEAR**—Fear that the moment they tell a supervisor they need help dealing with a critical incident or emotional trauma they will lose their gun, badge, livelihood and identity.*
>
> • ***LABELING**—Being labeled by their peers and/or family as being weak, not able to handle their "job." Labeling themselves: For officers to admit to needing help is to acknowledge to themselves that they are suffering.*
>
> • ***PRIDE**—When an officer does seek assistance, it comes with the knowledge that admitting the aforementioned will lead to self-accountability, acceptance of emotional vulnerability and ownership that they could not work through issues alone. This goes against every grain of an officer's makeup. They are the helpers, they are the sheepdogs, and they are the ones to rescue others. To admit needing help is one of the hardest things to do for many officers, especially men."*

This applies to getting help in our marriages. These are real fears, but there may come a time when you can't ignore the issues any longer. The longer you wait, the harder it may be. The good news is that you do have options.

When Conflict Gets Physical

Domestic violence became a topic of discussion everywhere when the video emerged of NFL player Ray Rice knocking out his fiancé in a hotel elevator. Domestic abuse is a reality that happens in the homes of approximately one in four police families. I was surprised by this statistic. Most of the officers I know do not seem like they would ever engage in such behavior. But anyone can put on a good act for others. You as officers see the crap that goes on behind closed doors, and it is terrible how people treat each other. But statistics show that police officers have a higher tendency toward this kind of behavior than the general public.

If there is physical violence going on in your home, you already know you've got a problem. Unless you do something about it, it will continue. There are also several other forms of abuse that are subtler, and could eventually lead to violence. Here are some questions to ask yourself if you are abusing or at risk of such:

- Do you embarrass your partner with put-downs?
- Is your partner or your child afraid of you?
- Do you find yourself controlling whom your partner talks to or where they go?
- Have you demanded your partner stop seeing family members or friends?
- Do you control your partner with money such as withholding it, taking it, or refusing to give them money?
- Do you make all the decisions, or do you discuss and decide together?
- Do you threaten your partner with taking away or hurting your children?
- Do you prevent your partner from working or attending other functions?
- Has your partner filed any charges against you?
- Have you threatened to commit suicide so that your partner would relent?
- Do you see your partner as your personal property?
- Did you witness domestic abuse in your home growing up?

- Have you threatened to kill your partner?
- Have you done any of this while under the influence of drugs or alcohol?
- Have you pressured your partner sexually for things he/she doesn't feel comfortable with?

If you've answered yes to any of these questions, there is help available.

If you turn these questions around, you may be a victim. Both men and women abuse.

On its face, domestic abuse seems to be about anger. But it is much more than this. It's more about learned and modeled behavior that you have been trained (intentionally and unintentionally) to treat as acceptable. It's about fundamentally viewing others as having less value than you. It's about seeing others as your property rather than your partner, and even sometimes it's about reducing that person to a sexual object.

It's really about the way you think that determines these actions. And it can be exasperated by difficulties at work, substance abuse, stress, and soul wounds.

Most often the programs available for preventing and protecting against domestic abuse are for the victims.

Programs and help for abusers exist as well. It will require an attitude change, professional therapy, a retraining of the mind, and time and patience, but you can stop this behavior. Resources for the abused and the abuser are in the Resource Guide.

Ready to Call it Quits?

When you've lived life with your family in a reactive way for too long, there are things that are broken that you and your spouse don't have a clue how to fix. You need a restoration.

I like Nicole Curtis of HGTV's Rehab Addict. It's not that she's a little blonde badass who loves power tools and runs marathons. It's not that she's stubborn with her vision, or that she sports a midwestern accent, or that she lives in Minnesota. It's that Nicole Curtis looks at old homes that others have deemed as doomed and is willing to put in the work to make them pretty again.

She braves old basements, salvages what she can, and pours new foundations. She is sure to comment that working with a shovel is a great core workout. She opens up walls to expose old brick, cleaning it up with a wire brush, and patching holes in the mortar. She designs the rooms around the brick, using it as a focal point. It's beautiful. She pulls up linoleum and exposes hardwood flooring, meticulously refinishing and repairing the old wood. The timeless beauty of the home emerges. She appreciates the splendor of old things, restoring them to let them shine in their craftsmanship, and adding both old and new to give a home the best of both.

Nicole restored a home damaged by arson. The fire had spread to the house next door. When the damage was left unaddressed, old homes throughout the street were boarded up as their owners abandoned them. These homes were damaged. Devalued. Decomposing. Ugly.

Much like the tendency to do in our own homes. When the fires of conflict or neglect torch a home and the damage is done, many choose to just scrap it all and walk away. But it isn't just the lone couple that suffers. Lasting damage breeds more destruction to those around them.

When there is reconciliation—when a couple decides to salvage their marriage, patiently doing the work to look at both the good and the bad in their relationship and purpose to restore it, there is something amazing that happens. There is a quality and beauty there, and a mature character that something (or someone) new just can't measure up to.

Whether we've been married three months or 25 years, our marriages could use a little tender loving care—sprucing up what's in good condition, repairing damage, and a few new changes.

"Do not think that love, in order to be genuine,
has to be extraordinary.
What we need is to love without getting tired."
Mother Teresa

Perhaps you've been reactive for so long, it seems there's nothing left in your relationship. You've been unable to move past the problems, and there is bitterness and separation. One or both of you are done. Think of your marriage as an old neglected house. The tendency is to think that your house is too far-gone. It should be condemned. But if one person comes in, sees the value and is willing to do the work, your "house" could be beautiful again. It spreads to the other person in the marriage and he/she joins in. Commitment, time, patience and hard work can get it there.

If your marriage needs restoration, please read on. Perhaps you'll find yourself in between the pages of this book or find a new resource in the back of the book. Perhaps you can pinpoint the damage, look at what caused it, and then do a renovation with new tools, renewed attitudes, and a new plan.

Brent and I know a couple that did this very thing.

The Second Marriage

There were problems from the start. Adam was a social worker who was laid off just a few months before his wedding to Kathy. He took the opportunity to do what he'd dreamed about as a little kid—to become a police officer.

Kathy had a very different expectation of the life she and Adam would share. She wanted to lead a quiet life with a nine to five job, steady income and white picket fences. A cop? Really?

To make matters worse, Adam's department had some budget issues soon after he was hired, and he was let go. Out of work for a time, Kathy tried to convince Adam to go back to social work. But he had gotten a taste of what he really loved and wasn't interested. He was a cop.

In time, he secured a position with a police department. As low man on the totem pole, he was assigned to the graveyard shift. From that time forward, Kathy developed a grudge against police work. She closed herself off to the department, his love for his career, and eventually Adam.

Seven years and two kids into their marriage, Kathy wasn't happy. They went to their pastor for counseling, but because of their tight budget, they couldn't afford what he recommended. Their pastor instead introduced them to Brent and I. We met with Adam and Kathy for about a year, mentoring them individually and as a couple. Things seemed resolved for a while.

At nine years and three kids, Adam was done. He'd grown tired of the "double life" he was expected to live—two different people at work and at home. One night, after a scuffle in a dark alley with a suspect, he showed up late at home. The way he remembers it, Kathy didn't ask about the cuts and bruises. She did ask, however, if he was given overtime for the hours away. Kathy, by the way, has no recollection of this interaction.

Sometime after that, he turned to someone else who understood— a female officer who was also experiencing marital issues. It developed into an affair. Adam spent his workout time with his new friend. This also created some workplace issues, but he didn't care. He finally felt understood.

Adam moved out. Kathy called us immediately. The four of us met together. It was awkwardly clear he was already gone. But he agreed to meet with my husband separately. I met with her as well. It was profoundly painful to witness.

Slowly but surely, they agreed to at least try one more time. They found a great counselor with financial assistance from her parents. Kathy read my book and realized that she was actually reading about herself. He ended the affair as he realized Kathy was finally ready to accept him as a police officer. Through a slow, sometimes grueling process, both came to realize they still loved one another.

Adam moved back home. Kathy went on a ride along. She met some of his co-workers. They are now continuing to build what they call their second marriage, even adding one more child to their new life.

"One small crack does not mean that you are broken;
it means that you were put to the test
and you didn't fall apart."
Linda Poindexter

Practical Steps to Restoration

If you and your spouse are in a difficult place, there are some objective things you can do to work towards making it better.

First, take inventory of what you've got that is salvageable. What is good about your relationship?

Second, pinpoint the problem. This is best done together, by the way. Both of you each have your opinions as to what is wrong in your relationship. You may need to have a third party present to get to the root issues.

When you're talking, determine if the issues or problems are outside factors, factors within, or both. Outside factors would be your living situation, job-related issues like schedule or hobbies that take precious time from you. If outside factors are the culprit, then you may want to do some restructuring. Is there something you need to subtract from your life together that will make a significant difference? A person or persons, a commitment that has taken priority, or perhaps children's activities? How about a TV Show or limiting time on the computer? What about adding something that will help? Like committing to meals around the table once a day (any meal)? Or adding a walk three times a week? What about date nights? Occasionally a little restructuring is all you need.

But what if the problems are inside factors? Like you're in the disillusionment stage? Or you are holding on to unrealistic expectations? Or your spouse did something that you just can't let go of? Some issues are relatively minor, and can be talked through and given a solution.

But what if it's more serious, like your partner is beating you? Or your alcohol abuse is taking its toll? An affair? Then you have a choice. Are you still committed? Enough to get help? According to marriage expert Dr. John Gottman, couples wait on average about six years too long to get help. By then the animosity is so built up, the couple is ready to call it quits. Get help now—don't wait.

Wherever your marriage is at, there is information, help, and resources for police families. In the Resource Guide in the back I've listed several seminars, books, organizations and support groups you may want to check out.

. . . .

Think: What is it that you and your spouse argue about? Is it resolved? Why or why not?

Debrief: Talk with your spouse about something that is a recurring problem that causes arguments. Take a look at why it is still not resolved, and see if any of the tools provided here apply.

Strategic Action: Does this chapter spark any new ideas or aha! moments that you might try to incorporate?

"If you think people are inherently good,
you get rid of the police for 24 hours—see what happens."
Sylvester Stallone

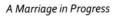

CHAPTER EIGHT

THE WOUNDED WARRIOR

*"I wish someone would've told me that you can do
everything right tactically, and still not have a good outcome..."*
Scott Brown, Sacramento deputy sheriff,
three days after he saw his partner shot and killed

At some point in your career, you will have to face something bigger than yourself. You've been involved in a combat shoot. You're first on the scene of a line of duty death. You've been recorded on someone's cell phone and it doesn't reflect what is actually going on. You are under investigation by Internal Affairs. Or you've just seen too many victims, too many stupid decisions, been in too many pursuits, and you're just sick of stupidity. In each of these situations, and others not mentioned, you are affected, and thus your family is affected. Whether you choose to share what happened with them or not.

Carla shared her sense about a difficulty her husband was going through. "I feel Brian," she confided. "He doesn't say much, but I feel it. I can sense the stress emitting from him."

Perhaps you've experienced this on duty. You have a feeling about a call. You and your partner look at each other and just know. You sense when something isn't right, no matter how subtle. It's the same thing with those who know you well.

I have been there often in my years with Brent. He doesn't have to say a word and I can sense his inner turmoil about something. I feel it—it's as real as words. If paying attention, your spouse can feel something is bugging you, too. There's no pushing it aside or denying it. It might be invisible to the eye, but it is very real. It's also a very good thing.

Job Stress and Burnout

"My cup is full of shit when I get off work," Gina commented from the back, holding up her coffee. "I can carry that home, and dump it all over my wife. Or I can choose to dump it out before I get home. Too many days I don't do that, and it really hurts her."

Gina elaborated. "It's kind of like a boat that picks up barnacles here and there as it sails through the ocean. After awhile, the boat needs a good scrubbing so it can move through the water better. We have so much negativity that comes in shift after shift. I think my mind needs a break. So I listen to positive music on the drive home. I also read positive books. This gets some good vibes coming in that helps flush out the bad thoughts."

Gina is right on. The stress of policing is ongoing and cumulative, and if there aren't ways to address the stress, burnout is inevitable.

There is too much to do, not enough time. Government red tape and politics gum everything up. People's egos and loss of mission/vision shape priorities, and then life gets really frustrating. Morale suffers from the boots on the ground on up.

Unless you have a plan and a practice to relieve the stress this causes, it is coming home with you, the very second you enter the door.

For family members, it can feel like walking on eggshells. There's heaviness in the room—a cloud that hangs precariously over interactions between spouses and children. The uncomfortableness threatens to erupt like thunder and lightening, and suddenly those in the house know without a doubt that there is something wrong, but are afraid or unsure of how to address it for fear of the reaction.

That's not a good feeling.

The way you deal with this stress makes all the difference. What are your coping mechanisms? Do you stuff and stuff until it comes spewing out in elevated emotion at the worst possible time? Do you just clam up and refuse to acknowledge you're bothered?

Do you douse it with a drink or two? Bury it with a large pepperoni pizza? Distract yourself with a trip to the nearest casino? Escape to that Internet site?

If so, these are defense mechanisms. You go into survival mode to deal with the immediate danger. You feel uncomfortable, maybe even pain. Coping mechanisms such as those just described give temporary respite from pain but create longer-term problems.

The first problem with unhealthy coping mechanisms is that they deal with symptoms, but not the cause. They are a temporary fix; masks to hide or silence the root cause. These coping mechanisms are often addictive, which compounds problems.

The second problem is that these may work as survival tactics for you temporarily, but they are detrimental to your relationships at home (and your health). Isolation and moodiness often result, which cause relational distance between you and your loved ones. The longer these coping strategies are used, the more your perspective gets warped. [The more destructive coping mechanisms take it further—not only the separation because of misunderstandings and mistreatment, but wounding those you love (gambling, substance abuse, emotional and physical abuse).] Cops who at one time were motivated to crush crime, save lives, and alleviate human suffering become the subject of criminal and internal affairs investigations for conduct that would have been unthinkable. That inner and outer stress creates problems at home.

It doesn't have to be this way. There are healthier ways to deal with the stress and residue. There are coping mechanisms that help and heal your body and mind. They can also help your relationships.

Exercise is a great start. It restores your body and your mind. Get out and take a run; lift weights. Work out aggression in intensified workouts. Walks and bike rides with your spouse and kids incorporate time together, reducing stress and building relationships at the same time.

Time away is good for the soul. It isn't just about time off; there should be a mental separation from the career. You can be "off", but not mentally. When you get away, turn off the phone, intentionally put work on a shelf for a time, and give yourself time to shed the residue. Time away gives respite from the stressors and can give you rest and fresh perspective. You may not have much availability in different seasons of your career, but make the most of what you do have. Protect your time off, and don't waste it in front of a screen.

Gina's idea of positive music is good because it's almost always accessible. Watch what you listen to though; music that is angry or hateful may serve to reinforce your pain, not ease it. As you think through issues while listening to positive music, you will be introduced to a different mood. You can exhale stress, forcing issues to take their lower place in the hierarchy of priorities. In the Appendix I've listed some song suggestions on a Playlist for the transition from work to home.

Talking out specific issues with a trusted friend is also healthy. This person is someone who understands you, knows you, and can give perspective. The one thing about stress is that it distorts thought processes. The issue can circle your head a dozen times, gaining speed with each turnabout. But when you talk it out, your confidant can give you a perspective that isn't readily apparent to you because your thinking is clouded or you're just in too deep. A really good confidant will ask questions, allowing you to break the cycle in your brain and pinpoint the issue, then determine a good course of action. Talking it out allows you to untangle your thoughts and iron out the thought process toward a solution. It's like the Christmas lights that we take out of the box every winter. They come out a jumbled mess. It takes some time to unravel, carefully and methodically. Then when they are straightened out, we replace the burnt out bulbs to get things bright again. Our thoughts are similar.

Another way to combat burnout and job stress is to find new ways of dealing with hurdles, people, and problems. Brent is a great example of this. He often quotes Einstein's definition of insanity—doing the same thing over and over but expecting different results. He consistently looks for solutions outside of the norm to benefit the greatest amount of people. He does this at work and at home. Some of the perspective-changing books that have been helpful to him are Leadership and Self-Deception, The Speed of Trust, Crucial Conversations, and Seven Habits of Highly Effective People. I've seen him refer to his library as he struggles through things. Soon he's got new or refreshed perspective and tools on how to deal with those hurdles, people and problems.

Burnout is normal, natural, and it is cyclical. Recognize it, plan for it, and avoid unhealthy coping mechanisms.

When Unhealthy Coping Mechanisms Take Control

If you consistently rely on drinking, drugs, sex, food, gambling, or porn as coping mechanisms, they become habits. These habits run the risk of becoming additions. There is much to be said about addictions. The most important point to make here is that addictions are destructive on relationships with those close to you. Addictions can cause financial instability, loss of trust and respect, undependability, and clouded thought processes that lead to arguments, destructive behavior, and wrong choices. All of these problems can ruin a marriage and destroy your relationships with your children.

The following are symptoms of addictive behavior and what to do. The Resource Guide at the back of the book offers several organizations that discreetly help officers who are in this situation.

To recognize if you have an addiction to alcohol, prescription and/ or illegal drugs, gambling, pornography, or food, ask yourself these questions:

- How important is this activity/substance to me? Can I go without it often without thinking about it or craving it? Is it a priority in my life?
- Do I feel better or more in control when I am consuming this substance or doing this activity?
- Do I feel that I need more? Have I found that the time I devote to it is never enough?
- Could I stop without an emotional attachment to it? Does thinking about not doing it ever again make me anxious?
- Has this activity/substance disrupted my life in some way? Has a loved one complained about it? Has it affected work or relationships?
- Have I tried to quit, only to revert back to it?

These are good questions to keep you on alert to the possibility of addiction. If you find that you're answering yes to these questions, then what?

- Acknowledge you have a problem that needs a solution.
- Decide that you will stop no matter how difficult. Commit to the process of scrubbing this addiction from your life.
- Understand you can't do it alone. You need accountability, comfort, and encouragement. Choose accountability partners wisely.
- Get rid of everything that is associated with your addiction. This may include some habits, places, and relationships that harbor/encourage this behavior.
- Recognize triggers and either avoid them or develop a plan to respond to them.
- Join a 12-step program. This program is helpful to reach the root cause(s) for the addiction, and then directs action that will deal with the cause.

Critical Incidents

A critical incident is an incident that has significance for you. This event can cause disruption in your work and/or your home. Critical incidents include shootings, injuries, death of children, and other calls that stay with you long after the fact.

In July 2003, Steve from Alabama stopped for some coffee to get through the remainder of the graveyard shift. As he stepped out of the convenience store, a pickup slid to a stop behind his patrol car. Steve recognized Chad, an EMT from the city's fire department.

"Quiet night so far?" he called out.

"Yeah, not much goin' on," Steve answered.

"Well, let's see if it stays that way," said Chad as he drove away.

Steve started his paperwork at the station, when dispatch waved him into the other room. A fireman on the phone had called in that Chad was threatening suicide and had stolen several vials of morphine from an ambulance. Immediately Steve was on his way to Chad's suspected location.

En route, dispatch advised him that Chad was mobile in his truck and armed. Further radio traffic indicated he had fired shots at a fireman and an ambulance. Steve attempted to intercept Chad and met him going the opposite direction on the highway. Chad fired a handgun out his window four times as he passed.

Steve advised dispatch of shots fired and turned to pursue Chad. Other officers quickly joined him. Chad drove his truck through various parking lots, firing his weapon at cars, windows and buildings. He ran over several highway signs and steered toward oncoming vehicles, often driving in the wrong lane. Several times he made U-turns and headed back toward Steve's patrol car, firing at him as they passed.

Chad got on the fire department's frequency via radio and declared, "Take me out whenever you're ready because I'm not going to jail!" He told dispatch to notify the coroner, as he would be checking out shortly.

The pursuit continued about 15 minutes at speeds over 100 mph. Several attempts to ram Chad's truck were unsuccessful because when they got close, he'd shoot. He kept rambling over the radio about visiting Ground Zero in New York and going on about 9/11. His speech became increasingly slurred and his driving more erratic. Then he said he was headed for the mayor's house to right some wrongs. Dispatch called the mayor and advised him of the danger. As they approached the mayor's home, Chad slowed his vehicle and Steve rammed him so he couldn't shoot at the residence.

"I'm not the same guy I was when I first went to war.
No one is. Before you're in combat, you have this
innocence about you. Then, all of a sudden,
you see this whole other side of life."
Chris Kyle, American Sniper

Chad's last words were, "Tell the doctor I'm going to drive into Central Fire Station and will have multiple bullets in my body at that time." He then drove down the wrong lane, and Steve T-boned his pickup as he crossed the road toward the fire station. Steve parked his unit perpendicular to the truck several yards away and ran for cover. Chad fired two shots into his own windshield and turned his handgun toward Steve.

That's when Steve shot and killed him.

Chad was dead, but the wheels of the truck continued to spin, filling the air with smoke. A fire extinguisher had discharged in the bed of his truck upon impact.

In addition to the fatal wound, Chad had a self-inflicted gunshot wound to his left thigh and there were five empty vials of morphine stuck needle down into the seat next to him. There were 89 empty shell casings in the truck, and a Ruger handgun was recovered from the floorboard.

After Steve finally left the station later that morning, he turned back a few miles from town. He felt he needed to go back to the fire station and face the men. He walked upstairs where the firemen were meeting with the city pastor and the mayor. The whole department was there. Half of them turned and went downstairs and the other half stayed. Steve doesn't remember what he said, but they cried and hugged.

The department held a mandatory critical incident stress debriefing a few days later. That was tremendously helpful. Then they placed Steve on paid administrative leave until the next grand jury, which was two months away. He had very little contact with anyone during that time. They took his weapon for evidence and did not give him a replacement. He felt like they had taken away his toys and put him in a corner.

That night changed Steve's life.

His family life deteriorated. He pulled away from his family and all but a few friends because he was afraid of letting anyone get close.

He couldn't play games involving guns anymore with his four-year-old son. No cops and robbers, no cowboys and Indians.

The smell of a fire extinguisher sickens Steve to this day.

Steve was engaged to the dispatcher that took the call. He had a couple affairs in the aftermath and their relationship fell apart. One of their biggest arguments happened when she attended Chad's funeral. Steve was hurt she would even entertain the idea of going. Now, Steve understands why she did, as she worked closely with the fire guys. He, however, wanted nothing to do with the funeral.

> *"There are victims and survivors: The victim is immobilized and discouraged by the traumatic event and may carry an unrealistic sense of responsibility for what happened. A survivor draws on the catastrophe as a source of strength and takes responsibility, not for the problem, but for recovering from it and moving past fear, anger, and guilt or thoughts of revenge."*
> Dr. Ellen Kirschman, I Love a Cop

"What helped me the most was talking about the incident, but there were few people that would ask. I trusted and confided in some close friends; the rest, if they did ask, just wanted the ghoulish details and 'wished' it was them that did the shooting," he says. "I had two friends that just let me talk and tried not to interrupt or interject anything into the conversation. They just listened. That was the most helpful."

Steve sought therapy but the psychiatrist wanted to put him on medications. He told the doc if he were going to work through anything, he would do it unaltered. He went to about six sessions, but doesn't think it helped as much as talking with his friends.

Years later, Steve is now Operations Captain at the same department. He took the individual and peer support Critical Incident Stress Management (CISM) classes and has participated in over two-dozen CISM debriefings across his state. He believes this helped him more than anything else, sharing his experience to limited extent. "I was helping others because I knew what they were experiencing. It helped us to know that we weren't alone in our feelings. Things would get better."

*"It's been several years now since our 'incident' but that doesn't
mean we don't have times when he gets an edge in his voice, or
his hackles stand up. Thankfully we both have come to recognize
the signs and can openly dialog about it. I will run interference
for the household and ask for a timeout, remind him we are on
the same team, not one of the parolees or street thugs he faces daily."*
Lola, CHP Wife

Steve's suicide-by-cop incident encompasses many of the symptoms and fallout of a critical incident. Relationships change. A tendency to isolate. Temptations to engage in unhealthy coping mechanisms. A need to make it right with survivors. Confusion, anger, and grief. Sight and smell triggers. No tolerance for light-hearted play with guns. Grand juries and trials. It all adds up to a long recovery from one fateful incident.

But Steve recovered. He is still working, has promoted a couple of times, and has built a successful career, even making changes in his department for better responses to future critical incidents.

His department provided a debrief, but broke down in their communication thereafter. Steve feels it's important to keep in contact during leave otherwise abandonment and punishment are negative adds to the list of already difficult circumstances.

Steve had a support system in place that was the most valuable resource he found during the fallout. He attempted counseling, which is recommended.

A key component with Steve's long-term healing was that he moved on in his journey through helping others. When a person who has been through something huge can move on to help or serve others with similar stories, it not only gives back, but brings about deeper healing along the way. This requires vulnerability, and courage to defy the enemy of isolation. The natural tendency is to pull away, feeling misunderstood and alone. Connection with those who've been there is crucial to moving on.

"...The 'shrinks' called us en masse to a get together and very briefly went over what we could expect in regard to our individual reactions and feelings as time went on. When it came time for questions, there were none. The mentality was 'cops don't talk to shrinks,' especially in front of a room full of your cohorts. So that was it—no individual briefing, just a few pointers, a business card and the opportunity to call them if we wanted to. To this day, I consider that a big glitch in the department's handling of the event. I feel we should have had compulsory debriefing by a behavioral specialist. I, for one, had never heard of post-traumatic stress disorder. I know that many would've not had quite the rough roads we did if we had been properly debriefed and educated a little more in-depth about what to expect."

John Caprarelli, Uniform Decisions

Responses to Trauma

In the last several years, I have encountered the emotional aftermath of trauma several times.

I saw it in the darkness that hung just behind the eyes of those who'd been to Afghanistan, as they recounted their painful stories.

It was in their tears as they described their nightmares.

It was in their shaking hands as they poured strong drinks.

It was in the strong language that was undergirded by anger and blame.

It was in the hard blinking tic of a six-foot-four, decorated warrior.

It was in the troubled silence of those faced with returning to Afghanistan.

It's in the sweating and anxiousness when recounting nightmares.

It was in the long hair and beard of a war hero who'd been plagued by loss and injustice.

It was in the admission of one who watched a colleague shove a pair of scissors into his neck, spraying him with blood.

It was in the utter rage of one who was stuck in a crowded theater, trying to escape the feeling of being trapped.

It was in the confusion and defensiveness when asked how post-trauma stress degraded into an illicit affair.

It was in the depleted confidence of a wife as she quietly admitted, "I am so tired."

It was in the icy stare of a Vietnam vet who claimed, "After I saw what I did in Vietnam, I realized that there is no God."

It was in the weighted shoulders of strong spouses as they silently bear the burdens of the heroes they love.

Responses to trauma come in many forms. If you have been through a critical incident, or a string of seemingly small but bothersome incidents, or memories plague you from years ago, understand that any of these symptoms you may be experiencing are normal reactions to something abnormal.

It is a relief that law enforcement culture is changing to understand and help those who've experienced trauma. Peace officers want to help people, and sometimes that just isn't possible. People die. Crime is destructive. Tragedies happen. It's part of the job, but you still feel the effects of trauma. You are bothered by it. That doesn't make you weak; it confirms you're human.

Dr. Langus explains it like this, "After trauma, we cops have a realization that we are vulnerable. There is helplessness, which equals a loss of control, which translates to 'I failed.' We're trained that way. And we care. Any cop worth his salt will end up in my office after trauma."

Post-Traumatic Stress Disorder (PTSD)

Reactions to trauma are normal, but if they persist over three months, become disruptive in your life, or cause you distress, then you may be experiencing the effects of PTSD.

Recognize what PTSD looks like. There are four types of symptoms that tend to be cyclical in nature:

1 | **Re-experiencing:** This includes nightmares and flashbacks that cause you distress. It also includes triggers—something that you hear, see or smell that takes your mind right back to the trauma.

2 | **Hyperarousal:** This is a result of a chronic state of re-experiencing the trauma—the body is in a constant state of hyperarousal. Symptoms include insomnia, anger, exaggerated startle response, problems concentrating, and hypervigilance. The body is in survival mode, taking on the fight/flight/freeze response when threatened.

3 | **Avoidance:** This is the behavioral response to triggers to avoid the pain and unpleasant feelings these triggers summon. This looks like avoiding crowded places and loud sounds, or depending on alcohol, drugs or other unhealthy coping mechanisms.

4 | **Emotional numbing:** Trauma can trudge up deep emotions that are very uncomfortable. Some will experience a numbing of sorts so to adapt to these intense feelings. For some it's fear; others it's a feeling of failure or guilt. This area is most difficult on relationships with others. Debby, whose husband suffers from PTSD, calls this "Poop Lasagna." His PTSD came from several incidents over his career. He experienced layer upon layer of unprocessed strong emotions that eventually resulted in emotional numbing.

If you are exhibiting any of these symptoms, acknowledge you may have PTSD. Grasp onto the idea that yes, something isn't quite right, and it needs to be dealt with. Despite the ignorant judgments of those who've either not been there, or deny it themselves, you are not crazy. You have a soul wound, and like a broken arm, you need to reset it and let it heal.

John Caprarelli, a retired LAPD officer who was given the Medal of Valor for his response during the infamous North Hollywood shootout in February 1997, describes the emotional toll on him and others in the months and years following the incident.

"The muzzle of his rifle is now squarely on me. Another second, maybe a half, and it will be all over...I glance at my weapon in confused amazement. I feel like I haven't drawn a breath in minutes. My head is spinning, my chest constricted, and I can hear the blood roaring through my ears...I give it one last chance and pull back on the trigger with all that I have...Nothing.

"Looking at his eyes, I can see under his sweat-sodden ski mask that the corners of his eyes are crinkled. He is smiling at me! With his leather-gloved finger curled around the AK-47's trigger, it seems as though his jaw is mouthing something from behind the mask...Panic courses through me and everything goes black as the world seems instantly yanked from me...Is this it?

"Drawing one long rasp of fresh air, I feel like I have just popped to the surface after too deep of a dive in some murky waters. It is dark, I am covered in sweat, and my heart is pounding like a jackhammer...Where am I?

"My wife touches my shoulder as she asks, 'You okay?'

"'Yeah, just another dream,' I reply. 'I'm fine.'

"We both know that is not true. There is an increasing menace, one we would not understand much about or know how to handle until it had already run its course."

Treating PTSD

There are several schools of thought as to how to treat those with PTSD. There are even different thoughts on the word, "disorder." It is thought that if we label it with the word disorder that it would bring shame to those who have it. There is a stigma with the word—it is a mental disorder, and therefore you're crazy.

But this isn't the case. Our bodies and brains have different ways of dealing with injuries. Some injuries need more intervention than others—and thus it is with PTSD. It can be cured, but not if it isn't acknowledged. "People believe that if you have PTSD that you have it forever and you cannot get better," says Becky Parkey, a counselor who works with veterans at the VA, and a cop wife. "Police departments believe this. That is not true.

You can get better, you can cope with it, and things will get better if you have the proper treatment. However, it will get worse without the proper treatment, especially if you stuff it inside and keep living and doing what you are doing. You will suffer, your family will suffer, but if you do the work, everything will get better."

Whether there is a trigger or not, PTSD can show up like an unannounced family member and stay for an unknown time period. Some triggers can be avoided, like staying away from crowds or having an escape route in close or crowded quarters (avoidance). Some veterans have a different way of celebrating Independence Day rather than the traditional fireworks show. But not all triggers are preventable.

The following is an excerpt from Selfish Prayer, a book I co-wrote with a war hero and CHP officer (since retired). It shows a little different perspective:

> "Post-traumatic stress is cyclical. I've talked with a police psychologist and I've gone through the counseling. I've been saturated with war and its carnage. There's so much residue. From time to time it just shakes out, and I have to deal with it.
>
> "My friend...a retired CHP officer and SWAT teammate, shared some poignant thoughts with me in a low moment. He was also a Marine Corps sniper and Vietnam veteran who suffered silently for forty years before he was able to speak of what he witnessed.
>
> "I was driving home one night, struggling with feelings and memories, and he just happened to call. I explained what I was dealing with and asked him if it ever went away.
>
> "'No,' he replied, 'it won't. It's not supposed to. It'll always be there.'
>
> "Believe it or not, this was a huge relief. It gave me comfort in a strange way. I didn't feel sorry for myself anymore. I finally realized post-traumatic stress from the war wasn't going away, and I had to make peace with it.
>
> "Anxiety-filled memories and nightmares come back once in a while. I say, 'Oh, there you are. I've wondered where you've been. I haven't seen you in a while, old friend.'

> *"The other key piece for me was talking with my friend and police psychologist, Dr. Todd Langus, who is a former cop and has been through many traumatic events. One night he said to me, 'Emmett, we're rescuers. That's how we're wired. We want to be able to fix things. We're fixers. We rescue; we fix; we want to make things better. But sometimes you can't, because it's a shitty situation. And it's OK to feel shitty about a shitty situation. That's normal.'"*

Dr. Langus highly recommends you see a counselor for PTSD and trauma-related issues that knows law enforcement, studies law enforcement, understands law enforcement, and has done research with law enforcement. Counselors that don't have the understanding of the tactical side of policing can miss places where you've been traumatized. Say you've been in a combat situation but didn't shoot—a regular counselor would not know to explore the guilt/shame/fear that comes with the law enforcement mindset in that situation.

Some have achieved great success in treating PTSD with Eye Movement Desensitization and Reprocessing (EMDR) therapy. The EMDR Institute, Inc. describes this therapy as "a psychotherapy that enables people to heal from the symptoms and emotional distress that are the result of disturbing life experiences. Repeated studies show that by using EMDR people can experience the benefits of psychotherapy that once took years to make a difference. It is widely assumed that severe emotional pain requires a long time to heal. EMDR therapy shows that the mind can in fact heal from psychological trauma much as the body recovers from physical trauma. When you cut your hand, your body works to close the wound. If a foreign object or repeated injury irritates the wound, it festers and causes pain. Once the block is removed, healing resumes. EMDR therapy demonstrates that a similar sequence of events occurs with mental processes. The brain's information processing system naturally moves toward mental health. If the system is blocked or imbalanced by the impact of a disturbing event, the emotional wound festers and can cause intense suffering. Once the block is removed, healing resumes. Using the detailed protocols and procedures learned in EMDR training sessions, clinicians help clients activate their natural healing processes."

Another thing to do is to educate yourself and your family. Your family needs to know what to look for, how to respond and diffuse difficult situations, and also to learn to communicate safely and effectively. We need to know what your triggers are.

Our son was diagnosed with PTSD after witnessing a horrific event in Marine boot camp. Our family went to a church service on Christmas Eve, having been given tickets right next to the stage. It was loud, unpredictable, beautiful, and almost everyone loved it. But not all. Afterwards our son stormed outside and when challenged, grew irate. It was very uncomfortable. In the silence on the way home, it occurred to me what was going on. I gently asked some questions, and then realized the outburst was a response to a PTSD trigger. At that point, our son had an aha! moment. He realized what was going on, apologized, and we resolved to sit in a place where a quick exit was possible, as well as distance from loud noises and surprising action. The following year we put these in place, and our son was fine.

Becky Parkey recommends when looking for a counselor, to see who offers evidence-based treatments for PTSD. Veteran Affairs counselors have had great success with veterans with these therapies. For more information on these treatments, see the VA's information on PTSD.

There are also several apps that are helpful for those with PTSD. They include coaching, breathing, mood tracking, etc. I've provided a list in the Resource Guide.

A fantastic book to have on hand is CopShock—Surviving Posttraumatic Stress Disorder by Allen R. Kates. This book is full of stories, resources, and excellent information compiled in one spot that will educate and direct you towards help.

PTSD can also take a serious toll on families. Adapting, learning, and applying what we learn are crucial. So is communication. Extending gracious understanding and forgiveness breaks up the confrontations and sometimes-uncontrolled responses. Like opening the door for someone who is on crutches, so it goes for those of us who live with those who suffer from trauma.

CODE FOUR BREATHING

One strategy for managing anger and other strong emotions is to slow down your breathing. This pushes out carbon dioxide and breathes in oxygen, helping your body to calm down.

Breathe in for four seconds
Hold four seconds
Breathe out for four seconds
Repeat three times

Treating Soul Wounds

Three of us sat in the busy restaurant, surrounded by the hustle and bustle of a Sunday lunch rush. Veronica introduced me to a police wife who had left her husband. The expectation was for me to talk some sense into Rachel so that her marriage could be saved.

But after a few moments of asking questions, it was apparent that there was much more going on than a choice to go or stay. Rachel had been deeply wounded by sexual abuse since she was an infant, and these wounds to her soul had never been healed. So, despite the expectations, we set the marriage talk aside, and spoke on an individual level. After more questions, I asked her why she didn't want to seek healing.

"Because it'll hurt too much," she answered.

"Aren't you in pain already?" I responded. That stopped her in her tracks. She looked me in the eye and said, "Every minute of every day."

We appealed to her to consider turning the pain that is destructive into pain that could count for something. We talked a bit more, and then left the restaurant. I have not seen Rachel again, but have heard that she decided to go deeper into the partying scene she was dabbling in at the time. You've seen what this kind of self-medication does. Perhaps you've arrested a Rachel.

*"Drinking, substance abuse, promiscuity, depression,
and gambling are symptoms of an underlying cause—
typically acute stress or emotional trauma—that has not
been effectively processed in a healthy manner."*
Captain Dan Willis, Bulletproof Spirit

There are, however, better ways of dealing with soul wounds.

First, we need to pinpoint the problem. Talk it out with someone compassionate and knowledgeable who asks really good questions. A counselor, a mentor, spouse, friend, peer support, or chaplain—these are all places to start, depending on the severity of the soul wound.

Second, we need to be educated on solutions. Understanding how we tick and why we are responding in certain ways is a great way to measure how we're doing and how to heal. Making sense of senselessness is a difficult thing—but knowing how it affects us is the key.

Third, we have to be patient. Healing from any injury takes time.

Fourth, we need to begin to nourish our souls with positive things like time with family and friends, faith, getting outdoors, and sleep. Resetting the mind with truth and thankfulness is crucial to long-term health.

*"Once the storm is over you won't remember how you
made it through, how you managed to survive. You won't
even be sure in fact, that the storm is really over. But one thing
is certain. When you come out of the storm, you won't
be the same person who walked in."*
Carlos, Police Officer, Kansas

Getting the Family Involved

Patricia, an officer in Michigan, attended a meeting to set up a peer support program in her area. She was surprised to learn that most of those present at the meeting who had been through critical incidents did not share anything about their experience with their spouses unless they were married to another officer. The main reason was they didn't want to bring work home. According to Patricia, they didn't want to talk to anyone but another officer who'd been through something similar.

Officers at a peer support training in California agreed. These were men and women who'd been members of peer support for about five years. Several said they had heard similar comments. But then a few of them countered.

"I can't imagine not sharing with my wife something that affects me so much. She's my best friend—why would I want to keep something this significant away from her?" said the soft-spoken giant in the back row with his arms crossed.

Then, a spouse who was present spoke up. "I told my husband that I really didn't want to hear about his day to day stuff—the brain matter, the gore, the filth—unless it was something that affected him. Then I would listen. One day that time came, and I sat and listened despite the fact it was very uncomfortable."

Did it affect her? "I cried for three days!" said the impeccably dressed businesswoman married 25 years to a seasoned officer.

A show of hands verified that these officers purposefully do not share stuff with their spouses for fear of this very response.

I asked the spouse, "How were you after the three days?"

"I was just fine," she responded.

You have the choice to talk or keep silent about the things that bother you on the job. I tend to agree with Strong not Silent in the back row—keeping things bottled up from the ones you love the most only separates and promotes isolation. If your spouse can't handle the details, don't share the details. But share something! You need to know you're not alone, not isolated, and that your human reaction is totally normal.

There may be a reaction. If she cries for three days, don't be afraid of that. She'll be fine. Police spouses are pretty strong people. Stronger than most. You have to be able to let your spouse process it through. If she asks a few days later about it, let her know where you're at with it. If you feel better, say so. If you don't, talk about the next step.

There is accountability with this. James confided that he just didn't want it to be brought up again and again. So communicate that. Set the expectation with your spouse—tell her what you need, what you don't need, and the best way she can support you. In a kind tone, of course.

Brent came home one night very troubled. We sat at the table as he told me of a coworker who had blatantly deceived him. I was livid, and let it all come out right then and there. After my outburst, he was silent.

I realized later that my response completely shut him down. We talked about it. He told me that although he felt the same way, he really didn't want to deal with my anger at the time, so he cut it off. He said he needed me to remain calm; otherwise he just wouldn't share anything. I learned from that—no more outbursts, just listening and clarifying questions. I'm an adult; I can adjust. I can respond the way he needs me to so that our communication continues. It is a tiny sacrifice for the reward—and entirely worth it. Your spouse can adapt with clear communication, too.

Wounded Officers

In the summer of 2014 I flew to Billings, Montana to spend the next four days with eight law enforcement families who gave just short of everything. They were wounded law enforcement officers and their wives, and were sponsored to attend the VOWS Retreat—a marriage retreat through Hunting for Heroes. What I learned was incredibly impactful; I won't ever look at policing in quite the same way.

We were met at the airport by a group of thankful citizens who held up signs of support. The mayor and his wife were there. Over the weekend, off-duty and retired officers, chaplains, and churches enthusiastically prepared special meals for this small group of officers who'd been injured in the line of duty.

Some of the men had limps. Many of them had head injuries. Some were heavy on pain meds, one retired officer sucking on a Fentanyl stick to deal with constant pain. The wives, well, they just looked tired. Profoundly weary.

> *"There really was no one that I knew who could relate to*
> *what I was going through, and I had to be there for Ladd,*
> *because what he was going through was physical pain on top*
> *of all of his own emotional and spiritual battles. Although at times*
> *I wanted to run in the opposite direction or crawl under the covers*
> *and not come out, I had to be strong for him and for the kids."*
> Heidi Paulson, Dependence Day

That night they shared their stories. The circumstances that caused their injuries were hard to hear. The aftermath was even worse. They described how their families had endured, not knowing if they would live or die. They talked about surgeries and learning to walk again, and the months of commuting back and forth to clinics and rehab facilities.

> *"The hospital part will be the easy part."*
> A pastor to Heidi Paulson,
> the night her husband was severely injured on duty

In each case, the Blue Line Family was there for the first several months, but then slowly but surely, that support faded. The wives became caregivers, and many of them still struggle with the toll of changing roles. Personality changes. Meltdowns. Nightmares. PTSD.

Many officers who are severely injured are forced to retire. It takes an emotional toll. They are still officers inside, but are no longer able to serve because of the physical limitations their trauma has caused.

Many described knock-down-drag-out fights they've had to endure for the benefits they thought they would receive for an on-duty injury. Most are profoundly disappointed by the lack of assistance and resources available when it comes to caring for their families long-term. They thought they were prepared, but were not. In the Appendix I have included a list of things to know and follow up on when you set up your disability insurance. It is worth the work to ensure your coverage if you should be severely wounded on duty.

Fortunately, these families found solace and community within the organization, Hunting for Heroes (H4H). Founded in 2010, H4H is a nonprofit organization that provides recreational therapy and counseling in the aftermath of a debilitating injury in the line of duty. H4H sponsors outdoor trips and retreats that give back that sense of brotherhood, all expenses paid. Wounded officers are encouraged and strengthened through contact with each other and their families.

Brent and I have been privileged to know a few officers who were severely wounded on duty with the CHP. One such officer was hit on the side of the road at an accident scene and lost both legs. He made it back to full duty with titanium legs, passing the physical test, which included a timed run. He has since become a motivational speaker.

Several other officers were able to return to work full duty; others have not.

Since on-duty injury is a real possibility, all law enforcement officers should consider the following:

- Make sure you have adequate disability coverage (see Appendix).
- Invest in your relationships. They may be the ones someday caring for you.
- Work out regularly—some of our wounded survived their ordeal or healed quicker because they were in great shape.
- Keep in touch long term with your buddies who've been wounded and had to retire. They are still cops and would really appreciate your friendship, especially in retirement. They would love to hear your stories from time to time.
- If you're looking for a great way to support wounded officers, please consider supporting Hunting for Heroes.

The following is an excerpt of a letter written by Shane, a wounded California motor officer. It aptly communicates the feelings of most officers who've been medically retired because of on-duty injury:

"I just want to say to the uniformed personnel that I am jealous you get to do your job and I don't anymore. I personally loved this career and had great plans for it. I may have only been able to work the road for five years, but each day was an awesome experience.

"On November 8th 2013, I was en route to the West Valley office, when a garbage truck made a right hand turn directly in front of me. I spent a month in the hospital with a lot of injuries. I've spent the last two years trying to recover, and wanted nothing more but to get back in the tan uniform and the motor boots I worked so hard to earn. Unfortunately my dreams were crushed, the carpet was ripped out from under my feet, and my life forever changed. I still have very limited movement of my left arm, shoulder, and hand, plus many other complications.

"I was officially medically retired. I still have a long road ahead of me, and I'll keep pushing forward, one day at a time.

"Words of advice for everyone. Stay in shape (the doctor told my wife one of the only reasons I survived was because of my strength and physical condition), keep training, don't take anything or anyone for granted, and listen and learn from the senior dogs. Max out your 457/401K, get life insurance, max out your vacation/sick/CTO banks. Treat the public like they were family; don't say anything to them that you wouldn't say to your parents. My goal on every stop was to get a thank you from the violator. I'd say 98% of the time I did. The other 2% we won't mention...

"Thank you to all those who helped my family and I through the last two years. Thank you to everyone who visited me in the hospital. Sorry for what you had to see; I don't have much memory of a lot of the visitors but you all made a huge impact on my family. You have all been a blessing. Please keep in touch."

For those of you who've been wounded in the line of duty, a few thoughts:

- Don't overlook the injuries to your soul. You've been wounded physically, but trauma also can injure emotionally and mentally, even spiritually. Seek healing for your soul as well.
- Take time to grieve for the things you've lost.
- An attitude of gratitude and humility will help you in the healing of body and soul.
- Understand that it takes time to learn who you are again. You still have the heart of a cop—but can't be that anymore. That's a tough thing to swallow. Look for other ways of satisfying that sheepdog heart.
- Appreciate your spouse—he/she has been through extreme difficulty and regularly makes sacrifices for your well-being. When you are tempted to complain about her, remember she's not perfect, but she's there. She deserves your love and expression of gratitude on a regular basis.
- Show your family that you love them in your unique way. Seek to unify in the midst of tragedy and move forward together. Those who are living with you are struggling differently, but they still struggle. Your words and acts of affirmation and love will soothe the rough spots.
- Check into Hunting for Heroes and what they have to offer. If you are able, pay the kindnesses you've been shown forward.
- Help others like you've been helped.

Thank you for your service and sacrifice.

Line of Duty Death (LODD)

"Whoa, will you look at this!" my coworker called out.

We went to the window and watched in awe as police cars filled the parking lot outside. They didn't use the white lines; there weren't enough spaces. They parked only inches from each other, filling the entire lot with little room to spare. As the officers emerged, I noticed they were dressed impeccably with shiny shoes and buttons and badges.

But their faces were grim.

This was the funeral of Fullerton Police Department (CA) officer Tommy De La Rosa on June 27, 1990. He was murdered in an ambush while engaged in an undercover drug buy. Over 5,000 uniforms showed up that day to pay their respects.

Since then, hundreds of law enforcement officers have perished in the line of duty, more than 100 each year. Just months before this book was published, Brent and I attended two LODD funerals in two days. Two others occurred that same week. Four LODDs in one week, just in California. That tends to wear on you.

> *"The deaths of Law and Gonzalez brought up horrible*
> *memories of our previous loss. My husband went immediately*
> *into cop mode, and looked for the facts in everything, not speculating*
> *on feelings. He's been abrupt with our children (ages two and five).*
> *While we watched the news reports, he snuggled closer on the couch*
> *as I cried. The fact that I, too, have friends grieving is almost beyond*
> *his comprehension, since it is a work-related experience."*
> Kristin, CHP wife

You knew when you took your oath as an officer the risks that were involved. We as police families hope against hope that death doesn't come knocking on our doors, or on doors of those who are close to us.

But, for some, it does.

Grief is real, and we can't plan for it. With every note from the bagpiper, every missing man formation by police helicopters, and the echoes of 21 gun salutes, there is a pain that resonates beneath that badge. It is a reminder of the frailty of life. A reminder that the uniform is in fact, fallible. We are reminded that we will lose some good men and women in this fight against crime.

"The officer who was gunned down this morning by a coward
did not deserve this. Without even knowing him, I knew him.
He was the kind voice in a time of need; he was the strong hand
when strength was required. He would set aside his safety and comfort
to provide safety and comfort. He was selfless, not selfish. He was the
reminder, to all who saw him, that we all have a responsibility to act
in a manner that reflects positively on the goodness that is America."
Mike, California

After two Sacramento area deputy sheriffs were killed in October 2014, many officers struggled to cope with this loss. There were those who shut down. There were those who went to the gravesite and sat for hours, trying to make sense of it. For those who may have been on scene either during or afterward, the images of a loved one lost is most difficult.

But it is not in vain.

Military veterans do not refer to themselves as heroes. Only those who died in combat are given that honor. They made the ultimate sacrifice—to take their oaths to the death. Similarly, peace officers that have died in the line of duty laid down their lives rather than swerved from the path of duty. That deep dedication and sacrifice is worthy of respect and celebration. We celebrate their lives and their careers. We mourn the person and the loss of a spouse/friend/parent, but we celebrate a life given to service to one's fellow citizens.

> *"We will go back to work, we will put the uniform on, get in*
> *the cars, and do our job everyday. And we will do it to*
> *honor Mike and other officers that have fallen victim to evil."*
> Sheriff Ed Bonner, Sacramento County, California

Grieving Alongside Others

The thunder rumbled and the room lit up. She sighed heavily, leaning over to see that her husband was not in bed. And then she remembered where he was. Sadness. Anger. Grief.

She pulled herself from under the covers. She couldn't sleep anyway. Between the physical storm that presently ripped through the sky, and the storm that had crashed in on their world just a few hours earlier, there was no peace in slumber. There was no peace anywhere. She and her husband were reeling from the loss of a Blue Line brother, and extended family member.

The days that followed were confusing, her husband dealing with not only a personal loss but also a professional one. Emotions alternated between shock, anger, and sadness. They went through the motions with arrangements, and protocol, and the overwhelming presence of uniforms, all with their confused children in tow. It was devastating.

"I don't know what to do," confided Kristin about her husband. "He's all business. He's short with the kids. I know he's hurting, but he won't allow himself to grieve."

> *"When it comes to the passing of those you love,*
> *laugh when you can, cry when you must,*
> *and don't ever forget to remember."*
> Chuck Norris

When you lose a brother or sister in the line of duty, give yourself permission to grieve. Here are a few ideas to work out the grief:

- **Talk it out with your spouse or another close friend.** Tell stories. Admit you miss them. Get angry at injustice. Whatever the stage of grief you're in, sharing these feelings does two things: It takes away the power to rule your thoughts, and brings you closer to those who listen. Grief is something to be shared.
- **Incorporate a characteristic, a quote, or something your loved one stood for into your own life.** "Let's roll!" became a household phrase after Todd Beamer said this before he died on Flight 93 on September 11, 2001.
- **Pay tribute.** Freeways named after the fallen, bike rides to DC in the fallen's name, a lapel pin or ribbon, scholarship funds, a trip—the list goes on an on.
- **Go to Police Week in Washington DC.** Attend the vigil. Get a name etching from the Law Enforcement Memorial Wall. Leave a note. Sit at the wall awhile. It's worth the time and money.
- **Be patient with the emotion.** As time passes, processed grief will subside. Sometimes feelings of loss will rise up here and there even years later. This is normal.

Supporting Survivors

When the grief of loss hits head on like a Mack truck, there are no words. The body is reeling from shock and numb with pain, the mind is a jumbled mess of questions, rationalizations, and disbelief, and the spirit is injured. Survivors simply can't hear anything. So, how can we help?

- They don't want to hear you're sorry. Everybody says that.
- They don't need to hear the upside view of things. At this moment there is no bright perspective—their lives have been forever changed.

- They don't need someone to force them to eat. The body shuts down the need for food in the initial stages of shock and grief. They will eat eventually. Hand them a bottle of cold water instead.
- They don't need advice. Solutions will present themselves soon enough. Let grief have its moments.
- They don't need you to pass judgment on how they grieve. Every person grieves differently. But being present means everything.
- They do need someone who will allow them to talk without interruption, cry as softly or loudly as need be, be silent and quiet as thoughts untangle, and to offer a comforting touch or hug if appropriate.
- They do want to hear short positive memories or compliments of the person lost when appropriate.
- They will appreciate photos of the deceased.

ITEMS FAMILIES NEED IN CRISIS

If you are the officer who picks up family members to take them to the hospital, take a moment to make sure they have the following:

✓ Cell phone and charger

✓ Purse/wallet

✓ A light jacket or sweater

✓ Comfortable and appropriate clothes and shoes
  (Make sure they understand many people will be at the hospital)

✓ Small toys, crayons and color books, and snacks for children

✓ Diaper bag and formula for infants

- Then, after the funeral and burial have passed and the world moves on, survivors will appreciate your acknowledgement that you are still thinking about them, they are not alone, and they are not forgotten. Cards are best sent a month or two after the death. Flowers at Christmas in memory of the person lost, a tribute of some kind, or a phone call—it's never too late to reach out to survivors.
- If survivors come into the office, look them in the eye, even if it hurts. Ask them how they're doing. Give a hug if appropriate. You don't have to soothe their hurts—you don't have to fix anything. You don't have to come up with something to say. Your acknowledgement and quiet care are enough.
- In recent years, officers have shown up in uniform to support the children of the fallen at daddy-daughter dances, graduations, career day at school—standing in for the deceased. What a beautiful way to grieve alongside survivors.

Grief, in all its anguish, is a normal, natural part of life. It is not something to avoid, but to make time to embrace and work through unhurried. Our heroes are worth it.

Hiking Life

It was a beautiful day in Yosemite National Park. Fifteen people decided to take an easy, one-hour stroll around Mirror Lake. Little did we know it would take us most of the day.

We started out, a motley crew of family and friends ranging in age from six weeks to 80 years, conversing along the paved way. We leisurely hiked about two-thirds around the lake when we came to a barricade that said, "Warning! Landslide damage. Trail ends here." Being the adventurous type and rationalizing it would take twice as long to turn back, we said to each other, "How bad could it be?"

We forged ahead until we came to the actual landslide. White rocks ranging in size from toasters to houses were toppled upon one another, with huge trees lying on their sides at the bottom. The area covered about three acres. To traverse over this seemed a daunting task with the small children and elderly present. Unbelievably, we went for it. Up and down, rock-to-rock, tree-to-tree, we got all fifteen of us across the debris safely. We regrouped on the other side, taking swigs of water and eating trail mix, chuckling about our ordeal, and amazed everyone made it with only a few minor scrapes.

On the journey through life and career, there will be critical incidents, loss, and soul wounds along the way. These difficulties may seem daunting, but the only way to go is through them. Here are a few principles gleaned from our Yosemite hike that are applicable to hard times.

First, we walked through the debris one step at a time. There were rocks upon rocks, and some of them were not steady. We had to test each rock as we moved forward and side-to-side, taking the most sure and stable route. When life is tough, maneuvering through pain and consequences can be pretty tricky. You may see where you hope to be at the end, but the path to get there may be riddled with detours. Taking each step slowly and steadily minimizes pitfalls that come with a difficult journey.

Second, some hikers needed help to get across. We took turns carrying the two-year-old and lending extra support to the mom who had the six-week-old baby strapped to her front. We also helped the grandparents. When things get tough, we need to lean on our support systems to get us safely to the other side. Sharing each other's loads is not only necessary for survival, but bonding can be a byproduct. By the end of the day we felt a special kinship with each other through what we'd been through.

One of the hikers was really fearful for the children. She was really angry we were in this situation. I was a little surprised at her reaction, because she is usually very levelheaded. My husband told me later that just a week earlier her son slipped and fell with his newborn son in his arms and dropped the baby. She saw the whole thing happen. The trauma of that situation carried over into seeing another grandchild in potential danger, and anger resulted. The third thing to remember is when we go through tough times, past hurts may ignite anger or fear. Past hurts tend to complicate things. Understanding, acknowledging the hurts, and communicating this will help navigate our response.

No sooner did we rejoin the trail, than we heard a huge crack and rumble from above. Thunder and lightening filled the sky, and then the downpour started. We were soaked to the bone by the time we reached our bus stop. Sometimes, when one trial ends, another one begins. And another. It's just the way life happens sometimes. We dealt with this by laughing. Most of us kept our sense of humor intact. Just moments before we got soaked, we were all sweaty from climbing over rocks and trees. We joked about not needing showers anymore. When life is one trouble after another, sometimes it's just good to laugh in the midst of it. Laughter is also contagious.

The final lesson comes from the fact that we never gave up. We kept moving forward, helping each other, talking it through. Afterward, we chuckled about the experience, thankful and even a little wiser.

Our on-duty and off-duty lives will be sprinkled with mountain peaks and valley lows. There may be an avalanche or a downpour or two. But when we have that support system to maneuver through, it makes all the difference.

. . . .

Think: Think of critical incidents you or your fellow officers have experienced. How have they come through it? Do you think any of this information could be helpful to you or them?

Debrief: Read this chapter with your spouse and then talk about an incident that bothered you.

Strategic Action: If you suspect you have difficulty in any of the areas in this chapter, follow up with resources that apply.

> *"Our nation's military and law enforcement personnel work hard to protect us. We must thank them for their continued vigilance. Without their sacrifice we would be less capable of protecting our nation."*
> Leonard Boswell

CHAPTER NINE

WHEN THE HURT SEEMS UNBEARABLE

"I don't know who I am anymore.
It seems I have lost something of myself."
Reagan, an officer who committed suicide three months later

Bob, a retired fireman, sat across from me at Starbucks, recounting the days leading up to his suicide attempt. Depression and suicidal thoughts had been a constant but unwanted companion, and an addiction to alcohol fueled his desire to end his life. His wife and children had left years earlier. He was alone.

He had it all planned out. He would use the very gun that his father had used many years earlier upon learning he had terminal cancer. The weapon had done the trick; it would do so again. He went out behind the garage, bringing with him a lawn chair and a beer. He was supposed to be at the station, but no one would think to look for him back there. The time for action had come. He placed the gun to his chin and pulled the trigger. But instead of death, he awoke moments later to intense pain. It didn't work. He was still alive.

After three hours of walking around spitting blood, he realized he needed to take a second shot. Then he started thinking about his kids, and didn't want them to think he died a long, horrible death. So he called 911 and then sat on the front porch. A fire friend showed up who'd been out looking for him, and then two more. Then the engine arrived, and everybody he knew was there. He learned later that the bullet went up through the roof of his mouth and lodged into his nasal cavity, stopping short of his brain. He was given a second chance.

In the days that followed, Bob was surprised to learn how many people actually cared about him. He went through surgery, and then spent several days in ICU. He later got help with the depression. He enrolled into a 12-step program to rid the drinking. His thoughts became clearer.

Over time, he realized there were better solutions to the problems in his life. He was grateful for the second chance. These days, he shares his story with first responders, cops, and military at the West Coast Post-Trauma Retreat. He also speaks at Alcoholics Anonymous meetings. He's been pleased to learn that his story has deterred other suicides.

In the United States, 125-150 officers commit suicide every year. Each is a unique situation with a particular story. But every one of those cops was dealing with some kind of pain, whether physical, emotional, mental, spiritual, or relational. Every one of those officers lost hope in life. Every one was convinced that it was better to die than to live another day.

Reasons Law Enforcement Officers Commit Suicide

Loss due to divorce or death
Marital problems
Terminal illness
Guilt over a partner's death
Legal problems
Feeling alone
Sexual accusations
Disability/retirement
Internal Affairs investigations
Financial problems
Arrest
Loss of employment
PTSD

Life can really be very difficult. Police officers are eyewitnesses to how true this is. You deal with the worst. You see injustices. You see the depravity of men and women, and how their choices hurt and even destroy those who are closest to them.

"Scars remind us of where we've been,
not where we're going."
Unknown

Like Gina in chapter eight, your cup is full of these thoughts and images after every shift.

"It seemed that a pattern was evolving with officers I had worked
with in the past taking their own lives, guys who had also been at
the shootout. Three whom I had worked the confines of a patrol
car with, whom I had joked with in the locker room and hallways
during different periods of time, had decided that life was just
too tough. These were guys who usually had smiles on their faces.
I couldn't understand it, and though I had heard others, including
the Chief, say that the shootout had nothing to do with it, I had
my doubts. With my own baggage from the shootout as a backdrop,
I easily saw how it could have played some part in the big picture.
For someone to resort to suicide it would require a lot of pressure
and stress, two things the shootout was generous in providing."
John Caprarelli, *Uniform Decisions*

If you are not flushing these thoughts and images regularly, and re-placing them with positive information, your view of the world in general will be very skewed. If you are not constantly communicating and caring for your loved ones, your view of your family (and their view of you) will also become skewed. Add to that an unresolved soul wound (or several), there can be a loss of hope, which leads to despair.

For Those Who are Struggling

Recently suicide hit my extended family. I listened tearfully to a loved one's cry. "I wish I would've known how he felt," she whispered. "He listened to me. Perhaps I could've helped."

A California officer said three local cops shot themselves in department parking lots—in a two-month period.

A grieving mother described hearing the shot upstairs, watching helplessly as her husband grasped his son, shouting, "Why?" She saw her son's blood pool on the bathroom floor before he ordered her downstairs. Their family suffers deeply as they mourn and struggle to move forward.

My daughter reasoned about a friend who was killed in a terrible car accident. "Perhaps she's with her dad, now. She used to tell me that when her dad took his life, she thought it was her fault. Maybe she knows now that it wasn't."

My mind goes back to a childhood friend who discovered his father after he took his own life. He has struggled with substance abuse his entire life. One night, in a drunken stupor, his grief tumbled out in a jumbled mess of cries, shouting, and despair. This was a decade after the suicide.

Some people equate suicide with mental illness. Perhaps that may be true for a few, but for most, it is a loss of perspective in the shadows of brokenness and pain. Alcohol and drugs fuel haywire thoughts, clouding thinking processes. Suicide begins to make sense.

Bob said that he didn't realize that something was wrong, and neither did 99.9 percent of those around him. He said there was only one co-worker who asked if he was OK about two weeks before his attempt. Of course, he lied.

Thoughts can be deceptive—we take facts and circumstances and filter them through our individual grids. Depending on the details and their emotional depth, our attitudes in the midst of struggles, and our inner fortitude based on upbringing/training, we come up with the conclusions all of these factors add up to in our minds. Yet our thoughts may be far from reality. This isn't necessarily mental illness—rather how our thoughts are filtered into distorted/confused arguments when we don't have all the facts. When life is overwhelming and unraveling, circumstances squeeze out answers, and the pain grows deeper still. It's difficult to want to go on. It seems relief will only come once life ends.

You may be contemplating suicide right now. Will you allow me to be a voice in your consideration? You may be listening to other voices—voices from the past that injure you, voices of anger that want to kill you, voices that say you are worthless, and voices that deceive you into thinking there is no hope, no solution, no end to the pain you now experience.

> *"Never believe the lie that no one cares whether you live or die.*
> *You may have made mistakes—we all have—but there are still*
> *people who love you. And even if the consequences of your*
> *mistakes appear insurmountable, believe this truth: there are*
> *people who will count it a privilege to help you and to walk*
> *beside you in whatever valley of shadows you find before you."*
> Clarke A. Paris, *My Life for Your Life*

There are some things you need to know. For those who consider suicide a viable option, here is a list of consequences that actually happen. If you kill yourself:

- Your life will end on earth.
- This last act may define your legacy.
- You will wound your children, no matter what age they are, and no matter what your relationship looks like.
- You will wound your spouse, even if you are at odds right now.
- You will break your parents' hearts.
- You will hurt your friends and coworkers.
- Some will be incredibly angry with you.
- Some who love you will be embarrassed and ashamed of the way you died.

- Some will take on guilt, and it will have a painful impact on their lives.
- Some will blame themselves, even though it isn't their fault.
- Some will say you were mentally ill. You won't be around to convince them otherwise.
- You will leave a lasting horrific picture for those who find you, which will be loved ones and possibly coworkers.
- You will let depression and despair have its victory.
- You will leave unanswered questions.
- If you are leading a secret life, it will be exposed. You will not have the chance to explain, nor apologize, nor make it right.
- Your life is interconnected with others; your suicide will leave a painful void. Even in people you wouldn't have guessed.

Call SafeCallNow—206-459-3020—right now.

"The night that you died, you made it clear that you had no intention of hurting anyone other than yourself. But your decision did hurt others because it caused pain to all the people who cared about you and that pain will never go away."
Chief John Pritchard, in a letter to Brian Resser after he committed suicide

As desperate and hopeless as things may seem, consider:

- Though you may not see it now, there is hope. Hope in love, hope in healing, hope in changes you can make in your life. Until you pull the trigger, it isn't too late to seek a different course of action.

- Though you may feel alone, you are not. Call out to others you trust even a little.
- If you are hearing voices that say you are worthless and you shouldn't be alive, this is a lie. The truth is that God gave you life and purpose and value.
- If you are weary of life, perhaps try something new—something selfless, something meaningful, something healthy.
- Depression is a symptom of unaddressed hurts and unresolved anger. It is a curable condition.
- Post-Traumatic Stress Disorder is a reality that thousands of military, civilians, peace officers, firemen, and first responders are dealing with right this minute. Bad things happened, and you witnessed it. You need to know that it's okay to feel awful about a horrible situation. It is a normal response to an abnormal event(s), and there are solutions to PTSD. Talk to someone who's been there.

Call SafeCallNow at 206-459-3020.

- Even if you are extremely angry with God or believe He's abandoned you, ask Him to meet you in your pain. In the Appendix, I've included a translation of Psalm 139 from the Bible. Read it now. The author was a warrior who experienced the plague of war and loss, and struggled with many failures in his life. Ask yourself, "Where is God in this pain?" The answer is there. Then reach out to someone you know who has a relationship with God. Don't know anyone? Send me an email, and I'll find someone to contact you ASAP. You can also speak to a chaplain by calling Serve and Protect right now at 615-373-8000.
- Life is a series of ups and downs. If this is a particularly bad season, give it time and connect with others. They will help you through it.
- Don't end your life in defeat—live your life strong! Understand your weaknesses as well as your strengths and accept both. There are those who love you, and those that need you. Don't let them down.

People to Contact NOW:

SafeCallNow: 206-459-3020

Serve & Protect: 615-373-8000

Why Cops Don't Seek Help
Denial
Avoidance
Anger
Fear

For Those Who Have Friends That Are Struggling

Bob had a co-worker who sensed something just wasn't quite right. His co-worker had the guts to ask about it. You are trained and experienced in sensing when something just isn't right. Here is a list of warning signs that show an officer may be contemplating suicide:

- Excessive Drinking
- Prescription Drug Abuse
- Finances in Turmoil
- In Need of Family Counseling
- Struggling with Addiction
- Marital Issues
- Depression
- Erratic Behavior
- Loss of Interest in Job
- Suicide Attempt
- Alienation
- Changes in Weight/Appetite

- Feelings of Hopelessness
- Unable to Sleep

If you suspect that someone you know may be contemplating suicide, what should you do?

- Ask them if they are thinking about hurting themselves.
  This may be the one time someone asks, and it might be the one chance to intervene.
  - ▶ If the answer is yes, do not leave the officer alone. Get them help immediately.
- Take all suicidal comments or hints seriously, even jokes.
- Don't judge, and don't panic.
- Listen intently.
- Offer your help to walk through the solutions with the officer.
- Do not keep this to yourself. Get help right away.
- Do not trivialize problems or tell them to "knock it off."
- Understand and implement your department's procedure for emergency suicide intervention. Many departments will have assistance units or peer support that are trained to help quickly and confidentially.
- If your department doesn't have resources to offer, call SafeCallNow at 206-459-3020 for guidance. They have a vast network of resources and help all over the country. It is confidential.

When a Co-worker Commits Suicide

Losing a Blue Line family member in any manner is a difficult blow, worthy of contemplation, appropriate grief, and celebration of life. Here are some thoughts and suggestions to adapt in the wake of losing a co-worker to suicide:

- Give yourself permission to grieve. The manner in which they died does not diminish your loss.
- Reserve judgment. It's been said that suicide is a selfish act. Closer to the truth, suicide is a painful act. The person was

unable to see any alternative to death.
- Don't take responsibility for the suicide or for not preventing it. It wasn't your choice.
- Support survivors. They are hurting. It's not their fault. They need your support.
- Prevent future suicides. Learn to recognize the symptoms and warning signs in yourself and others. Commit to personal prevention by implementing emotional care in your off-duty hours.

· ·

Think: Am I practicing good emotional care in my life?
Do I have suicidal thoughts?

Debrief: If you are having suicidal thoughts, share this with your spouse.

Strategic Action: Work on getting some new perspective from spouse, friends, peer support, or a therapist. Depression, PTSD, and substance abuse are curable conditions; suicide is not.

*"We have an incredible warrior class in this country—
people in law enforcement, intelligence—
and I thank God every night we have them standing fast
to protect us from the tremendous amount of evil
that exists in the world."*
Brad Thor

CHAPTER TEN

WHO'S GOT YOUR SIX?

*"Trust is hard to come by. That's why my circle is small and tight.
I'm kind of funny about making new friends."*
Eminem

In the fall of 2014, I asked Brent about the feelings of the troops in light of the movement of hatred toward police officers brought to the forefront in the Michael Brown shooting.

"Just another day on the streets," he replied. He reminded me that California is no stranger to this attitude. When Brent was a new cop on the streets of Los Angeles 27 years ago, CHP issued an officer safety bulletin because the Bloods and Cripps had declared war on the police. They had already shot at police from overpasses several times.

Brent was shot at while conducting a DUI stop. He'd been part of the law enforcement response to the Rodney King riots in 1992. Law enforcement responds to problems in Oakland as well as Los Angeles on a regular basis. And last year, when Christopher Dorner went on a killing spree in Southern California, social media blew up in support of his murderous rampage. This madness has been lurking beneath the surface for a long time.

But since that conversation, it's gotten worse. Brent's dad, a CHP officer for 37 years, said "Things have changed and not for the better. There's a different attitude than there used to be."

Protests spread to other cities. Accusations run wild whether they are based on fact or not. There are casualties of this war on authority—those who've lost their lives, their jobs, promotions, and some their joy of the work or confidence in what they do. Ferguson, New York, and Baltimore are painful reminders—it's spinning out of control. Officers are ambushed. Government leaders have to choose sides, public safety is suffering, and we've got ourselves a bonafide mess.

In all of this confusion it's been forgotten that police families are part of the community. We live and learn and love amidst the general public. We buy groceries, pay taxes, vote, attend church, watch baseball games, concerts, and parades and go to the farmer's market. We are not an occupying force. We are fellow citizens, part of the larger community.

Who Can You Trust?

The theme of this book is about training for off-duty life. You've been trained not to trust those you come into contact with on duty—you never know who you'll pull over, who will answer the door, who is hiding in the bushes, or who drives by. It's probably been your experience that most people are lying to you—and you know that because their lips are movin'!

Your training, and even more so your experience on patrol and in the community, has made you suspicious of everyone. It's part of why you go home after each shift.

That lack of trust spills over into your off-duty life. It dictates who you spend time with, who your kids' friends are, what neighborhood you live in, even where you sit in a restaurant. Because you know how people can be, you are not quick to trust anyone.

Since the war on authority that Ferguson ignited, this is even more important. You need to know who to trust. In a time when there seems to be much criticism, second-guessing, and hatred, you need to know that there are many who support you.

Is There Anybody Out There?

Throughout this book are quotes from people across the nation that are a part of the quiet majority who still support law enforcement, despite the verbal few who accuse and attack our officers. Cops need encouragement, more now than ever.

When we had a shooting in nearby Roseville, California in October 2013, the church I attend invited involved officers and their wives as guests at a Thanksgiving Banquet. Our pastors publicly thanked them and their wives for their sacrifices and gave them a gift bag with gift cards, a hotel stay, and a copy of my book. Though humbled, these officers were greatly encouraged.

Every Memorial Day, Fourth of July, and 9/11 churches have military, law enforcement, and first responders stand and then applaud them enthusiastically.

After two officers in October 2014 were killed, a church high school group put together goody bags for the Placer County Sheriff's deputies that included candy, gift cards, and best of all, thank you notes written by the high school students. Over 200 kids wrote notes.

Chick-Fil-A supports police officers by printing the slogan, "Back the Blue" on the backs of their employee's uniform shirts.

Operation Safety 91 is an organization that exists to instill an appreciation and commitment to honor first responders, law enforcement, and military. They pray for you and distribute free Psalm 91 (prayer of protection) cards.

Many people show up with signs of support at funeral processions and vigils. They put blue light bulbs in their porch lights. They quietly give to foundations that support police. They write letters of thanks to specific officers, and drop off baked goods at the holidays.

There are blue lines on the back windows of cars, blue ribbons in front yards, and individuals who will approach officers on duty and quietly thank them for their service. One elderly lady decided to visit a police station to simply hug an officer.

These listed here are not the ones you're arresting again and again. They're not the ones you see out and about after midnight causing trouble. They are the quiet majority—and they support you.

The quiet majority are not the ones who are marching in protest and accusation. These protestors are sometimes peaceful, many times offensive and destructive, but always loud. You hear them chanting and screaming in person and on TV. So do your loved ones. These people make it easy to forget about the quiet majority.

Law Enforcement Chaplains

I spent several months going through Sacramento's Law Enforcement Chaplaincy (LECS) training headed up by Mindi and Frank Russell. It was several months of training on how to administer emotional first aid in the face of trauma. We were trained to give death notifications, how to listen well, and what to do and what not to do when people are experiencing loss or devastation.

As the course progressed, there were four of us selected to be trained specifically as law enforcement chaplains (LECS also trains community chaplains and school chaplains). The list of requirements for this specialty were higher than the other two—there had to be demonstrated maturity, an explanation of motives to work alongside law enforcement, a requirement to be ordained by a church (for confidentiality protection), and most had some kind of knowledge or positive familiarity with police.

Sacramento law enforcement chaplains serve the local law enforcement community by administering death notifications for them, are present at scenes to help console survivors or victims, and provide food and assistance at DUI checkpoints and briefings. They serve in practical ways at funerals, and talk with officers, spouses, and others who attend police functions. They also hold critical incident debriefs with families.

Law enforcement chaplains exist to serve you. These people have compassion for what you endure as a cop, and they want to help. They are part of the quiet majority who support you, and most (I can't speak for all) can be trusted.

There are chaplains of all religions. LECS chaplains are trained to stay neutral, listen, and are not to pressure cops to join churches or to preach. They are trained listeners who will keep their mouths shut. When there are questions about where God fits into what people are dealing with, they are trained to provide answers and comfort.

The California Highway Patrol has recently begun recruiting retired law enforcement to serve as chaplains for officers and other retirees. It is important to the organization that who they have on hand to respond in crisis is learned in the ways of law enforcement, and has a deep understanding so that they are effective.

A great example of an involved and supportive chaplaincy is found in the town of Elkhart, Indiana. Chaplain Jim Bontrager, a retired Marine, has a desire and passion to help officers in his department, and beyond. Over two decades ago, he met with a few cops around a picnic table and fed them lunch. This evolved over the years to become the Law Enforcement Appreciation Day for law enforcement families, and is held the first weekend every October. Local restaurants serve delicious meals. There are bounce houses, face painting, and go-carts. There are shooting competitions, a zipline, and helicopter rides. Every family leaves with a donated basket of free goodies. It is set in the heart of Amish country, and staffed by volunteers who appreciate and love police officers. The best part? Everything is free—services, food and expenses are donated by many members of the quiet majority. Four years ago, Bontrager implemented a faith-based conference, Breaching the Barricade, to be held the day before the festivities. Lt. Col. Dave Grossman and J. Wallace Warner are two of the speakers in recent years. This weekend provides safe events in a safe place for officers and their families to get out for a day and build some great memories.

Your Off-Duty Support System

Your life off duty is naturally affected by a general mistrust on duty. You know when people are lying. And you know that many people just aren't trustworthy.

But when it comes to your personal life, you must have an inner circle of people who understand and support you. Who disagree with you sometimes. Who encourage you. Who call you out when you're being stupid. Who make you laugh. Who love you. Who give you perspective. People you can trust.

First and foremost, your spouse and children are your primary support system. They are the ones with whom you spend most of your off-duty time. They know you, live life with you. As you build trust together through the seasons of your marriage and family, they'll have your back.

Extended family and friends are next. Sarah has two very close friends in her life that are both named Michelle. The first is the spouse of another officer, and she herself is married to an officer. This Michelle totally gets the job and its life. There are times when she needs to vent or gather understanding from someone who really understands. The second Michelle is a woman who has nothing to do with law enforcement. The friendship gives perspective from a non-law enforcement view. This helps to keep her balanced.

Brent and I strive for this same balance. We have family in law enforcement and family that have nothing to do with policing. We have many friends who are law enforcement, and others that are business owners. We have friends in the computer business, and some in the medical field. It has been a well-rounded group of people we've built relationships with through the years. People we trust. People we love and who love us. People who make us laugh, and yes, people who are not afraid to ask some hard questions. There are many not in law enforcement who have the potential to be awesome companions and friends.

Relationship with God

Whether you believe in God or not, I assure you that God believes in you. God is pro-law enforcement.

There has been a war between good and evil since time began. You see this war played out on our streets and in our homes. There are those who are for life, goodness, restoration, and peace. And then there are those who are for anarchy, revenge, selfish gain, and destruction. You've seen it. You've smelled it. You fight it. That's what you do.

In the Bible, Romans 13 talks about how God appoints "avengers" to bring wrath upon those who do evil. He establishes the authorities of the people, and equips these men and women to uphold the law, to administer justice, and thus keep the general population safe and peaceful. In essence, God Himself appointed you into service.

When speaking specifically of this passage at a solemn assembly for law enforcement officers, Nicolas Sensley, then Chief of Police of Truckee (CA) Police Department said this: "You are ministers of the will of God in a service of sacrifice whether you know it or not, whether you like it or not, and whether you believe it or not."

God not only appointed you, but He equips you and supports you.

I realize that for some, God is associated with judgment and abandonment. For me, God has healed me in very deep places of my soul, and is a constant source of encouragement, strength, and wisdom. I consider God a friend who I talk with every day, not someone who is scrutinizing my every move or motive, waiting to zap me at every mistake. There are many police officers all over the world that have decided to invest in a relationship with God, and have found Him to be worthy of their trust. They have found strength, protection, understanding, and even healing in the process.

For more information, the Resource Guide lists books and organizations for law enforcement that are faith-based.

Something in Common

Brent and I drove back through the trees of Maine, feeling thankful and content. We had just spent time with a group of officers and their families over the weekend and came away greatly encouraged. There was beauty everywhere, from trees and lakes to the smiles of little kids on bikes. The mood was relaxed, comfortable, and jovial. Those we met at the Christian Law Enforcement Officer Retreat in Danforth became dear to us in just a couple days. One couple confided in us about their marriage struggles and how they overcame them, speaking freely in front of their teenage girls. There was a sense of grace and freedom. They'd been through hard times as a family, and they survived the rough stuff together. A few years after the fact, we saw the evidence of forgiveness, renewed commitment that overcame separation, and recharged trust. The joy within their family was an encouragement to us.

As we go through this life, there will be those who have law enforcement in common, and they understand. There is a bond there. They get it. There are also those who are united in faith, and those who are close through surviving something difficult. Those people we live life with, even if we're hundreds of miles away, have our backs. We hold on to those friendships over time, and they bring stability and comfort.

The Support Goes Both Ways

If you are a younger officer, build your support system with not only family and friends, but a mentor or two. Choose someone who is trustworthy and has invested his/her life well. This is someone you and others respect, and is not afraid to speak directly into your life.

As a seasoned officer, are you building into others? Are you actively speaking life and possibility into the lives of young officers, teenagers, or troubled kids? If you are a peace officer, you have experience and wisdom that others can benefit from.

Your support system is not a one-way deal. Relationships are give and take. As a peace officer, you need people in your life. But those same people need you just as much.

There are officers that would do anything for another officer—at the expense of their family. Sometimes that is necessary. But is it a habit? There are cops that spend their time, money, and attention on their jobs way beyond the shift. That communicates the most valued priority. Do you engage at home? Do your kids talk to you? Do you remember what they say when they do? Does your spouse feel supported by you? Does he feel respected? Does she feel loved? These are good questions to ask. If you don't like the answers, perhaps it's time to be more intentional in supporting those you love.

· ·

Think: Who is my support system? Is this adequate? Do I have my family's back?

Debrief: Who is our support system as a family and as a police family? Talk about ways they have come alongside of you in the past.

Strategic Action: Take some time as an individual and as a couple and thank those who are supporting you. Bring up the specifics through a card, a coffee date, or even in the hallway before shift. They may not even be aware that what they did or said made an impact.

"I know a little bit about law enforcement because my father was a police officer. I'd watch him put on his uniform every day...He always let me put on his jacket first before he put it on. I remember I was so little the jacket went all the way down to the floor...And I watched him put his shield on his chest and walk proudly out of the door. That gave me the deep respect for our law enforcement officers and also for their families."
Arnold Schwarzenegger

CHAPTER ELEVEN

PROVISIONS FOR PRIORITIES

"You're not rich until you have something money can't buy."
Shilpa Tripathi

Many of the concepts in this book must be tailored to your relationship. There are things you can do or not do that are appropriate for your specific situation. There is no specific formula for success—it's about choosing, adapting, growing, and changing as your relationship progresses through the years.

But when it comes to your money, there is a formula that works. This is an area of your marriage that you can apply a formula, and with some patience and discipline, see the results you want.

Basics for Your Bucks

The formula for long-term financial well-being is 10-10-80. You take your paycheck after taxes, give ten percent to your favorite charities, put ten percent into the bank as savings, and then live on the rest. Over time you will see your money grow and your security increase. Guaranteed.

Can you live on eighty percent? I know there are many jurisdictions that are struggling financially and your pay reflects this. Money is tight. But there are still ways that you can make this happen.

The first practice is to adhere to a budget. We can't expect to get ahead in our finances if we don't know where our money goes. If there is no planning, bills surprise us and we find ourselves with too much month at the end of the money. Some people try to keep track on the money in their heads, which is dangerous. Something is always forgotten, and that unexpected expense is what sabotages the checkbook.

At one time I was a teller at a bank. Occasionally I'd have an irate customer come in and accuse the bank of stealing their money. "I checked my account two days ago and it said I had this much," they'd complain. "I didn't spend a thing, and now it says I have this much! How does that work, huh? You took my money!" After helping a couple of these customers, I understood exactly what happened. People didn't subtract the checks they wrote from their balance. They assumed once they wrote the check, the money was taken out. They didn't allow a few days for the check to clear. Even as much as electronic banking has become the norm, if you stick to a budget rather than spending from your ATM balance, you'll avoid a lot of headaches.

The other benefit to budgeting is that you are forced to prioritize your income ahead of time and set limits on spending. If you don't have the money, you don't spend it!

> *"Winning at money is 80% behavior and*
> *20% head knowledge.*
> *What to do isn't the problem; doing it is."*
> Dave Ramsey, The Total Money Makeover

Brent and I use an envelope system to keep our spending under control. We budget all of our responsibilities first. Then we budget for spending in different categories, such as clothing, eating out, and recreation. Some put the cash in the envelopes and pay from that, which is a great system. But we'd rather not carry cash around, so we keep receipts in the appropriate envelope and a running total of what has been spent and the balance on the corresponding envelopes. This system has worked for us for years.

Consumer debt will curb any efforts to make your money work for you. Once you go into debt, you begin to turn over control of your financial future. The bank is the one in charge at that point, and they set their price, and usually it goes up. To stay out of debt, we've got to deal with something within our own character: impatience.

We want things now. We may even argue we need it now. After all, dealing with the unique stressors that a career in law enforcement brings, don't we deserve it?

> *"All too often, people see their financial situation as one of desperation. They feel lost and alone. They see people around them and make assumptions that all their ducks are lined up perfectly in a row. Frequently, those people they are making assumptions about are making the very same assumptions about everyone else."*
> MotorCop Blog, *Is Your Financial Situation Unique?*

Our daughter wanted to buy her own car. She put together a plan where she took 40 percent of her earnings and deposited it into savings. Soon she had a few thousand dollars! She looked for a car for that amount, and realized she needed more to get what she really wanted. She then increased her saving budget to over 50 percent. She also was nearing graduation, and knew that she would probably receive some gift money. Within a few months, she had amassed over $5000, and bought a cute little Honda Civic. The main thing that kept her going was patience, knowing that she grew closer with each paycheck.

Bree and Hector went into their marriage with a relatively small amount of debt and no budget. Over time that debt grew because they were not committed to paying the debt off immediately. Then Bree quit her job to have their first child and they were down to one income. They made minimum payments and the debt grew even more. Several years later, they were in crisis. Credit companies were calling, they had to use credit cards for groceries, and it all came to an ugly realization that they were failing miserably.

> *"Debt in any form is a form of repression.*
> *Nationally or personally, debt is bondage,*
> *plain and simple. When we're not in debt,*
> *we're free to live, move, and enjoy our being."*
> Chuck Norris

At that point they instituted a budget. Realizing where their money was going was huge. They had to make some cuts based on their priorities. At first it was easy—subscriptions, luxury items, using coupons and discount stores, even going to the thrift store for needed items. Then they had to make some deep cuts that hurt more—cutbacks on smart phones, downsizing cars, cancelling their gym membership, and not going out for dinner. For two years it was tough, living paycheck to paycheck, as they paid off more and more credit card debt. Gradually the burden lightened, and they've been able to replace the beater cars, reinstate the gym membership, and go out to dinner occasionally. The recovery was made possible because they are budgeting those costs now. This was all done on one steady law enforcement income.

In addition to budgeting, it's also important to have an emergency fund—money that serves as a safety net when life's unexpected events occur. When our daughter took all the money out of her savings to buy her car, she suddenly felt a little insecure with no savings. What if the car broke down? She then decided to keep putting aside the 50 percent, and built up a safety fund right away. Start with a thousand dollars if you have nothing saved. Then build your reserve to at least three months living expenses. The peace of mind this brings is tremendous. It also greatly benefits your relationships.

Relational Aspects of Money

A friend recently shared about a small crisis he and his wife were having because of their money. They maintained separate bank accounts, so each was responsible for paying certain bills. He had thought through how much of his paycheck needed to go towards bills, and had about a hundred dollars left over for his meals for the following two weeks. Then, last minute his wife realized her check was short for that pay period. He would need to give her the hundred dollars to cover rent and eat peanut butter and jelly the rest of the pay period. He was angry. He felt that she didn't care about him needing to eat. Thus the argument began.

Communication about money is crucial. This is an area I have really faltered in over the years. Brent makes a great living, but several years ago with four kids and one income, we were struggling to make ends meet. Working from home, I always got the mail and so would see the bills that were coming up. But somehow I got into a bad habit of putting those bills into a folder and assuming that Brent was checking the folder. Bills fell through the cracks. We talked about it, and I vowed to do better. Then life got busy, and I would forget to tell him about a bill coming up, and then I'd feel guilty that I let it happen once again. Then I'd pay it myself to make sure it wasn't late. All without explaining anything to Brent.

He got angry because it was one surprise after another. I broke his trust, and really for no good reason. I didn't want to upset him with big bills because we were strapped, but inevitably I made him more upset by not communicating.

Communication about money and trust go hand in hand. I learned the hard way. Now we put together a budget and have a system of seeing bills, and our communication has improved greatly. And what a surprise— our money situation has improved, as well as our relationship.

There's another way to break down trust when it comes to money: how to handle overtime. There are some of you who don't disclose it to your spouse. You've decided that you've earned that money and you want to spend it on whatever you wish. You figure what she doesn't know won't hurt her. Wrong.

She ran the house without you so she had to make sacrifices for that overtime check. Second, the simple fact that you have to keep something hidden from her is enough to break down trust right there. You've separated yourself from her with a secret.

But what if you talked with her about it? Hey, Babe! I've got some overtime pay coming and was thinking I'd use it to buy a new gun. Whaddya think? Okay, I know, she may put up a fuss. Especially if things are a bit tight and you really should use the extra cash to make up for shortages in the household budget or build up that emergency fund. But at least you wouldn't have secrets that separate you from her. Perhaps you could meet halfway—put half of the overtime towards bills or savings and the other half to the gun. A little delay, a little more trust between you, and you'll still get what you want.

Which brings me to another way overtime can be a problem in your relationship.

> *"My divorce was because of money, although it was more complicated than that. We needed money, so I worked very detail on the planet, so I was never home, so our relationship died, which led to, shall we say, problems that couldn't be recovered from."*
> Aaron, New Hampshire

Lydia and Steve built a large home on the outskirts of town. They liked to shoot. He liked to restore old cars. They had several kids. Pretty soon, the bills got out of hand and debt built. The overtime that he earned on a regular basis became a needed part of their income. They came to depend on that income each month.

Money pressures and the time apart began to be a problem. Issues mounted, and their relationship began to suffer.

At that point, they decided this wasn't going to work. The stress was too much. They ended up selling a bunch of possessions to pay off debt. Then they decided they really didn't need the huge house, its care, and the heavy mortgage. They sold it and bought a home in town, one that was close to schools and required a lot less work.

These choices improved their relationship tremendously. They are a lot less stressed, and the overtime goes toward fun, non-budget items.

Hypervigilance and critical incident stress factors found in law enforcement have their effects on money management as well. Dr. Gilmartin says, "The behavioral and marketing researchers on Madison Avenue have ... clearly established that certain individuals, when feeling mildly depressed or unfocused, can find themselves feeling more energetic if they purchase something. This form of 'retail therapy' does have distinct gender differences. Women tend to make small ticket purchases ... Males do not appear to like to go shopping, but they do enjoy 'buying stuff' ... big-ticket items like boats, cars, pickup trucks, motor homes, campers, and maybe some power tools."

Retail therapy, if not budgeted for, results in debt. Debt becomes a burden that adds a tremendous burden to any relationship.

This spending affects our marriages. More and more pressure is heaped on to the rollercoaster, and can rob us of financial security. We are constantly behind, working harder and harder to catch up. Dr. Gilmartin adds, "This cycle robs the officer of any sense of financial security across the span of the occupational career. Many officers, without having a sense of proactive control of their finances, experience significant distress economically..." A sense of desperation and frustration takes over.

> *"If I'm not satisfied with what I have,*
> *I'll never be satisfied with what I want."*
> Greg Laurie

There are many stresses in this law enforcement life. Money will become one of them if we do not budget our resources, communicate with our spouses, and be wise with our spending.

Mutual Accountability

Typically, every couple has a spender and a saver. Unless we agree upon goals and budgets, the constant push and pull of the money can be destructive to our marriages. The best way is to acknowledge our short-comings, our pitfalls, and both get involved to solve the problems. These questions, when discussed honestly, will promote marital (and financial) health:

- Are we both committed to improving this area?
- Are we both committed to paying off debt?
- Who is the saver, who is the spender?
- What are our individual responsibilities (who pays bills, who makes the budget, who calls the companies when there are discrepancies)?
- What are our financial goals?
- Where can we cut our spending to invest in our future?
- When do we waver in our control of spending?
- How did we get ourselves into the debt we have?
- Are we a slave to our home, striving to make the payments?
- Is our money working for us, or against us?
- How deep are we willing to cut to ease financial stress?
- We have no debt, but can we do better?

When we are proactive about communicating when it comes to money, it has an accumulating effect, much like the emotional bank account. Brent's and my situation was that these early conversations were prickly—we were embarrassed as individuals as to how we had gotten ourselves into trouble financially. There was resentment and blame going on. But the bottom line was we had to improve. So, as we worked through the tough realities and agreed on the cuts and a new spending plan (budget), those conversations got easier. As the burden of debt lifted and we experienced relief, it actually became a joy to talk about our money.

There was another benefit to getting our financial affairs in order. Our kids learned valuable life lessons in the process. We were candid with them about the mistakes we made and what we were doing to correct them. We explained why we had to say no to many things that they wanted. If they wanted to go to summer camp or selected an expensive pair of shoes, they had to come up with a lot of the money themselves. In hindsight, it was the best education they've received as far as spending. They appreciate the things they have, and they understand that consumer debt is dangerous, and avoid it. They've learned to do without so that later they can use their money for things that really matter.

"Stupid things are always going to be done in families unless the wiser member learns to stand up to the forceful one."
Dave Ramsey, *The Total Money Makeover*

Backup Plan

Just like you train for the possibilities of calls going bad, we as police families have to plan for the worst with our money. We face higher risk for injuries and death on duty, so it is imperative to take care of ourselves just in case the worst happens. The safety net I mentioned earlier in this chapter is a start. We also need to have individual life insurance and disability insurance policies that cover you and your family in the event of a debilitating injury, or worse. While you're at it, make sure you have a written will and an advanced directive.

As far as life insurance is concerned, it is best to get your policy with a reputable company early on. Shop around and you'll likely find a highly affordable policy. Be sure to update your beneficiary information anytime there is a change (e.g., marriage, children, or divorce), and meet with your agent periodically to make sure your coverage is adequate.

Line of Duty Disability

This type of insurance differs greatly depending on where you are, but more often than not is inadequate when a significant injury takes place, even on duty.

Brent and I had a conversation with one of our officers who we almost lost when he was hit on his motorcycle on-duty. He said the most frustrating struggle was the fact that workman's comp was questioning whether his injury was work-related or not. He was speaking to us from a wheelchair, paralyzed from the waist down.

We have been shocked to learn about how some workers' compensation adjusters and departments fail when it comes to providing for those who've been wounded in the line of duty. I've heard several horror stories from the people I've met through Hunting for Heroes. Sometimes these battles go on for years.

In light of this reality, you've got to protect yourself now. There is a checklist in the Appendix to make sure you are covered adequately in case of debilitating injury. Don't assume that your department will completely take care of you.

Funding the Future

I asked a group of police officers if they had a vision for their marriage. Only one or two raised their hands. Afterward an officer approached me and shared that he and his partner had the goal of retiring in Palm Springs with a beautiful home. They are planning and saving for it. This has become even more important as he has suffered the effects of multiple sclerosis. His speech is affected and he walks slowly with a limp. Although he can still work in the office, the vision and goal of what they continue to work towards is all the more important. It keeps them moving forward, and hopeful in the midst of his disease.

As a law enforcement officer, the age you retire will be typically lower than other careers. You will still be relatively young and able when you hang up that uniform. Ask questions now, and then instill a vision for who you want to be and what you want to do when you retire. Then create a plan to fund it. Here are some questions to consider:

- When do you want to retire? When will your spouse retire?
- Will you have a second career after you retire from law enforcement?
- What do you want to do when you retire?
- What are your passions and abilities and how do they relate to your future?
- Have you considered volunteer work or a way to help others? This may have been the reason you chose law enforcement; that inherent desire won't change once you're retired.
- Who do you want to spend time with when you retire?
- What are your retirement benefits? Are they adequate for your plans? Have you calculated it out?
- Will you have adequate health insurance?
- Are you making good choices in your lifestyle, so that you'll be healthy enough to accomplish your plans?
- How can you cut expenses to save one percent more of your income to put towards retirement?
- What is the worst disaster that can happen after you retire? Are you prepared financially if this happens? Before you retire?
- If you are close to retiring, have you met with someone who can help you maximize your employer's benefits?

MotorCop, a California motor officer who has a great blog on policing and finances, wrote an article for PoliceOne magazine. He compares the discipline of keeping his head and eyes focused on where he wants to maneuver his bike rather than concentrating on the cones he had to avoid during motor school. He writes:

> *"Just as I needed to develop the habit of turning my head to look to where I wanted to go as opposed to looking at a much closer threat, the same is true of my approach to personal finance. If I only look at what is in front of me and not further down the line, I am running the risk of crashing.*
>
> *"If I ignore my long-term goals with regard to finance, I may*

be short-circuiting them for short-term pleasure. If I am not budgeting with the rest of the month in mind or if I focus on my checking account balance instead of allocating my salary, I may overspend or, at minimum, spend without direction.

"Consequently, when faced with financial obligations or challenges, I may have spent my way into trouble instead of adhering to the plan (read: budget) which is in place with long-term goals in mind."

MotorCop also has an eBook called Badges and Budgets, a free webinar, and is a financial coach specializing in helping cops with their finances. I've listed his information in the Resource Guide in the back of the book.

The size of your salary is not what matters—it's how you spend it. Having a vision/goals, a patient plan, and consistent discipline will add so much to your marriage and family wholeness.

· ·

Think: Where can you improve in your money management?

Debrief: Go through and discuss the list of questions in the Mutual Accountability section.

Strategic Application: Implement goals and a plan for your money. What is the first step?

> *"I'm super-obsessed with law enforcement.*
> *I'm what you'd call a 'cop-fan.'"*
> Pauley Perrette

CHAPTER TWELVE

A MISSION FOR MARRIAGE

"Real life doesn't travel in a perfect straight line;
it doesn't necessarily have that 'all lived happily ever after' bit.
You have to work on where you're going."
Chris Kyle, *The American Sniper*

One of the greatest memories of my childhood is playing with my brothers underneath the old Hooker Oak Tree. Located in a park near my home in Chico, California, this oak tree was almost a hundred feet tall with a trunk 29 feet in circumference. The massive tree was a draw to many, and especially children, who played under its canopy. I have vivid memories of swinging from the branches that curled downward almost to the ground, some with large cement markers propped up beneath to keep them from breaking. Experts at the time considered this to be the oldest valley oak in the country, approximately 1,000 years old.

When I was eleven, the Hooker Oak fell. As tree experts were called in to examine why this occurred, a shocking discovery was made. The Hooker Oak was not one tree, but actually two trees that had grown together over 300 years earlier.

Two trees that grew together over time, creating one large tree that brought life and beauty to those around, and children frolicked beneath its shade. It was a picture of timeless strength. When I think of what marriage should and could be, I think of that old Hooker Oak.

Healthy marriages are like the Hooker Oak—two individuals that grow together over time, creating one life that brings life and beauty to those around, and children frolic underneath its protection. A great marriage is a picture of timeless strength.

"Sign on the way out the door:
'You may only love once, but if you do it right,
once is enough.'"
Anonymous Survey Response

I witnessed a marriage like this just a few miles from that old Hooker Oak. My grandparents were married for almost 73 years. They were inseparable for most of that time, raising four generations before they both passed in 2014.

The final separation was painful, yet peaceful. My grandma held my grandpa's hand, sang a hymn in his ear, and gave him permission to go.

Not only did they live a legacy of love and faithfulness amidst really trying circumstances over the years, they both demonstrated the ultimate act of loyalty at the end—Grandpa hanging on because he didn't want to leave his lifelong love, and Grandma releasing him because of his pain and suffering. What a beautiful way to end a life well lived.

My parents have followed in their footsteps—they've been married 51 years, and they are each other's best friends. Their lives together represent a loving home, a safe place for kindness where their community, children, grandchildren, and extended family enjoy. Brent and I are another generation behind them, celebrating over 27 years at the time of this publishing. We are blessed to carry on this legacy.

"You know that look old married
people give each other?
How they communicate with their eyes
from across the room? It's not because
their life was so happy all the
time and easy. It's because they went
through hell, and made it through together."
Chief Brent Newman

The title of this book is A Marriage in Progress. The reason is because relationships are always changing, and with the right attitudes, commitment, and training, can improve with time. Even in law enforcement marriages.

Life is like an investment account—you invest early and consistently, hang in there during the ups and downs of the market, and reap the benefits in time. You spend so much time investing in your career—but that is good for 25-30 years. A good marriage will last a lifetime.

Your career is a segment of a long journey. It's a great job—but it's still just a job. Retirement is another chapter. In twenty years, your department won't care about the investments you put in. But your kids care. Your spouse cares.

What is your vision for your marriage?

Will you have that partner who knows you, has been with you through thick and thin, and has grown old with you, hobbling together towards the sunset in a strong and victorious finish?

"After 25 years, whom are you left with? If you've abused your time with family for those 25 years, now you have no spouse and your kids don't even know you. It's like that Cats in the Cradle song. It repeats the cycle. Your career is important, but you put in those 8-12 hours and you do the best you can, walk away feeling good, and then come home and enjoy your family as best you can. Because at the end, it's all about family. You have to see the big picture. You have to look at the finish line. What is it you want at the end of the finish line—a wall full of accolades saying how good you were in uniform? That lasts about twenty minutes; then you gotta dust 'em so those end up in a box and then you've got an empty house. You keep the 'I Love Me' wall, and I'll keep my family."

Anne, Retired Officer, California

Do you want to spend your retirement celebrating your hard work together, and enjoy the twilight years as a strong tree-like protection to your children and your children's children?

Will you celebrate the survival of a crisis-driven career, surviving mid-life confusion, reevaluating and reinterpreting relational principles to fit the seasons and circumstances along the way?

You will be glad you didn't quit...the best is yet to come!

One last thought. In chapter five I mentioned four kinds of love. There is yet another Greek word for love—pragma. This type of love describes the deep understanding and mature love that develops between couples who've been married a long time. The idea is to stand in love—to make an effort to give love rather than just receive it. This kind of love is made up of patience, compromise, understanding, and perseverance. Two individuals, one life, standing in love, growing together.

*"What you leave behind is not
what is engraved in stone monuments
but what is woven into the lives of others."*
Pericles

May you and I hold true in the seasons of joy and pain to our spouses and our children. May we be examples of unselfish living—and dying—leaving legacies of loyalty, commitment, and unconditional love.

. . . .

Think: What is the vision you have for your marriage? Your family?

Debrief: Talk about what you want your marriage to be. What have you invested already? What can you do now to improve your marriage?

Strategic Application: Follow through on this discussion by implementing your own ideas. God bless your efforts, and your family.

*"I love police. I love firefighters.
I try to bring them as much joy as they bring to me."*
Shaquille O'Neal

COMIC RELIEF:

POLICE STORIES
FROM AROUND THE COUNTRY

DEPUTIZING LUMBERJACKS

Many years ago I was a Field Training Officer in Sacramento. One of my new officers, Clint, and I were walking the beat downtown, talking about the drug problems in the area. We walked to the crest of some railroad tracks near 16th Street, when we saw two guys walking up the steep grade. One took a hit off of a joint and passed it to his buddy when they spot us looking down on them.

Smiling, I called down to them, "Come on up." They complied, although one started looking around. I knew what was coming.

He bolted, and I gave chase, running down the tracks under the railroad trestle. As I ran, my nightstick went flying. (Never saw it again.) Didn't slow me down.

He jumped up on a wall with a cyclone fence, when I drew my pistol and ordered him down or I would shoot. "No, you won't!" he called out, and then took off again. He ran through an abandoned industrial area, and I paralleled him on the other side of a fence. He then hopped another fence into a lumberyard where there were very large men working in the yard.

When I reached the fence, I saw the lumberjacks watching him, and then spot me. "Go get 'im!" I yelled, and like a pack of Rottweilers, they took off after the suspect. I ran to catch up, but laughed because there were four giant lumberjacks chasing after this little dude in the distance. I finally made it over the razor wire fence, and caught a glimpse of the suspect throwing packages into a culvert (five packs of marijuana).

About the time I hit the ground running, Clint screeched the car in sideways. "Hop in!"

When we arrived, the little dude was against a fence with four lumberjacks beating him down. "Okay, guys! Thanks, I'll take it from here." All four immediately did an about face and walked away.

"Good job, guys!"

As I put the cuffs on the runner, I couldn't shake the feeling that he was glad I rescued him.

HOW THEY ROLL IN PHILLY

My partner and I were chasing a guy in the cruiser, doin' 137 miles per hour. As we go around this really sharp turn, I propped my feet on the dashboard. My partner, Mike, yells, "Dude, if the airbag goes off, your knees 'll go through your face, asshole!"

I shot back, "What are yous lookin' at me, for? Drive the car! Keep your eyes on the road!"

We pursued this guy until he crashed. But when we tried to stop, the brakes were so hot they didn't work. Mike drove the cruiser up onto the sidewalk a couple of times to slow down, using the curb and the wall to bring it to rest.

We took off on foot like a shot, chased the two guys down the street and recovered the gun. We locked 'em up, when the radio asked if we see a white car on fire in the area.

We go back up the block to the cruiser, and all we see is white smoke rising from the wheels. The fire truck pulls up and they wash down the tires.

We then drove the car back to the station. The mechanic replaced the brakes—good as new!

WORK COLLARS ON!

A K-9 officer in New Hampshire is married with two darling little girls. Because he is on call at all times, he brings the cruiser home, leaves the house with uniform on, with the appropriate dog in tow (he has three dogs).

"The dogs go on alert when his phone rings," said his wife, Yvonne. "They switch into work mode in the blink of an eye. At home, they have their home collars on. When it's time for work, they are changed into their own uniform—their work collars. Whatever the call entails, the K-9 that is trained for the task will get a work collar, and then head for the car, ready for action.

"One day, my husband was getting dressed to respond to a call. My daughters were trying to get his attention, wanting to show him something from their own little world. He wasn't responding. The younger daughter was disappointed, but the older daughter encouraged, 'Oh, don't worry—Daddy already has his work collar on.'"

SWAT TEAM REDECORATING

SWAT was called to assist an allied agency in Orland, California. The surrounded murder suspect had apparently dispatched with great prejudice his fellow entrepreneur and business partner, likely over a sales, manufacturing, or marketing dispute. He was also wanted in connection with a recent kidnapping; no doubt a strategy in dealing with a competitor in a niche market (the methamphetamine business can be brutal). Our methed-up and sleep-deprived businessman was an HIV-positive three-striker. He claimed he had explosives, many firearms, and would not be taken alive.

On arrival, his apartment was already surrounded by allied SWAT teams. They had taken turns on the perimeter, and it was exhausting. We were briefed in detail and immediately tasked with relieving the perimeter team, who had been there for hours. I set up behind a Ford Mustang where I could see his front door of the six-plex. Within five minutes, as I stared over my MP5-40, he tossed out a throw phone (used by police negotiators to communicate with bad guys) and shot it a couple times. I guess negotiations have officially broken down...

Throughout that day and into the night, the suspect periodically fired off errant rounds just to keep us on our toes. The immediate area had been evacuated, but we knew a stray round could clip an "innocent" at any time.

After about thirty hours of this crap, the TOC command decided it was time to go in. We went over the plan and everyone knew his or her role. I was tasked with throwing the initial flash grenade through the rear window as fellow teammates were to shove a bang pole (a pole that had several grenades attached) through the same window and run around to the front to flush him out. Three-two-one...green light!

I rushed in with the guys behind me, pulled the pin, and threw it hard. That damn grenade hit the center of the window with all that I could muster— right square into a metal strip that separated the glass. It ricocheted off the *window, bounced onto loose landscape pebbles at the team's feet and exploded. Flash—bang! Shit!*

Peppered with rocks and blinded, the team pressed forward and in went the bang pole. I stood there for a second all kinds of pissed off, and then barraged the apartment with flash bangs and tear gas grenades. Smoke billowed out as the suspect began firing in all directions not ten feet from me. All I saw were flashes of gunfire and the suspect's smoky silhouette.

Hell, maybe he'll hit me and the pain of the divorce will go away.

Our team sergeant ran toward me out of the darkness. "It's time to go," he coaxed.

The plan worked. The gas and bangers pushed him out the front door, where the allied team shot him with nonlethal beanbag rounds. They twisted him up and took him into custody.

I'd thrown so many gas and flash bangs the apartment caught on fire, and then really caught on fire. Once the scene was secure with the criminal in handcuffs, the firefighters on standby put the wet stuff on the red stuff, extinguishing the fully engulfed room.

HALLOWEEN VAMPIRE

Beth was sent to an upper class area of her city. After locating the residence, she exited her cruiser and was met quickly by a 30-something man running out of the house yelling, "It's in the living room!" As she entered the home, her partner came in a side door off of the kitchen. He had the presence of mind to grab a lacrosse stick out of a stack of similar such items by the door.

They made their way through the massive house to the living room, which was decorated in white carpet, white leather furniture, and a white marble fireplace. The only items that weren't white were the glass-topped tables throughout the room. It was easy to find the suspect—a small bat hanging off of the fireplace mantle.

Beth told her partner she was getting a towel to throw over the animal when it decided to take flight. Her partner, out of reflex, swung that lacrosse stick for all he was worth. It collided with their furry friend and sent it flying straight up, where he met his demise in one of the rotating ceiling fans.

You wouldn't think that little bat had much blood to shed. But in a completely white room, it looked like something out of a horror show.

Beth stood there in complete shock. Her partner muttered, "See ya!" and exited quickly. He left her to deal with the irate homeowner who now had to clean up her mess, and pointed out repeatedly that it was her responsibility to clean it up as he paid an exorbitant amount in property taxes for sub-par police services. But Beth had a really hard time drumming up sympathy for a 30-year-old man afraid of a little bat. It was with great relief that she ultimately referred his complaint to her lieutenant and cleared the scene.

The clincher to this story? It happened October 31st.

CAPTAIN UNDERPANTS

Thomas was an investigator for the Sheriff's office. Each night he arrived home, he'd take his pants off and lounge around the house in his underwear and work shirt.

One hot summer night, the air conditioner was out. All outside security lights were off so they could open doors and windows without letting in a massive amount of bugs.

Around midnight, Thomas went outside to water the newly planted grass. While outside he heard two male voices talking about "cops this and cops that." He went back in the house, grabbed his gun, and then returned to stake it out.

He heard them attempt to enter his vehicle, so crossed the yard in the shadows, coming to a stop just behind the perpetrator. He shoved the barrel of the gun just behind the guy's ear and commanded him to put his hands up. He led the perp by the belt loop up the driveway while giving commands to the other.

Soon he had two teenage boys lying face down on the driveway between the cars, security lights on. He called out for his wife to call 911.

Once officers were on the scene and were advised of the situation, Thomas asked if he could go put some pants on. From then on, he was given the nickname of Captain Underpants!

In memory of Deputy First Class Thomas A. Nash, Jr., 9/27/60-6/18/13

SHE'S GOT A POINT!

Daughter: You work on Thanksgiving?
Dad: Yes.
Daughter: Why?
Dad: Because there's still crime on Thanksgiving.
Daughter: They should make crime illegal on holidays.

K-9 COMEDY

It was the end of the day when I parked my police van in front of the station. As I gathered my equipment, my K-9 partner, Jake, was barking, and I saw a little boy staring in at me.

"Is that a dog you got back there?" he asked.

"It sure is," I replied.

Puzzled, the boy looked at me and then towards the back of the van. Finally, he said, "What'd he do?"

HORSING AROUND

Someone stole a horse and transported him to the ninth floor of a North Miami apartment building. The only way to get the horse down was on the elevator. Most likely he went into the elevator without much of a fight the first time. But when we arrived the horse had pink frosting all over his face, and we had a heck of a time getting him back in the elevator.

My sergeant wanted to ride down with him (he obviously knew nothing about horses). I told him he was not going to do that unless he wanted to die.

I went down to the lobby in the other elevator, and told him to send the horse. The elevator stopped on the fifth floor, and when it got to the lobby...NO HORSE. I can only imagine what the poor person in the middle of the night on the fifth floor must've thought when a pink frosting-covered horse bolted out of the elevator. Three hours later, we got the horse to the lobby.

DID HE REALLY JUST DO THAT?

My husband, Roger, and I were at the house with some fellow law enforcement friends. He quickly ran to the store to grab something.

When he returned, Roger threw the change in the desk drawer by the door.

"Feed the pig!" I called out, referring to our new piggy bank on the desk. He looked at me puzzled. "What?"

"Feed the pig," I repeated.

He then walked over to me, picked up a few gummy worms and stuck them in my mouth.

LOSING ONE'S HEAD

On the night of a big fight, there was lots of drinking. One guy got really belligerent so the host drove him home. On the way, this dude demanded to be left on the side of the road so he could walk home. The host reluctantly obliged. Problem was, the road was dark, and an oncoming car didn't see the drunk until it was too late. The car struck him right at the neck with the A-pillar. Cops were dispatched to the scene, but when the coroner went to bag the body, the head was nowhere to be found. After a fruitless search, the graveyard guys passed it on to the next shift.

The next morning, day shift found the head. It had rolled down the incline and came to rest against a chain link fence, right side up. It looked like he had been buried up to his neck. They called for the coroner, and waited.

Cops with time on their hands is a dangerous thing. Their wheels got to turning, so a radio was hidden next to the head.

The unsuspecting coroner (who was rather new to the job) made his way down through the iceplant (wearing wingtips). "Where is it?" he called back. Suddenly, the head called out, "Over here! Over here!"

The coroner shuddered hard and almost lost his balance. "Shit!" Chuckles and snickers were heard round about.

Almost to the bottom the coroner realized he'd forgotten a body bag. He improvised with an old cement bag he found near the head. Gloves on, he reached for the head.

"NOT BY THE HAIR! NOT BY THE HAIR!" screamed the head.

The coroner lost his composure. "You guys are seriously f*%$*d up!" He found the radio and threw it at the closest cop, who was now blowin' snot bubbles.

SPECIAL SECTION FOR LEADERSHIP

"The day soldiers stop bringing you their problems is the day you have stopped leading them. They have either lost confidence that you can help them or concluded that you do not care. Either case is a failure of leadership."
Colin Powell

It was a night to celebrate a long career in law enforcement of a great friend we knew through the CHP. Conversation at the table was easy, getting to know a law enforcement couple we'd just met that were about to be married. Through the evening things were said that were both positive and negative about our department. As you know, this is usually the case with cops.

After some time, a friend we knew approached Brent and greeted him with "Chief!"

The officer we'd been speaking with went white. "Oh my god, is he a chief?" he whispered to me.

I nodded. He began to backtrack, apologizing profusely for saying the things he had said.

I assured him that he was fine. "He didn't take offense at anything you said," I countered. "He purposefully leaves the detail of his rank out of conversations so that he can actually have a truthful and real conversation. You'd be surprised how officers act when they learn he's management."

This story isn't unique. It has happened over and over, with people in various places and with different departments. There's just something about rank that puts some officers off. Some think that those with bars and stars have gone over to the dark side—and by default, aren't trustworthy.

The difference between an officer and a lieutenant is a little brass, a little more salary, and a little more power. With that power comes increased responsibility, inside knowledge, increased accountability, and a lot more stress.

Brent and I know about the stresses of bars and stars. It's in our home. The hardest years in our marriage have been the years since Brent made captain. At times he almost wishes he didn't know what he knows.

As management, you know that every rank has to answer to someone. The pressure from those above and the needs of those on the road are a constant balance act—and at times very delicate. Since Ferguson, we've seen leaders accountable to politicians make some tough choices, and some have even lost their jobs. Like those on the road who put their lives on the line, you as a leader may have to put your career on the line.

> *"Be more concerned with your character than your*
> *reputation, because your character is what you really are,*
> *while your reputation is merely what others think you are."*
> John Wooden

The following is a list of recommendations for management who want to be effective leaders. Emmett Spraktes, a retired CHP officer and National Guardsman who earned a Silver Star for bravery in Afghanistan, compiled this list by talking with law enforcement and military leaders from all over the country:

Leadership Under Fire

Every day you are asked to send out men and women with weapons. They wear ballistic vests to protect themselves from severe injury and death. You ask them to confront the most dangerous people in your community. With this in mind:

- Lead by example.
- Do not ask anyone to do something you would not do yourself.
- Arrest someone once in a while. You must continually dispel the notion that you're nothing but an out of touch bureaucrat by those you lead.

- Listen to the radio and back up an officer on a call occasionally.
- Go on patrol occasionally as a ride along.
- Ask officers about their beats (problem areas, trends, successful solutions).
- Wear your uniform with ballistic vest.
- Teach your department's history, know your demographics, and demonstrate a sense of pride.
- Communicate: Of all the rules, what are the most important?
- Have a mission statement that reflects the priorities of the department/community.
- Stay in great physical shape.
- Give everyone a job during a crisis even if it's simply having them cover an area; give them ownership, purpose, and hope.
- In extreme circumstances, when things look dark, talk about what has to be accomplished now and after this crisis.
- Know and follow your own rules, rules of engagement, and use of force.
- Train with the troops and train with SWAT. Train, train, train. Train responses to bank robberies, riots, demonstrations, looting, and terrorist attacks, rather than shit like MORE diversity training.
- If an officer is hurt on the job, check on him, go to the hospital, and call the spouse. Let him know you're glad he's alive.

"It is hard for police officers to properly serve the public when they believe themselves to be poorly supported by their agencies... In fact, much of the time, they experience the terrible dilemma of being simultaneously powerful and powerless: powerful because their every action has potentially critical consequences; powerless because they are constantly scrutinized, supervised, and reined in by their own department and by the community in ways that can be irritating, humiliating, and sometimes irrelevant to their actual job performance."
Dr. Ellen Kirschman, *I Love a Cop*

At a dinner for officers in preparation for this book, the discussion turned to how leaders could better support the troops. It became a very animated discussion that had similarities across several different departments. Their thoughts are below, even though this falls into the on-duty category. Leadership affects not only officers, but their families as well.

• Communicate, communicate, communicate. This was the main beef—officers (and a sergeant and lieutenant) felt they were in the dark most of the time. Their departments were going in directions these guys just didn't understand. One officer said, "Even if we don't like the direction, it would really help to hear the reasoning behind some of these decisions. We may not like it, but at least we can support it, seeing the perspective." Others agreed. When there isn't clear communication, the tendency is to misunderstand, misinterpret, and mistrust.

• Think we, not me. There are leaders who make decisions based on personal gain and/or fear at every level. This will never result in respect from those around you, and will many times backfire. One former officer called it, "success versus suck-cess—there's a difference depending on who you suck up to. Is it about you and your career, or the rest of us?" Making wise and courageous decisions for the good of the organization will generate respect, and build morale on-duty and off. You also have the power to put good leaders in place, not those who are motivated by personal success.

"I hire strong horses, and then let them run."
Bob Kraning

• Never lose touch with the boots on the ground. As a leader, you aren't out on the streets much, so your physical risk level has decreased. You're not wrestling with a suspect on the ground, or taking verbal abuse from motorists or staring into the eyes of those opposite the police line in a protest. Robert, a chief, believes that although he's not laying down his life out there on the road, he may have to lay down his career path for the sake of the troops. In the current climate of cop hate, there are those who are demanding changes in policing that are detrimental to not only our communities in the long run, but also for the safety of our officers. And unfortunately, we've seen law enforcement leaders cower to these demands. If you've been in the office for so long you've forgotten what it's like to be out on the street, one officer suggests "you get your ass out in the field once a month on ride alongs. That way your ignorance won't lead to bad decisions."

Leadership for Off Duty Life

There are two schools of thought for department leaders when it comes to the personal lives of officers. Some leaders feel strongly that it is not the department's responsibility to provide help for personal problems, even if these problems are related to the job. There is a job to do and it is the responsibility of the officer to figure it out. Come to work to work—toughen up and get it done. This thought has been around for a long time, and was the norm until the last decade or so.

Other leaders see it differently. It is still the officers' responsibility to come to work ready to serve. But if officers are supported during times of personal difficulty, this engenders loyalty and builds morale.

The California Highway Patrol is one of the leading organizations when it comes to wellness on duty and off. They have a competent Employee Assistance Program that includes employees who respond to critical incidents, line of duty deaths, and shootings. They conduct critical incident debriefings and refer officers and their families to other resources. They have hundreds of trained peer support volunteers. They have begun a new program with our chaplaincy, enlisting retired personnel to come alongside others in this capacity. They have an orientation for families before the academy, and a family panel the day before graduation. But there is still more to do.

One of the most organized and thorough models for training in emotional and relational wellness is San Diego Police Department (SDPD).

They have a Wellness Unit that consists of three sworn officers who assist in day-to-day operations of the unit. It consists of varying components including Peer Support, Chaplaincy Program, Focus Psychological Services (an organization that serves those in public safety through counseling, training and critical incident response), San Diego Law Enforcement Officer Wives Group, a drug and alcohol abuse unit, and the Member Assistance Program. These resources are available for all SDPD officers and their direct families.

A Psychological Preparedness Day is a mandatory training day for the newly graduated officers and their families. The Wellness Unit discusses the challenges the officer and the family will face and offers awareness of the assistance available to them. On this training day, they hear from other officers who were involved in critical incidents or other life challenges, what happened to them, and how they dealt with it (good and bad). This shows the newer officers to set aside ego and not to lose focus of the whole wellness of themselves and their families. They talk about each and every component of the Wellness Unit and provide the families with resources. There is also a question and answer time.

Chief Sarah Creighton of SDPD is the driving force behind this program. Their department had experienced a season of misconduct and low morale. Agreeing that this approach might help, her boss gave permission to try some of her ideas. She started with an internal survey, seeking feedback from the officers. Then she and her team put together a Wellness Center, first meeting offsite for the first year, then creating a coffee library that resembled a living room. It was the place to hang out. If an officer has an issue, they close the door. The place is open Monday through Friday. They had to do much marketing from the beginning, but eventually the Wellness Unit became part of the culture. At the time of this writing, they have 19 chaplains, 50 peer support members, five psychologists, and a critical incident team. This is to serve 2400 law enforcement personnel.

But what if your department is unable to offer such comprehensive resources? Major Travis Yates, Tulsa Police Department, said they placed a blood pressure machine on the wall in the squad room, do a mandatory spousal panel for spouses before the academy, and give officers a copy of Emotional Survival for Law Enforcement. They conduct yearly training on emotional survival and private, officer-led meetings away from the department where officers can talk. This approach may be more realistic for most departments.

You as a department leader have an opportunity to show your troops how much you support them as officers and as people. Investments into these areas are positive reinforcement of the humanness and wholeness as officers, and can generate loyalty and camaraderie.

Ways Leaders Can Support Families

There are relatively easy ways that you as a leader can support officers and their families without too much time and money.

The first is to **acknowledge** the important role families have in the wellness of officers. The job affects families, and families affect the job—it is a reality. To communicate that when you have the chance is huge. Our CHP Commissioner, Joe Farrow, is a great example. He always takes time in his speeches to point out the importance of loved ones in the lives of officers. Graduations, funerals, time with cadets in training, speeches to different groups that support officers—every chance he has, he acknowledges and encourages spouses, parents, and loved ones. In addition to speeches, you can support families in written communication, appointing people to put together spousal academies, and one-on-one conversations with families. All get the point across.

The second is a close cousin—**appreciation**. You can't say thank you too often. A lieutenant decided he wanted to buy signed copies of my book for his officers for Christmas. He collected the names of his officers and their significant others for over 25 books. Another leader handwrote personal thank you notes to spouses for their support during particularly rough patches with the department, such as mandatory overtime. These kind gestures are always welcome and appreciated, and will result in greater respect for you.

The third is **atmosphere**, which is created by your attitude and proactive implementation of the first two mentioned. These thoughtful acts create an atmosphere of teamwork between department and home. This is so healthy.

The last is **assets**—programs and events you can put into place through your leadership to support families. Spousal academies, conferences, family fun events, seminars, availability of chaplain and counseling services, and support of spouses who want to create a task force for families are all great ideas. A department in Arizona put on an academy for the spouses that educated them on what their officers did on their shifts. They had shooting at the range, spins in the patrol cars, testimony from officers, and tactical demonstrations. All of the families came away with a greater appreciation for what their officers were a part of, and in response were more supportive.

Departments and chaplaincies have responded to needs of families and developed family academies, spousal boot camps, question and answer panels, and even emotional survival and relationship seminars. In parts of Canada, emotional and relational training is considered to be a valuable and needed part of their education, and therefore officers are paid for attending.

On a trip to the Philippines a few years back I met with wives from the Philippine National Police (this was organized by a respected general). We spoke succinctly and directly about the struggles of the family of police officers. The wives, shy at first, eventually opened up and joined in the conversation. At the conclusion, one beautiful woman said in broken English, "It is good to speak of such things."

It is good to speak of such things. If we want to thrive in our marriages, it's imperative to speak of such things.

> *"Little things are easy to do. They're also easy not to do."*
> Unknown

There are two phases on how to educate and assist families to thrive within a law enforcement career. The first is to prepare the family as they begin. The second is to provide tools for the family once they've lived with the affects of the career for a while.

Family Readiness

At the beginning of an officer's career, life changes in the home. Drastically. Shift changes and long hours, low seniority, extended shifts, a steep learning curve and holidays missed are a huge change for a family. The officer is elated; the spouse is fearful. The officer can't wait to crush crime; the spouse is hesitant. The officer feels confident and motivated, but the spouse is insecure and adjusting to the changes in scheduling and perhaps a shift in responsibilities at home. It can be overwhelming.

At this time, education on managing expectations realistically and guidance in how to maneuver the changes from someone who's been there is extremely helpful. This is where spousal academies come in.

New police officers go through training at length. They've learned codes, the law, and enforcement tactics. They've been trained to drive at high speed, use weapons, and officer safety. Our CHP academy crams over 1300 hours of training into 27 weeks; the equivalent of earning an associate's degree in six months. It is a grueling process, and one that is done absent from time with family. Other academies have different lengths of time and are completed while the officer is coming home at night, but there is still a transformation that occurs.

While the officer is undergoing this process, most spouses don't receive any training to deal with this crazy career. They are thrown in and expected to go with the flow without any pushback. But with everything changing, they've got to have some heads up. They, too, need to know what to expect, how to maneuver, and how to change.

The day before graduation, our department conducts training for the new officers' families. They bring in three to four seasoned CHP wives who have different but positive outlooks on being a cop wife. It takes four packed hours. They cover gun safety in the home, the break-in process, health and wellness tips, hypervigilance, information on resources that are available through the department and beyond, a question and answer time, and of course, humor, cookies and coffee, and a little reality check.

Not only spouses attend, but parents, grandparents, siblings, and even representatives from other departments, coming to get a peek at what the CHP does so they can start their own program. The purpose is to educate families so that they will choose to understand, adapt, and support the officer in this new endeavor.

The response is very positive overall, but mixed. I've met with gals who are crying at the end of it, crazy with worry and dreading the changes. Others are totally looking at the experience as an adventure. Still others are unsure but hopeful, grateful for the heads up. Whatever the response, it is still the best thing for families—to prepare for what's ahead.

Family Resiliency

After the law enforcement officer has been at this awhile, families again have a need for information and perspective. Many officers aren't married at the time they became a cop, or they remarry someone who's not familiar with this life. Once a family has settled into the daily routine, there may be resentment, or lack of understanding. Kind of like advanced training techniques you learn once you've been a cop for some time.

Amy was married to a trooper. He'd been in a critical incident, and their marriage was struggling. She described mood swings, silence, over-protectiveness, rudeness toward her and the kids, nightmares and chronic impatience. She felt like she didn't know him anymore. He'd changed from the happy man she'd married, and it was getting really difficult.

Amy's experience is along the lines of what many other spouses experience. The symptoms were identical to others who'd been there. She was surprised; she'd never heard this before. She was relieved that others had been there before and that there were solutions. She wasn't alone.

These are common themes that many law enforcement families experience. I am always excited to see spouses come alive when they realize they're neither alone nor abnormal when it comes to life with their officers.

Officers, although they've been trained to be cops, more than likely haven't been trained for off-duty life. Most try to make it work with family, doing the best they know how. Some grew up in a healthy family, operating pretty well, applying what was modeled. But chances are there's still some guesswork.

Taking advantage of law enforcement relationship information that has been produced in the last fifteen years is vital to a thriving relationship. Two pioneering books, *I Love a Cop* by Dr. Ellen Kirschman, and

Emotional Survival for Law Enforcement by Dr. Kevin Gilmartin laid the foundation for seminars, survival training, chaplaincies, ministries, community groups and programs tailor-made for law enforcement families. The Resource Guide lists many helpful resources, but there are always new ideas and tools popping up. This is a great thing—the more resources, the better we are able to respond to the needs of all families.

The goal for family resiliency is to strengthen the family within the realities of law enforcement life—growing together while moving through the career. With education, officers, spouses, and children can gain a deeper understanding of the hurdles, gain tools with which to apply in different seasons, solve problems, learn to communicate, and build trust along the way.

If you read through the chapters in A Marriage in Progress, you caught a glimpse of my heart for law enforcement families. As the wife of a Chief, I also appreciate you as a leader. You have the privilege and responsibility to lead your department in a crucial and difficult time in history. I know from experience how time consuming and sacrificial it can be on you and your family. But the rewards of influence in the lives of those you lead is significant, and in some ways life changing. My hope is that you will lead with confident humility, and learn along the way.

If I can be of assistance to you and your department, such as providing bulk rates for multiple book copies or speaking to your families, please contact me at victoria@how2loveyourcop.com.

ENDNOTES

Page 36: California code for Officer Needs Help.

Page 38: http://www.iaedjournal.org/content/turnover-factor
http://www.iaedjournal.org/content/turnover-factor

Page 46: *Emotional Survival for Law Enforcement*, Kevin Gilmartin.

Page 47: Ibid.

Page 47: Ibid.

Page 48: *Switch on Your Brain*, Dr. Caroline Leaf, p. 35

Page 52: Dr. William C. Dement, The Promise of Sleep, pp. 56-57

Page 55: A book I co-wrote for a flight medic in Afghanistan.

Page 66: *Warriors At Home*, a poem written by Victoria M. Newman

Page 72: PTSD—A Spouse's Role, http://firelink.monster.com/training/
articles/9167-ptsd-a-spouses-role?page=2

Page 76: *A CHiP on my Shoulder*, page 45

Page 101: Used by permission. Excerpt of chapter 13 of *Blue Line Baby—
Chronicles of a Cop Kid*. Christa Waaler-Trinchera. Sacramento, CA. 2015.

Page 103: In-laws, exes, badge bunnies, etc.

Page 103: http://answers.yahoo.com/question/
index?qid=2008042404517AAJv1Fj

Page 106: https://en.wikipedia.org/wiki/Greek_words_for_love

Page 158: http://uniformstories.com/articles/opinion-category/suicide-
ptsd-addiction-the-law-enforcement-stigma

Page 159: http://womenandpolicing.com/violencefs.asp. There are differ-
ing views on statistics of police family violence because of the discrepancies in reporting. Many cases are handled off the record or filed differently
to help the officer keep his job. See also http://www.policeone.com/health-

fitness/articles/1350610-Domestic-violence-in-police-families-Causes-effects-intervention-strategies/.

Page 159: Adapted from www.manupcrusade.com.

Page 164: *Why Marriages Succeed or Fail...and How You Can Make Yours Last*

Page 172: http://www.monash.edu.au/lls/llonline/writing/medicine/reflective/2.xml

Page 179: http://www.ptsd.va.gov/public/PTSD-overview/basics/symptoms_of_ptsd.asp

Page 180: John Caprarelli, *Uniform Decisions*, pp. 15-16

Page 181: *Selfish Prayer,* pages 301-302.

Page 182: https://www.emdr.com/general-information/what-is-emdr/what-is-emdr.html

Page 183: The first is Cognitive Processing Therapy (CPT), which includes education about PTSD symptoms, thoughts/feelings awareness, skills to deal with these thoughts and feelings, and then understanding how to live after trauma. The second is called Prolonged Exposure (PT) that includes education, breathing retraining, exposure practice, and then talking through the trauma. The third is Cognitive Behavioral Therapy for Insomnia (CBT-I) that addresses sleep behaviors. She also recommends Cognitive Behavioral Conjoint Therapy, which is couple therapy.

Page 183: http://www.ptsd.va.gov/

Page 184: Adapted from VOWS Retreat curriculum, by Becky Parkey.

http://www.ptsd.va.gov/apps/ptsdcoachonline/tools_menu.htm

Page 189: https://www.huntingforheroes.org/support.html

Page 201: Excerpt from *My Life for Your Life*, Clarke A. Paris, p. 76

Page 202: http://www.badgeoflife.com/currentmyths.php

Page 202: "Not One More Suicide Prevention Training" 2007, Beth Dansie, MFC

Page 206: Excerpt from *My Life for Your Life*, Clarke A. Paris, p. 142

Page 207: victoria@how2loveyourcop.com

Page 208: "Not One More Suicide Prevention Training" 2007 Beth Dansie MFC

Page 208: List from SafeCallNow.

Page 213: www.os91.com.

Page 227: *Emotional Survival for Law Enforcement.*

Page 227: Ibid.

Page 231: http://www.policeone.com/police-jobs-and-careers/
articles/7404033-Use-this-1-simple-tactic-to-maximize-your-police-salary/

Page 236: http://www.yesmagazine.org/happiness/the-ancient-greeks-6-
words-for-love-and-why-knowing-them can-change-your-life

Page 242: Used with permission. SSG Emmett Spraktes. *Selfish Prayer*,
Sacramento, 2013.

Page 252: If you would like to contact Chief Creighton at SDPD, email her
at screighton@pd.sandiego.gov.

RESOURCE GUIDE

This is the most comprehensive resource list I've compiled, but there are constantly new additions. For the most current list, see my website, www.how2loveyourcop.com.

<u>Chapter One</u>

A CHiP on my Shoulder, Victoria M. Newman, available on Amazon, Barnes & Noble, and my website, www.how2loveyourcop.com.

On Combat, Lt. Col. Dave Grossman.
On Killing, Lt. Col. Dave Grossman.
Bulletproof Spirit: The First Responder's Essential Resource for Protecting and Healing Mind and Heart, Dan Willis.
Emotional Survival for Law Enforcement Officers, Kevin Gilmartin, PhD
Hearts Beneath the Badge, Karen Solomon
Warrior Mindset, Michael J. Asken and Lt. Col. Dave Grossman
Selfish Prayer, Emmett W. Spraktes with Victoria M. Newman
Women Warriors: Stories from Behind the Thin Blue Line, John M. Willis
Daring Greatly, Brene Brown
Cadet Blues, Rob Krider.

SAFETAC Training: Seminars on Officer Safety, Wellness, Relationships and more. www.SAFETAC.org.

Seminars/Training by FranklinCovey: Specifically for Law Enforcement. Includes 7 Habits of Highly Effective People, Speed of Trust, Nobility of Policing, and Leadership skills. Trainers are current and former law enforcement professionals.
http://www.franklincovey.com/tc/solutions/law-enforcement-solutions/the-7-habits-of-highly-effective-people-for-law-enforcement.

Dave Smith and Associates: The Winning Mind courses and workshops for law enforcement. www.jdbucksavage.com.

Street Smart Force: Videos and resources for law enforcement officers by Dr. Joel F. Shults, retired police chief from Colorado. www.streetsmart-force.com.

Public Safety Training Institute. Training for law enforcement. www.psti-site.org.

Calibre Press. Training for law enforcement. www.calibrepress.com.

MotorCop/The Crossover Show: Hilarious postings from a motor cop in California.

Law Enforcement Appreciation Day: For Cops and their families only—a day of fun, shooting, helicopter rides, zip line, food, prizes set in Indiana. Held the first weekend in October every year. https://www.facebook.com/nationallawenforcementappreciationday2015/

Chapter Two

Dr. Kevin Gilmartin, *Emotional Survival for Law Enforcement Families.* www.emotionalsurvival.com. Book; seminars.

Special Olympics Torch Run information: http://www.specialolympics. org/Sections/Donate/Special_Olympics_Torch_Run.aspx

Police Marriage Resource. Resources for Law Enforcement Marriage specifically for police officers. www.policemarriageresource.com

Blue Wall Institute: Officer Wellness Seminars. www.bw-institute.com.

Cops Alive/The Law Enforcement Survival Institute: Information, strategies, and tools to help cops plan happy, healthy and successful careers, relationships and lives. www.copsalive.com

10-33 Foundation: Providing Prevention, Intervention, and Post-Intervention Services to those in uniform. www.1033foundation.org.

SAFETAC Training: Seminars on Officer Wellness, Relationships and more. www.SAFETAC.org.

Chapter Three

Resources for Police Spouses:

Wives Behind the Badge. www.wivesbehindthebadge.org – Perhaps the largest organization for wives, providing resources, support and networking. Retreats began in 2014.

The Police Wife Life. www.policewifelife.com – Online organization for wives, blog.

How 2 Love Your Cop. www.how2loveyourcop.com. Resources for police families.

National Police Wives Association. www.nationalpolicewivesassociation. org. Support and assistance for families of law enforcement.

Police Wives Inc. www.policewives.org – Offers support forums and charitable efforts for families of law enforcement officers.

Wives on Duty. www.wivesonduty.com – Faith-based encouragement for cop wives, now in five states.

Cops Wives. www.copswives.com – Offers support and encouragement for wives of police officers.

COPS. www.nationalcops.org – Concerns of Police Survivors – an organization that assists families who've lost a family member in the line of duty.

Hidden Partners – www.hiddenpartners.org. Several departments have created their wives' groups with the help of Hidden Partners, including Los Angeles Police Department. See their website for details.

Conferences/Classes for Law Enforcement Couples:

Christian Law Enforcement Officer (CLEO) Retreat, Danforth Maine. Hosted by Living Waters Bible Camp and held every second weekend of September. Call 207-448-2310 for more information.

P.O.L.I.C.E. Families Class – Excellent class for police families by Stephen and Mendi Keatts of Virginia. Contact them through Wives Behind the Badge website.

Backup for the Home – Four and eight hour seminar for police families by Victoria M. Newman. www.SAFETAC.org.

Books for Law Enforcement Spouses:

A CHiP on my Shoulder – How to Love Your Cop with Attitude. Victoria M. Newman
I Love a Cop, Ellen Kirschman, PhD
Bullets in the Washing Machine, Melissa Littles
Crazy Lives of Police Wives, Carolyn Whiting and Carolyn LaRoche
Under Fire, Kristi Neace
Lives Behind the Badge, Kristi Neace
Standing Courageous, Kristi Neace
Because I'm Suitable – The Journey of a Wife on Duty, Chaplain Allison P. Uribe.

Chapter Four

Children's Books on Policing:

Policeman's Safety Hints (Board Book), Giovanni Caviezel
Daddy, I Worry About You, Clarke Paris.
Police Officers on Patrol, Kersten Hamilton.
Feeling Safe with Officer Frank, Linda Mobilio-Keeling
Cops' Night Before Christmas, Michael Harrison and David Miles
Officer Buckle and Gloria, Peggy Rathman
Adventures of Hoover the FBI Dog: Hoover Travels the World, Joe Altman and Jon Chad

Books on Cops as Fathers:
Blue Line Baby – Chronicles of a Cop Kid, Christa Waaler-Trinchera

Chapter Five

Disability Insurance Checklist – see Appendix.

Dave Ramsey's Life insurance search link: https://www.daveramsey.com/elp/health-insurance.

For sex-related issues in marriage, here's a faith-based website that promotes healing in that area of life. Excellent books available. www.barbarawilson.org.

Excellent book on forgiveness, especially in extramarital affairs: Forgiving the Unforgiveable, by David Stoop.

Chapter Six

Excellent Books for Communication in Marriage:

Crucial Conversations, Kerry Patterson & Joseph Grenny
For Men Only and For Women Only, Shaunti Feldhahn & Jeff Feldhahn
Arresting Communication, Jim Glennon
The Five Love Languages, Military Edition, Gary D. Chapman & Jocelyn Green
The Art of Dancing with Porcupines, Bob Phillips

Personality Test Links:

http://www.16personalities.com/
http://www.humanmetrics.com/cgi-win/jtypes2.asp
http://www.proprofs.com/quiz-school/story.php?title=gold-orange-blue-green-which-color-are-you

Chapter Seven

Crucial Conversations, Kerry Patterson & Joseph Grenny
Leadership and Self-Deception, Arbinger Institute

Domestic Abuse Resources for Victims:

Police Domestic Violence: A Handbook for Victims. http://www.smashwords.com/books/view/388395

S'entraider. Help for law enforcement spouses that are victims of domestic abuse. www.sentraider.webs.com.

Man Up Crusade. Created by a deputy sheriff. Provides awareness, financial and educational support for domestic violence, using the cowboy ethic as a backdrop. www.manupcrusade.org

Behind the Blue Wall: Blog for domestic violence victims married to police officers. www.BehindtheBlueWall.blogspot.com.

Domestic Abuse Resources for Abusers:

Emerge. Education, Anger Management Courses, Accountability and Counseling for those who batter. www.emergedv.com.

Amend. 26 session program for men who abuse.
Ohio: http://www.ywca.org/site/pp.asp?c=agLGKXNOE&b=3990275
Pennsylvania: http://www.dvscp.org/AmendProgram.html
Colorado: http://www.amendcounseling.com/

Chapter Eight

The Will to Survive, Bobby E. Smith, PhD.
I Love a Cop, Dr. Ellen Kirschman
Emotional Survival for Law Enforcement Families, Dr. Kevin Gilmartin
Ruby Shoes – Surviving Prescription Drug Addiction, Michele Zumwalt

Substance Abuse Programs for Law Enforcement Officers:

Confidential Recovery. Substance abuse outpatient recovery program for first responders in San Diego, California: www.confidentialrecovery.com

The Champion Center, Heroes Program. Substance abuse recovery center for first responders in Lompoc, California: http://www.championrecovery.com/heroes-program

Brattleboro Retreat, Uniformed Service Program. 1-800-738-7328. Vermont. http://www.brattlebororetreat.org/usp.

Hazelden Betty Ford Foundation, Springbrook Treatment Center. 1-800-866-4662. Newberg, Oregon. Specializing in addiction treatment and co-occurring trauma disorders.

Alcoholics Anonymous: No dues or fees, just a desire to stop drinking is needed. www.aa.org

Peace Officers Fellowship: Meetings for men and women to share solutions to problems with alcohol. Facebook page for more information: https://www.facebook.com/PeaceOfficerFellowship/info/?tab=page_info. Call 818-760-6966 for meetings and information.

Post-Traumatic Stress Disorder:

CopShock, Allen R. Kates
Surviving the Shadows, Bob Delaney with Dave Scheiber
When Cops Kill, Lance LoRusso.

PTSD apps:

Mindfulness Coach: http://t2health.dcoe.mil/apps/MindfulnessCoach
Breathe2Relax (Diaphragmatic Breathing Exercise): http://t2health.dcoe.mil/apps/breathe2relax
PTSD Coach: http://t2health.dcoe.mil/apps/ptsd-coach
mTBI Pocket Guide: http://t2health.dcoe.mil/apps/mtbi
Tactical Breather: http://t2health.dcoe.mil/apps/tactical-breather
BioZen (Biofeedback): http://t2health.dcoe.mil/apps/biozen
Positive Activity Jackpot (Pleasant Events Scheduling) http://t2health.dcoe.mil/apps/positiveactivityjackpot
Virtual Hope Box (coping skills): http://t2health.dcoe.mil/apps/virtual-hope-box
T2 Mood Tracker (mood tracker): http://t2health.dcoe.mil/apps/t2-mood-tracker
Parenting2Go: http://t2health.dcoe.mil/apps/Parenting2Go
Stay Quit (for those who have quit smoking): http://t2health.dcoe.mil/apps/StayQuit

Badge of Life Canada: www.badgeoflifecanada.com

Residential Retreats for PTSD and other job related issues:

West Coast Post-trauma Retreat, California. A five-day confidential program for first responders who are overwhelmed by job stress. http://www.frsn.org/retreats/wcpr.

On-Site Academy, Massachusetts. A three-day confidential program for first responders and military who are suffering from effects of their job. www.onsiteacademy.org

Wounded Officers:

Dependence Day, Heidi Paulson.
The Price They Pay, Karen Solomon
Visions of Courage, Bobby E. Smith, PhD.

Hunting for Heroes. Nonprofit organization that provides services and counseling for disabled law enforcement. www.huntingforheroes.org.

Chapter Nine

My Life for Your Life, Clarke A. Paris.

SafeCallNow: Confidential 24-hour crisis referral service for members of public safety and their families. www.safecallnow.org.

Serve & Protect: Confidential 24-hour crisis hotline and chaplain/therapist alliance for law enforcement families. www.serveprotect.org.

Badge of Life: Organization that provides psychological survival awareness and education, data collection, and training for law enforcement officers. www.badgeoflife.com.

The Pain Behind the Badge: Books, seminars, movie all designed for Suicide Prevention for Cops. www.ThePainBehindtheBadge.com.

Langus, Pike & Associates. Provides psychological services, training, and critical incident debriefing services for law enforcement. California. www.drtoddlangus.net

11-99 Bridge: Nonprofit corporation dedicated to reducing law enforcement suicide. Information, counseling and opportunities that help prevent LE suicide. www.1199bridge.com.

Chapter Ten

Faith Based Books for Law Enforcement:

Spiritual Survival, Cary Friedman
Cold Case Christianity, J. Warner Wallace
The Book of Proverbs Through the Eyes of a Cop, Charles Gilliland
The Book of Matthew Through the Eyes of a Cop, Charles Gilliland
The Peacekeepers, Michael Dye
Take Up the Shield, Tony Miano
Devotions and Prayers for Police Officers, Steve J. Voris
The Servant Warrior, Kevin McGinnis
The Spirit Behind Badge 145, Jim McNeff

Faith-Based Organizations for Law Enforcement:

Ten-Four Ministries: Practical and spiritual help for police officers. www.tenfourministries.org.

Heirs of Restraint Ministries: Faith-based ministry to correctional officers. www.heirsofrestraint.com

CODE 3 International Ministries: Equipping police officers for Christian leadership. www.code3im.org.

Cop Church Chattanooga: Church for Cops, Chattanooga, Tennessee. www.copchurch.com.

Fellowship of Christian Police Officers: Helps peace officers develop a Christian mindset using biblical truths to meet their spiritual needs. www.fcpo.org.

Centurion's Faith: Provides resources designed to encourage, strengthen and support the First Responder's spiritual, professional, psychological and physical well-being. www.centurionsfaith.org.

Centurion Law Enforcement Ministry: Christian law enforcement outreach, newsletter, Bible studies. www.thecenturionlawenforcementministry.org

Peace Officer Ministries: Christian law enforcement chaplaincy program. www.peaceofficerministries.org

Covered Law Enforcement: Promoting faith and solidarity with police officers. www.coveredlawenforcement.org.

Christian Police Association: Encouragement and support for Christian police officers. www.cpa-usa.org.

Badge of Hope Ministries: Christian peer support for law enforcement families. Seminars, newsletter, books, and more. www.badgeofhopeministries.com.

Off Duty Partners for Life: Faith-based support, education, and encouragement for law enforcement families in Canada. www.offdutypartners.ca

Law Enforcement Chaplaincy of Sacramento: Named "The Model Chaplaincy In the Nation" because of its exceptional organizational structure, extensive training requirements,
and rapid response capability. www.sacchaplains.com.

Breaching the Barricade Conference: Christian law enforcement conference held the first Friday of every October in Indiana. For more information, contact Jim Bontrager at jim.bontrager@elkhartpolice.org.

<u>Chapter Eleven</u>

GPS Financial Coaching: Operated by a motor officer in California. Offers financial tips, classes, and coaching, especially for police families. http://gpsfinancialcoaching.com

Dave Ramsey: Books, programs, financial advice. www.daveramsey.com

Sheep Dog Impact Assistance: Sheep Dog IA provides assistance to military, law enforcement, fire & rescue, and other emergency personnel and their families in times of need and personal hardship. They also provide assistance to communities during disasters with a volunteer relief force, and educate people on the importance of disaster preparedness and survival. www.sheepdogia.org.

APPENDIX

Checklist to Protect You and Your Family in Case of On-duty Disability

• Discuss with your spouse about your faith, eternity, DNRs (Do Not Resuscitate), organ donation, etc. Keep necessary paperwork in a safe place where your spouse can locate it.

• Make sure you have long-term disability coverage; don't assume the department has this covered or that Social Security Disability will apply or be available.

• If your department opts out of Social Security, you are not eligible for any FICA disability coverage, not one penny, even if you have paid into Social Security in a previous job/position. You have to be paying into it at the time of disability.

• If your department has alternate disability coverage in place, count your blessings. Check out the details and know what it covers, what the amounts are and if you can live on that if you can't return to work. Even if you get disability retirement, this is often at significantly less than current wage (i.e., 50%) and you may have to pay expenses the department used to cover out of that retirement amount. This could include health insurance. Do not count on disability retirement being enough to live on.

• If your department offers alternate/additional disability coverage, take it, even if there is a co-pay or employee premium involved.

• If your department does not offer alternate disability coverage, look into other options. This can be difficult because many companies will consider law enforcement officers high risk, which makes the premium very high for individuals.

• If something does happen, talk to a workman's comp attorney before settling anything.

• Make sure you have things like a Health Care Power of Attorney, DNR, Living Will, Organ Donor, etc. completed, notarized and in a place easy to find. Our hospital keeps these on file electronically, so they are already in place should the need arise. We actually have them on file at both hospitals in town because trauma doesn't allow a choice.

• If you pay child support or alimony, check with your attorney about how that would be handled in the event of disability. One officer gives up almost half of his disability to alimony, even though his ex now makes more than his disability retirement.

• Disability policies vary from state to state and department to department. Some states, like California, have a state disability payroll deduction/tax. If your state has this, you may be better off than others.

• Many departments have honor guards and specific guidelines for handling line of duty deaths, yet have no protocol for handling permanent disability.

• Some departments have rules on the books that if an officer can't return to work within a year, they can be fired. Don't assume that you will be taken care of if you are critically injured/disabled in the line of duty.

• While there is federal legislation under the Alu-Ohara act that says departments are to provide medical insurance coverage at the level and rate that the officer had at the time of injury, the legislation is full of loopholes. Many agencies take advantage of these loopholes to avoid providing insurance to disabled officers. Work Comp should cover issues related to the on-duty injury, although many officers have to fight for years to get the treatment their doctors recommend. These officers and their families need insurance for other medical issues that may come up later. As an example, Ladd's disability retirement is half of his pre-injury pay. He pays almost half of that for insurance, leaving a quarter of his pre-injury wage to live on.

Playlist Suggestions for the Commute From Work to Home

Fight the Good Fight – Triumph
Hero – Skillet
American Soldier – Toby Keith
Shake it Off – Taylor Swift
Stressed Out – 21 Pilots
War Inside – Switchfoot
It's My Life – Bon Jovi
Dear X, You Don't Own Me – Disciple
Meant To Live – Switchfoot
I Won't Back Down – Johnny Cash
Dare You to Move – Switchfoot
Going Through the Motions – Matt Redman
Always Look on the Bright Side of Life – Monty Python
Sometimes You Can't Make it On Your Own – U2

Home – Chris Daughtry
Just the Two of Us – Will Smith
Little Toy Guns – Carrie Underwood
Can't Feel My Face – The Weeknd
Stay Like This – James Morrison
Watching You – Rodney Adkins
Close Enough to Perfect – Alabama
God Gave Me You – Blake Shelton
My Little Girl – Tim McGraw
Have I Told You Lately – Van Morrison
Wonderful Tonight – Eric Clapton
One Hot Mama – Trace Adkins

With a Little Help From my Friends – Beatles
Stand By Me – Ben E. King
Kickin' Up Mud – The Lacs

Psalm 139

Oh Lord,
> You have delved into the deep recesses of my soul and you know who I am.
You are aware of how often I lay down and when I rise up to fight,
> And you understand my thoughts of joy, grief, fatigue, desire, and contentment no matter where I am.

You have watched me day after day, and you are intimately familiar with what motivates me, makes me angry, and what brings me joy.
Even before I speak, you know what I'm going to say, you know me so well.

You have my back, and You know where I'm headed, and hold me firmly in the grip of your hand.

> I can't even begin to understand how you do it –
you are unfathomable.

Where can I go from your Holy Spirit? Where can I escape your Face?
In my happiest moment, You are present.
> In my deepest failings, You are present.
If I am healed, or if I am drowning in sin,
> You pursue me.

You will lead me with Your hand. You will catch me when I fall.

When I am sinking under the weight of depression, and I do not see any way out,
I am reminded that this darkness does not obscure Your view.
> Because even though You are with me in this pain, You are not bound by it.

Because You made me who I am.
> You wove me together in my mother's womb.

Thank you, Lord, for making me who I am – because You make beautiful things.

You are amazing, and the deepest part of me knows this.
Even though no other saw me growing inside my mother,
You were crafting my body, and my personality
From the time of conception.
You saw who I could be even before my fingerprints were formed
And You wrote my story in your book
Every day of my life – the good, the hurtful, the amazing and terrible
Before I ever even took a breath.

How valuable your thoughts are to me, O God!
I cannot fathom all the details that You came up with in Your unlimited creativity and artistry
I am human, bound by so many things;
But You are not bound by anything except Your promises made in Your faithful love for me.

Please deal with wicked people, O God; Keep me away from those who kill and maim! They speak against You, and Your character. I despise them, I loathe them, I hate them; They are my enemies.

Look into my heart again and again, O God, and take notice of me.
Let me be tested, and show me what I fear and what makes me anxious;
See if there is something that still pains me, or something I do that hurts others
And lead me to healing,
forgiveness, and
ultimately more of Your presence.

(Written by vmn, based on study of the Hebrew account of Psalm 139)

MEET THE AUTHOR

Victoria M. Newman is Founder and CEO of How2LoveYourCop, an organization that creates encouraging and supportive resources for police families. Married over 27 years to a Chief with the California Highway Patrol, she authored *A CHiP on my Shoulder*, a realistic but positive book to help police wives in their marriages. You can find more of her writing in her blog on www.how2loveyourcop.com and postings on Facebook and Twitter.

Victoria speaks to audiences throughout the United States, Canada and the Philippines. Her seminar, Backup for the Home, is available in four and eight hour increments through SAFETAC Training. She has been instrumental in shaping and improving spousal academies for several departments. She partners with Hunting4Heroes to create and present at the VOWS Retreat, a marriage conference for wounded law enforcement officers and their spouses. She also speaks with her husband, Brent, who is a seasoned trainer/presenter for the California Highway Patrol and FranklinCovey. Trained as a law enforcement chaplain, Victoria personally mentors several officer wives and has come alongside families in crisis for over fifteen years.

Victoria has operated a book consulting business for the past thirteen years, collaborating, editing, and ghostwriting works on business practices, prison survival, special needs children, fantasy fiction, marriage, and a memoir from a World War II prisoner of war. She collaborated with SSG Emmett Spraktes to write *Selfish Prayer: How California National Guard DUSTOFF Changed the Face of Army Medevac amid the Chaos, Carnage and Politics of War.* The research of this controversial book took Victoria to several states of the Union, culminating at the White House for a Medal of Honor ceremony. The project also gave her an opportunity to see firsthand the emotional toll of war.

Victoria has four children, one daughter-in-law, and resides near Sacramento, California.

You can reach her via her website email, at victoria@how2loveyourcop.com.

ACKNOWLEDGEMENTS

The process of writing A Marriage in Progress was long and difficult. Although I had the title and outline in 2013, I actually started putting words to paper just after Ferguson in 2014. Since then, the Blue Line Family has been through the fire on every side.

Nationally, issues with cop hate invaded our thoughts, social media, leadership, and everyday calls. Many days I dealt with not only the fears and justified anger of spouses and family members, but my own inner processing.

In October 2014, what was to be two weeks of intensive writing came to an abrupt halt when an illegal alien and member of the Mexican drug cartel killed two deputies in a several hour crime spree here in the Sacramento area. I learned that several of my friends' husbands were involved, and one was on scene when the whole thing began. This manuscript took a back seat to the grief, loss, and fears of police families in this region. Life has since moved on, but many officers and their families have not recovered.

Over fifteen months of writing, our family endured several of our own personal and professional trials that were extremely difficult. It felt like I had to fight for every word.

There were many people who I leaned on for support, information, accountability and feedback. I could not have written this work without them.

Several officers came to dinner and answered my questions thoughtfully and enthusiastically: George, Bryan, Ross, Emmett, John, Scott, Kevin, Chad, Jake, Jason, Ryan, Michael, Jay, Caleb, Kym, Scott, Mel, and Sondra. There were those who met with me face to face or by phone for personal interviews: Chief Sarah Creighton (SDPD), Sgt. Susan Feenstra (SPD), Dr. Todd Langus, Dr. Gary Lowe, Sacramento Bob, Mike Abbott, Karen DiMatteo, Stephen & Mendi Keatts, and John Maxfield.

There were police families who connected with me on Facebook, Twitter, and email: Tristina, Patti, Heidi, Heidi, Melissa, Colette, Steve,

Lori, Crystal, Beth, and Kara.

A few helped me with miscellaneous but crucial details: Cory Howard, Emmett Spraktes, Sondra Christian, and the Roseville Police Department dispatchers.

Some spent time discussing available resources: Skip Carter, Scot Panfill, Chief Sarah Creighton, Heidi Paulson, Maria DiGiovanni, and Becky Parkey.

There were very busy people who provided invaluable feedback on my manuscript: Jonathan Parker, Travis Yates, Emmett Spraktes, Barbara Upham, Kevin Bernard, Eddie Reyes, Becky Parkey, and Carl Franklin.

Nick Matalonis was willing to model for an afternoon for the cover. Kyle Johnston gave creative and patient photography. Dave Eaton created the cover and layout designs. All represented the visual excellence of A Marriage in Progress.

Many friends sent notes of encouragement or verbal support: Elizabeth Dansie, Arlene & Darrel, Mom & Dad, Aunt Carol, Donna, Linda, Dave & Rose, Rachel, Kara, Aunt Viola, Melissa Littles, Scott, John & Christy, Lorelei, Heidi, Teddi, Cindee & Tim, Laura, Francis, Erin, Roz, Christa, Kristi Neace, and Barbara Morgan, Brinda, David, Diane, Kathryn, Michael & Kathryn, Carol, Melissa, Norm, Rob, Dale & Judy, MC, Debbie, Christa, Sondra, Christine, Sylvia, Jim, Orval & Jeannie, Mike & Nancy, Nina, Donna, Greg, Jim, Paula, Sarah, Valerie, Chuck, Corey, Keith, Maria, Debra, Joel, Kyrie, Travis, Eileen, Judi, Jack, Joyce, Mary, Kevin & Deborah, Cretia, Liz, Brandii, Tina, Debby, and Dale.

Michael & Kathryn Redman offered their longtime friendship, encouragement, and marketing/business expertise.

There were 934 individuals who spent time on my online survey, and several were kind enough to answer follow up questions.

My parents, Gary & Mary Campbell, listened to my woes, and prayed until their knees hurt. Along with Aunt Viola, they have been my champion prayer warriors, doing battle for me for many years. Mom and Dad never cease to tell me they believe in me and what I do, which I won't ever take for granted. Aunt Carol sent clever words of wisdom in very low times, and this was dear to my heart. Grandpa Bernie and Grandma Helen's words and excitement continue to resonate even though we buried them both during this writing journey. I'll never forget Grandpa's question the last time I talked with him, "So! What mission are you on, now?" I cherish that exchange.

My kids, Kyrie, Ben & Christina, Annika, and Dave were very supportive, giving encouragement, talking me out of bad attitudes, helping with cleaning and dinner, and giving up time with me so that I could write.

Brent was my biggest supporter and at times my biggest pain as he meticulously read through my manuscript for months. His input and critique raised the level of excellence to where it needed to be. His encouragement and willingness to be put on the page for the sake of others was incredibly generous and absolutely crucial. He also is my biggest cheerleader. Thank you, Babe.

And the last whom shall be first, the Lover of my soul, and my closest Friend, Jesus Christ. All that I am and have yet to be, I owe to Him.

For all of you mentioned here, I am incredibly grateful for the support and work you've given. May God richly bless you for your contribution, and the results this manuscript will generate.

Bibliography

Newman, Victoria. *A CHiP on my Shoulder.* OK: Tate Publishing, 2011.

Kyle, Chris. *American Sniper.* New York, NY: William Morrow, 2012.

Glennon, Jim. *Arresting Communication.* Villa Park, IL: Lifeline Publishing, 2010.

Brown, Cynthia. *Brave Hearts.* Cambridge, MA: American Police Beat Publishing Group, 2010.

Willis, Dan. *Bulletproof Spirit.* Novato, CA: New World Library, 2014.

Kates, Allen R. *CopShock.* Tucson, AZ: Holbrook Street Press, 2008.

Patterson, Kerry, Grenny, Joseph, McMillan, Ron, and Switzler, Al. *Crucial Conversations.* New York, NY: McGraw Hill, 2012.

Phillips, Bob. *The Delicate Art of Dancing with Porcupines.* Ventura, CA: Regal Books, 1989.

Paulson, Heidi. *Dependence Day.* Bloomington, IN: Crossbooks Publishing, 2010.

Gilmartin, Kevin M. *Emotional Survival for Law Enforcement.* Tucson, AZ: E-S Press, 2002.

Chapman, Gary. *The Five Love Languages, Military Edition.* Chicago, IL: Northfield Publishing, 2013.

Stoop, David. *Forgiving the Unforgivable.* Ventura, CA: Regal Books, 2003.

Wilson, Barbara. *Kiss Me Again.* Colorado Springs, CO: Multnomah Books, 2009

Kirschman, Ellen. *I Love a Cop.* New York, NY: Guilford Press, 2007.

Arbinger Institute. *Leadership and Self-Deception.* San Francisco, CA: Berrett-Koehler Publishers, Inc., 2010.

Paris, Clarke A. *My Life for Your Life.* Las Vegas, NV: Pain Behind the Badge, 2011.

Nila, Michael J. *The Nobility of Policing.* Salt Lake City, UT: FranklinCovey, 2008.

Norris, Chuck. *The Official Chuck Norris Fact Book.* Carol Stream, IL: Tyndale House Publishers, Inc., 2009.

Dement, William C. *The Promise of Sleep.* New York, NY: Dell Publishing, 1999.

Spraktes, Emmett W. *Selfish Prayer.* Dixon, CA,: Create Space, 2013.

McInnes, Kevin. *The Servant Warrior.* Calgary, Alberta: Off Duty Partners for Life, 2008.

Rogish, Stephanie & Grossman, Lt. Col. Dave. *Sheepdogs: Meet Our Nation's Warriors.* Jackson, WI: Delta Defense, LLC, 2013.

Covey, Stephen. *Speed of Trust.* New York, NY: Free Press, 2006.

Leaf, Caroline. *Switch on Your Brain.* Grand Rapids, MI: Baker Books, 2013.

Gottman, John & Julie. *10 Lessons to Transform Your Marriage.* New York, NY: Three Rivers Press, 2006.

Ramsey, Dave. *The Total Money Makeover.* Nashville, TN: Thomas Nelson, 2003, 2007, 2009.

Mackall, Lisabeth. *27 Miles: The Tank's Journey Home.* Minneapolis, MN. 2013.

Caprarelli, John. *Uniform Decisions: My Life in the LAPD and the North Hollywood Shootout.* Los Angeles, CA: End of Watch Publishing, 2011.

Gottman, John. *Why Marriages Succeed or Fail.* New York, NY: Simon and Schuster Paperbacks, 1994.

Chan, Francis & Lisa. *You and Me Forever.* San Francisco, CA: Claire Love Publishing, 2014.

Made in the USA
San Bernardino, CA
15 November 2016